GrowLab™

Activities for Growing Minds

GrowLab™

Activities for
Growing Minds

National Gardening Association

180 Flynn Avenue
Burlington, Vermont 05401
(802) 863-1308

Authors:	Eve Pranis
	Joy Cohen
Contributing Writer:	Jimmy Karlan
Editor:	Deborah Burns
Cover Design:	Randall Leers
Design and Production:	Battery Graphics
Illustrator:	Grant Urie
Administrative Coordinator:	Lois Reynolds
Project Managers:	Eve Pranis
	Joy Cohen
Project Director:	Tim Parsons

Fourth printing, 1994.
Library of Congress Catalog Card Number: 90-60652
ISBN: 0-915873-32-X

This project was supported, in part, by the
National Science Foundation
Opinions expressed are those of the authors and not necessarily those of the Foundation

To curious and growing minds everywhere.

Table of Contents

Preface viii
Acknowledgements x

Introduction

Overview of Guide 2
   Chapters 2
   Background Information 2
   Activities (Suggested Grade Ranges) 3
   Activity Format 4
   Record-Keeping Reproducibles 6

The Process of Science 7
   Science Process Skills 7
   Problem Solving 8
   Plant a Question, Watch it Grow 9
   Problem Solving for Growing Minds 10

Science Teaching Tips 12
   Effective Questioning 12
   Fostering Healthy Attitudes 12
   Student Grouping 13
   Assessing Students' Learning 14
   Classroom and Materials Organization 15

Planning a Yearly Calendar 16
   Sample Horticultural Themes 17
   Sample Conceptual Themes 19
   Sample Topical Themes 20

Activities

Chapter 1: Plants Alive! 27
   Teacher Background: Beginning with Seeds 28
   Activities: Journey to the Center of a Seed;
   Yo Seeds, Wake Up!
   Teacher Background: Basic Needs 39
   Activities: Magic Beans and Giant Plants; Make Room
   for Raddy; Enough is Enough
   Teacher Background: Transport and Support 52
   Activities: Root Watch; Why Root for Roots?; Root Loops;
   Earthgrippers; What a Sy-Stem!
   Teacher Background: Plants as Food Makers 74
   Activities: Look Out for Leaves; Puzzled by Photosyn-
   thesis; A-Maze-in Light; Lighten Up
   Wrap-up Activity: What's in a Name? 97
   Teacher Background: The Soil Connection 101
   Activities: A Soil-a-bration!; Soil Sort; MockSoil

Chapter 2: Generation to Generation 117

Teacher Background: Plants from Seeds 118
Activities: Plant Cycles; Flowers: Up Close; Petal
Attraction; Plant Parenthood; Fruit for Thought
Teacher Background: Plants from Parts 139
Activities: Plantenstein; Slips, Snips and Growing Tips;
The Eyes Have It

Chapter 3: Diversity of Life 153

Teacher Background: Diversity 154
Activities: Plant Private Eyes; Diverseedy; Lettuce Be
Different; Mystery Family Ties; Order in the Class;
Designer Crops; Rainforest Stories
Teacher Background: Adaptations 188
Activities: Go Seeds Go!; Seed Busters; To Weed or Not
to Weed?; Turning Over a New Leaf

Chapter 4: Sharing the Global Garden 207

Teacher Background: Interdependence 208
Activities: FungusAmongUs; Getting Hooked on
Worms; Aphid Pets; Salad Celebration; Plants 'R' Us
Teacher Background: Human Impact 238
Activities: Grass Blast; Pollution Solutions; PlantAcid,
Global ReLeaf

Appendices

Appendix A: Specific Activity Reproducibles 263
Appendix B: General Reproducibles 281
  Plant a Question 282
  Problem Solving for Growing Minds 283
  My Plant Journal 285
  Observation Journal 286
  Create-a-Chart 287
  Garden Calendar 288
  GermiNation and Growth Journal 289
  Futures Wheel 291
Appendix C: OnGrowing Ideas 293
Appendix D: Fast Plants Growing Instructions 295
Appendix E: Resources (annotated) 297
Appendix F: Seed Sources 303
GrowLab Program Resources 304
Index 306

Preface

Plants, like people, have basic needs that must be met if they are to thrive and grow. They've evolved with an amazing array of structures, responses, systems, shapes, colors, and smells to ensure survival. They function as power plants, hydraulic lifts, and air filters. They're essential to life on Earth. These familiar marvels are natural tools for stimulating students' sense of wonder about their world.

As students watch a seedling unfurl, witness the response of a neglected plant, or try to influence the direction a root grows, questions inevitably arise. With guidance, these questions can lead to exploration and discovery. Once students experience the joy of using their senses and problem-solving skills to investigate their own questions, they realize that they can be scientists themselves. They find that science is not dull, scary, or "just a bunch of facts," but fun and engaging.

As a non-profit membership organization, the National Gardening Association's mission has always been to promote gardening for all ages because it adds joy and health to living and encourages an appreciation for the environment. Through our youth gardening programs, we've been particularly aware of the power of plants and gardens to stimulate young minds. When we discovered in a national survey of teachers that 78 percent of all teachers engaged in some type of gardening and were comfortable using plants as teaching tools, we decided to go ahead with our ambitious GrowLab Indoor Gardening Program. With support from the National Science Foundation and many others, we developed this curriculum guide to complement the other Grow-Lab Program Resources described on page 304.

GrowLab: Activities for Growing Minds reflects a new thrust in hands-on science curricula, intended to help teachers make science inviting and relevant to students' lives, and to make connections between science and other disciplines. Activities in this guide draw on students' own experiences, encourage open-ended questioning, and help students then turn their own questions into active investigations. We see the teacher as co-explorer, collaborating with students and gently guiding their explorations.

Whether you're new to plants or a proven "green thumb", the activities in this guide help you use the indoor classroom garden to explore plants both as individual organisms and in the context of the "global garden." As students come to understand basic needs and the interdependence of living things, the Grow-Lab becomes a natural springboard for exploring some of the current environmental problems that face us all. Using this curriculum guide, a class might create an indoor tropical rainforest, conduct classroom acid rain studies, or raise tree seedlings to complement studies on global warming.

But the GrowLab Program is much more than this curriculum guide and the other products described on the back page. We've found that the most successful school gardening efforts involve others in the community. Botanical gardens' staff may provide technical assistance to teachers, local businesses may help purchase supplies, 4-H leaders or garden club members can become classroom consultants. We've developed the GrowLab Partners Program, briefly described on page 304, to support these efforts.

Our goal is to spark students who have confidence in their ability to tackle problems, who appreciate and respect the natural world, and, above all, who enjoy learning. To do that, inspired educators, like you, must have the tools to accomplish the job. This curriculum guide is one of those tools.

Acknowledgements

GrowLab: Activities for Growing Minds has benefitted from the vision and expertise of educators reflecting a wide range of experience, demographics, and perspectives.

Sincere thanks to members of our Curriculum Design Team who provided initial guidance in shaping the curriculum, as well as ongoing feedback and support: Russell Agne, University of Vermont, Burlington, VT; Jan Altobell, Harris Center for Conservation Education, Hancock, NH; Roberta Jaffee, Life Lab Science Program, Santa Cruz, CA; Jimmy Karlan, Wild Ideas, Brattleboro, VT; Karen Worth, Educational Development Center and Wheelock College, Boston, MA.

The collaborative efforts of the following classroom teachers were invaluable to the early stages of activity conceptualization and development:
Jeff Brohinsky, Martin Luther King School, Hartford, CT; Bonnie Bush, Charlotte Middle School, Rochester, NY; Thea Fry, Douglas Grafflin School, Chappaqua, NY; Dot Gorenflo, Academy School, Brattleboro, VT; Jo Piotrowski Hendry, Science Consultant, Goffstown, NH; Gregg Humphrey, Mary Hogan School, Middlebury, VT; Molly McClaskey, Monkton Central School, Monkton, VT; Hannah Morvan, Northfield Falls Elementary School, Northfield, VT; Chip Porter, Edmunds School, Burlington, VT; Lynne Stinson, Graham & Parks Alternative Public School, Cambridge, MA; Pat Pierce, Bristol Elementary School, Bristol, VT; Charlotte Stetson, Academy School, Brattleboro, VT; Phil Veysey, Dearborn Middle School, Roxbury, MA.

Our heartfelt appreciation goes to Jimmy Karlan, who creatively wove together ideas generated by the teacher teams and wrote initial activity drafts. He has been an ongoing source of creative inspiration.

More than 120 classroom teachers tested GrowLab curriculum activities in their classrooms during the spring and fall of 1989. Many thanks to the teachers and administrators at the following schools for providing feedback and fresh ideas to help make the final guide a useful resource for their colleagues:

Academy School, Hartford, CT; Apopka Middle School, Apopka, FL; Auburn Union School, Auburn, CA; Baldwin School, Pennsauken, NJ; Barbour School, Hartford, CT; Beech Tree Elementary School, Falls Church, VA; Beechwood Elementary, Fort Lewis, WA; Bingham Middle School, Kansas City, MO; Boys & Girls Club, Encinitas, CA; Breckinridge Elementary, Louisville, KY; Bristol Elementary, Bristol, VT; Champlain School, Burlington, VT; Charlotte Central School, Charlotte, VT; Chattanooga School of Arts & Sciences, Chattanooga, TN; Childlight Montessori, Delhi, NY; Cornwall Elementary School, Middlebury, VT; Deerfield Valley Elementary, Wilmington, VT; Delmar Hills School, Del Mar, CA; Developmental Research School, Tallahassee, FL; Douglas Grafflin School, Chappaqua, NY; Edmunds Elementary School, Burlington, VT; Fairsite School, Galt, CA; Fillmore U.S.D., Fillmore, CA; Folsom School, South Hero, VT; Glen Forest Elementary School, Falls Church, VA; Graham & Parks Alternative, Cambridge, MA; Holland School, Fort Wayne, IN; Horace Mann Lab

School, Salem, MA; Key School Option Program, Indianapolis, IN; Lamprey River Elementary, Raymond, NH; Mallets Bay School, Colchester, VT; Martin Luther King School, Hartford, CT; Mary Hooker School, Hartford, CT; Mead Elementary School, Wisconsin Rapids, WI; Missouri City Elementary School, Missouri City, MO; Moretown Elementary, Moretown, VT; Noah Webster School, Hartford, CT; Northfield Falls Elementary, Northfield, VT; Oakmont Elementary, Columbus, OH; Orchard School, South Burlington, VT; Park School, Brooklandville, MD; Providence Day School, Charlotte, NC; PS 205, Queens, NY; Rawson School, Hartford, CT; Santa Ynez Elementary School, Santa Ynez, CA; Santa Catalina School, Monterey, CA; Savannah Grove Elementary, Effingham, SC; School 98, Indianapolis, IN; Serena Hills School, Chicago, IL; Sheldon School, Sheldon, VT; South Street Elementary, Fitchburg, MA; St. Albans Town School, St. Albans, VT; St. Ambrose Catholic School, Godfrey, IL; St. Mary's Catholic School, Centerville, IA; Sutton Elementary, Sutton, MA; Sweethaven Farm, Salisbury, CT; Thomas Quirk Middle School, Hartford, CT; Ukiah High School, Ukiah, CA; Underhill ID, Underhill, VT; Vine Street School, Hartford, CT; Waverly School, Hartford, CT; Wheeler School, Burlington, VT; Woodrow Wilson School, Daly City, CA.

We're grateful to Carol Ann Margolis, Peter Horvath, Charlie Nardozzi, and Lynn Fontana for lending horticultural expertise to the project.

Special thanks to National Gardening Association Education staff: Nell Ishee, for her ongoing review and input; and Lois Reynolds, whose administrative support and mastery of in-house publishing made the project's completion possible.

Many thanks to Sharon Levin for carefully reviewing and annotating student fiction and non-fiction books for the annotated resource section.

Thanks to Sue Storey for design support; to Barry Genzlinger for valuable computer consultation; and to Alison Watt, James Evans, and Julie Nordmeyer for final-hour production assistance.

Our appreciation to the sharp reviewers who provided valuable feedback in the final stages of curriculum drafting: Sig Abeles; Jan Altobell; Sharon Behar; Maura Carlson; Cindy Carwell; Cheryl Charles; Ted Chittenden; Clint Erb; Nancy Gallagher; Joe Griffith; Jack Hale; Lois Haslam; Debi Hogan; Gregg Humphrey; Paul Johnson; Nancy Johnson; Robert Koenig; David Kramer; Debra Lehrer-Epstein; Denise Martin; Ellen McCurdy; Casey Murrow; Pat Pierce; Chip Porter; Malvina Pranis; Chuck Roth; Lynn Rupe; Diane Syverson; Kathy Topping; Darlene Worth; Karen Worth

Finally, our special thanks to the National Science Foundation, the Jessie B. Cox Charitable Trust, The George Gund Foundation, the Wallace Genetic Foundation, and Corporate Associates and members of the National Gardening Association for their generous funding of the GrowLab Program.

Introduction

How do you decide if a tomato is ripe? How do children discover whether an earthworm's skin is moist or dry, or how a burdock seed "rides" on a sock? We are all scientists, explorers, and problem solvers, continually using our senses and minds to understand the natural world. Your indoor garden offers a rich opportunity to spark your students' curious minds and engage them in active explorations. You will be partners in a dynamic learning process, sharing questions and discoveries while you garden in your classroom.

By sharing the joy of discovery with your students, you provide them with a model for solving problems in all contexts. When a student asks: "What would happen if a bean plant had no flowers?", and you respond: "Gee, I'm not sure—how could we find out?", you impart a key message—knowing how to find an answer is as important as knowing an answer. Throughout your GrowLab adventures, consider yourself facilitator and guide, rather than the source of all gardening wisdom. This book provides suggestions for turning your students' questions into vital, fruitful learning experiences.

GrowLab activities are designed to assist you in your role as facilitator. The teaching strategy they reflect encourages inquiry, the active use of science skills, and creative and critical thinking. They help you teach key life science concepts, and they support the positive development of students' attitudes toward science and the environment. They can be a springboard, providing a model for integrating a hands-on indoor gardening program into your classroom. The explorations, strategies, and questions can be adapted to meet the needs of your own classroom.

"One of the best things about a garden, large or small, is that it is never finished. It is a continual experiment."

—Margery Bianco, Horticulturalist

Overview of Guide

This guide contains four chapters, each with background information and sections of related activities. The "Activity Summary" matrix on page 22 outlines the activities in each chapter, including topics and science process skills covered, duration, and grade ranges. Reproducible worksheets are found in Appendices A and B.

Chapters

The activities in the four chapters represent a number of key life science concepts. The chapters are:

Plants Alive! Students investigate the miracle of life, from seed to plant. Explorations examine some important basic needs that must be met if plants are to thrive and grow. Students discover how plants' structures and responses to their environment help them meet these needs. Some activities focus on soil; others explore green plants' unique ability to make food.

Generation to Generation. Students observe plant life cycles and discover the structures and processes involved in plant reproduction. They consider the amazing adaptations that allow plants to create new generations both from flowers (sexually) and from plant parts (asexually).

The Diversity of Life. Students explore the tremendous diversity of life and how we make sense of this diversity. The chapter also focuses on how specific plant adaptations to different environmental conditions help create diversity.

Sharing the Global Garden. All of the elements in the "global garden" are interdependent. Students examine a few simple relationships that involve plants directly. They'll investigate how humans use plants, how our actions can affect them, and how we can lessen our negative impact in the global garden.

Background Information

Comprehensive **background sections** precede related activities. The time and materials box at the beginning of each activity indicates where to find relevant background information. Key terms and vocabulary in the background are highlighted with **bold** type. We recommend giving new words meaning through concrete experiences. Vocabulary words will have more relevance when they are part of hands-on, inquiry-based explorations.

Additional resources to supplement the background information are listed in Appendix E. Always refer to *GrowLab: A Complete Guide to Gardening in the Classroom* for basic planting and plant care information.

Activities

The activities in this book are only a sampling of the types of lessons you can use to support life science concepts in an indoor gardening context. They are intended to model different approaches, reflecting a range of teaching styles, learning styles, and classroom conditions. Some activities are long-term projects, others can complement a thematic garden project, and others can be done in sequence as a series of science explorations. See the "Activity Summary," on page 22 and "Planning a Yearly Calendar," on page 16 for help in developing units and sequencing activities.

Suggested Grade Ranges. Symbols are given for each activity. These generally correlate with grade ranges: K–2; 3–5; 6–8. *Do not let the grade range indicated deter you from reading and using an activity.* Instead, adapt activities to meet your unique needs. For instance, if you or your students have had little experience with growing plants or with hands-on science, we recommend beginning with lower-level activities, adapting them where appropriate to your grade level. In some activities, you'll find sidebars suggesting adaptations for different grade ranges.

K–2　　　　　3–5　　　　　6–8

Activity Format

Each activity's format reflects a multi-step teaching cycle. The steps build on one another, helping students use science skills to construct understanding. The descriptions below highlight the type of information you will find in each section of the activities.

Grade Level/Range

These symbols represent the general developmental level (K–2, 3–5, 6–8) for which the activity is appropriate. Adapt activities to your needs and your students' ability level.

Overview

This statement summarizes what students will do during the activity.

Time

The time allotments suggested are based on experiences in field-test classrooms. Adapt them to your own classroom needs. Making Connections is always indicated as "ongoing." Vital to effective science teaching, it is an ongoing process that will vary with your approach to the activity.

Materials

This lists recommended materials and reproducible worksheets. We suggest materials that are readily available, in GrowLab starter kits or in the classroom. The quantity listed is generally per exploration setup. You'll have to adapt the amounts depending on whether students conduct the explorations individually, in small groups, or as a class. For open-ended investigations with student-generated ideas, materials will vary.

Background

This section lists where to find background information that supports the activity.

Advance Preparation

Some activities require preparation in advance. In some cases, this section recommends doing other activities first as preparation for the current activity.

Plant Cycles

Overview: Students compare plant and human life cycles, and observe the life cycles of their GrowLab plants.

This is a good activity to do in conjunction with any long-term garden project. Whether students are growing a salad garden, have their own special pots, or are engaged in another project, they can observe and understand changes during plant life cycles. It's particularly valuable when flowering plants like beans or tomatoes are used.

Time:
Groundwork: 45 minutes
Exploration: 6-plus weeks ongoing observations
Making Connections: ongoing

Materials:
• GrowLab plants (plants that easily produce seeds such as tomatoes, beans or peas are preferable)
• "Garden Calendar" reproducible, page 266
• "My Plant Journal" reproducible, page 265

Background: Page 116

Advance Preparation: ...t enough plants in the GrowLab ...r each pair of students to have one ...o adopt.

Laying the Groundwork

Objective: To consider how both plants and humans change throughout their life cycles.

1. Ask students to think about how humans change during their lifetimes. *How are you different now than you were as a baby? How are you the same? How do you expect to change when you're an adult?* Incorporate answers onto a class chart. Ask: *What similarities do you notice in the ways we all change over time?*

2. Having stimulated thinking about human life cycles, turn the discussion to plants. *In what ways do you think plants change throughout their lives? What have you observed to make you think this? How can you tell whether one plant is older or at a later life stage than another?*

Exploration

Objective: To observe and record how certain plants change throughout their life cycles.

1. Have students work in pairs to "adopt" a plant from the Grow-Lab to observe throughout its cycle. (More than one group can use the same plant.) The activity should begin when seeds are planted, so students can observe the complete life cycle. Students can use personal journals, or the "My Plant Journal" reproducible to record regular observations of changes in their plants. Remind them to notice such things as changes in leaf number, leaf size, height, new parts, and the order in which changes occur.

2. While plants are maturing, refer to "OnGrowing Ideas," Appendix C, for suggestions for interdisciplinary activities to sustain students' interest and curiosity. Students can use the "Garden Calendar" reproducible to record events or changes during plant life cycles.

Plant Cycles 123

 **Plant Cycles**

Overview: Students compare plant and human life cycles, and observe the life cycles of their GrowLab plants.
This is a good activity to do in conjunction with any long-term garden project. Whether students are growing a salad garden, have their own special pots, or are engaged in another project, they can observe and understand changes during plant life cycles. It's particularly valuable when flowering plants like beans or tomatoes are used.

Time:
Groundwork: 45 minutes
Exploration: 6-plus weeks ongoing observations
Making Connections: ongoing

Materials:
• GrowLab plants (plants that easily produce seeds such as tomatoes, beans or peas are preferable)
• 'Garden Calendar' reproducible, page 288
• 'My Plant Journal' reproducible, page 285

Background: Page 108

Advance Preparation:
Start enough plants in the GrowLab for each pair of students to have one to adopt.

Laying the Groundwork

Objective: To consider how both plants and humans change throughout their life cycles.

1. Ask students to think about how humans change during their lifetimes. *How are you different now than you were as a baby? How are you the same? How do you expect to change when you're an adult?* Incorporate answers onto a class chart. Ask: *What similarities do you notice in the ways we all change over time?*

2. Having stimulated thinking about human life cycles, turn the discussion to plants. *In what ways do you think plants change throughout their lives? What have you observed to make you think that? How can you tell whether one plant is older or at a later life stage than another?*

Exploration

Objective: To observe and record how certain plants change throughout their life cycles.

1. Have students work in pairs to adopt a plant from the GrowLab to observe throughout its life cycle. (More than one group can use the same plant.) The activity should begin when seeds are planted, so students can observe the complete life cycle. Students can use personal journals, or the 'My Plant Journal' reproducible to record regular observations of changes in their plants. Remind them to notice such things as changes in leaf number, leaf size, height, new parts, and the order in which changes occur.

2. While plants are maturing, refer to 'OnGrowing Ideas,' Appendix C, for suggestions for interdisciplinary activities to sustain students' interest and curiosity. Students can use the 'Garden Calendar' reproducible to record events or changes during plant life cycles.

Plant Cycles 123

Life Cycles: From One Year to Many
Not all plants will complete their full life cycles during their time in your GrowLab. **Annuals** are plants that flower and complete a full life cycle from seed to seed, in one year. Common GrowLab annuals are beans, cucumbers, lettuce, peas, peppers, potatoes, tomatoes, and annual flowers. (Some of these, like lettuce, probably will not flower in the short time they are in your GrowLab.) **Biennials** complete a full life cycle in two years. During the first year, the plant puts energy primarily into roots, and it flowers during the second year. Common GrowLab biennials are beets, carrots, onions and parsley. **Perennials** continue to flower, produce seeds and grow for many years. They often have adaptations such as dormancy and dropping leaves to help them survive year-round in a changing environment. Perennials that you might raise in your GrowLab include tree seedlings and garden flowers like black-eyed Susans.

3. As plants mature, discuss student observations. Ask: *What tended to happen to leaves and plant height over time? Did the fruits always follow the flowers? What similarities are there in the ways different plants change throughout their life cycles? What happened to your plants after they produced seeds?* (You may want to follow this activity with **FungusAmongUs**, which illustrates how dead plant materials are also part of the cycle of life, decomposing and providing nutrients for new life.) *How were changes in your plants similar to changes to humans during our life cycles? How were they different? How does this compare with your predictions?*

Making Connections

1. Have pairs of students do a short class presentation about the life cycle of their adopted plant. Encourage them to prepare visual displays, short stories, poems, or skits.

2. Play Plant Cycles. Select six students to represent parts of a plant's life cycle: seed, sprout, mature plant, flowering plant, fruiting plant, another seed. Randomly position the students in a circle. Ask other students to rearrange the parts of the plant's life cycle into an order that shows a plant growing from a seed to the next generation of seeds.

3. Working from their observation journals, have pairs of students draw a number of the life cycle stages of their adopted plant. Mix up the drawings and share them with another pair. That pair must decide on the appropriate sequence for the drawings. Wrap this activity up by binding each set of drawings into a flip book.

Branching Out

• Save seeds from GrowLab plants for replanting (see sidebar, page 121.)

• Identify and explore other things in the environment (or in our lives) that follow cycles, such as water, seasons, or holidays.

• Take a walk outdoors and try to identify different life cycle stages of plants. Consider having a scavenger hunt for plants at different life cycle stages (e.g., flowering, sprouting, dying).

• Research differences between plants that complete their life cycles in one year (annuals) and those that take two (biennials) or many years (perennials) to complete life cycles (see sidebar).

124 Generation to Generation: Plants From Seeds

Laying the Groundwork
This section engages students in the concept. The Groundwork helps tie the Exploration to familiar concepts/experiences in students' lives. It includes questions and creative activities to help identify students' current understanding and ideas on the topic or concept. This allows you to structure the exploration to guide students effectively as they examine new ideas.

Objective:
This states the purpose of different sections of the activity in terms of content understanding, process skill, and/or attitudinal outcome.

Exploration
This section provides opportunities for students to explore phenomena actively. It includes explicit yet flexible suggestions for facilitating hands-on explorations. It has procedural hints, suggests classroom management strategies and recording and reporting techniques, and includes results to expect, when appropriate. (See page 15 for more on classroom and materials organization.)

Making Connections
This section is vital for effective science teaching, and should be given adequate time. It offers ideas for helping the students process the Exploration for meaning. This includes interpreting data, reflecting on experiments, identifying patterns, clarifying concepts, seeing "the big picture," communicating results with others, applying understanding to other contexts, and raising new questions. This is also an important opportunity for you to assess what students have learned.

Branching Out
This section suggests optional activities both in science and other subject areas that extend the concepts covered or processes used.

Record-Keeping Reproducibles

After many years of painstaking scientific research, a scientist discovered a process for producing artificial insulin. He had to spend another two years repeating his efforts, however, because he never wrote down the successful procedure. Without records, he was unsure what it was that had worked.

Keeping ongoing records of observations, ideas, and other information gathered is an important part of the science process, integrating science, math, and language skills. Records help students make sense of explorations and build understanding. Reproducible record-keeping sheets are found in Appendices A and B. We encourage you and your students to develop your own record-keeping sheets to supplement those included in this guide.

In addition to providing record-keeping sheets for specific activities, we've provided some general reproducibles to be used for a range of activities. These include the following:

• **My Plant Journal** (page 285). This can be used by primary-level students to record observations, drawings, and measurements during plant investigations.

• **Observation Journal** (page 286). This can be used by intermediate- and advanced-level students to record observations, drawings, and measurements during investigations.

• **Plant a Question** (page 282). This reproducible, described in detail on page 9, will help guide primary-level students as they ask questions and set up investigations to explore their answers.

• **Problem Solving for Growing Minds** (page 283). This reproducible, described in detail on page 10, is for students ready to conduct controlled investigations. Using the template provided, they can record the planning and results of their experiment.

• **Create-a-Chart** (page 287). This suggests a variety of ways to use charts and graphs to present data.

• **GermiNation and Growth Journal** (page 289). This reproducible, attached to a letter from the National Gardening Association, invites students to record information about their growing experiences to be shared with classrooms throughout the country.

The Process of Science

For your students, learning about and "doing" science can range from watching a zinnia bloom to testing a cucumber plant's response to salt water. When allowed to explore in an atmosphere that promotes imagination and discovery, students will experience science as an essential and exciting part of their lives.

During this "age of information" your students have an extraordinary amount of information available at their keyboard fingertips. Science is more than the sum of those facts, terms, and definitions. It is using existing knowledge, our senses, reasoning, and communication skills to explore questions and solve new problems. Students at work in the indoor garden already use such skills as observing, measuring, and predicting.

How students use these skills varies with their developmental stage. Younger students rely largely on their senses to experience the world around them. Students' increasing use of science skills reflects their increasing ability to think abstractly. While younger students can carry out simple investigations to confirm or refute predictions, older students are able to design experiments, control variables, and quantify results.

Science Process Skills

observing	Smelling leaves of different plants.	Examining stomata with a hand lens.	Observing changes over time when stomata are clogged with petroleum jelly.
raising questions	"What will happen if I grow my plants in the dark?"	"How can I make my bean plant grow faster?"	"What makes a plant bend toward the light?"
predicting/hypothesizing	"The larger the seed, the bigger the plant."	"The warmer the water, the faster the seeds will germinate."	"Plants raised under red filters will have more flowers than plants raised under blue filters."
finding patterns and relationships	Sorting seeds by shape.	Developing a list of characteristics that make a fruit a fruit.	Noticing how soil temperature affects germination rates of different types of seeds.
designing/conducting investigations	Growing two plants in a closet and two in the GrowLab.	Experimenting to examine how different music affects plant growth.	Experimenting to determine how the amount of fertilizer applied affects growth rate.
inferring	"Plants must need water to grow."	"The beans probably didn't germinate because the soil was too wet."	"The beans probably didn't germinate in the wet soil because they didn't have enough oxygen."
communicating	Sharing drawings of bean sprout development.	Presenting a graph showing the effect of salt on the growth of ryegrass.	Debating the advantages and disadvantages of genetic engineering.

Problem Solving

Although we're typically taught that scientific exploration requires "the scientific method," the actual method used by scientists is not a linear, rigid, step-by-step process. The problem-solving process of science consists of an ongoing cycle: questioning, exploring, experimenting, often backtracking, and developing new questions.

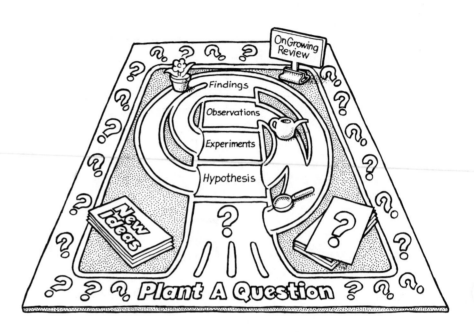

As with any science skill, a first grader will investigate a question very differently than will a seventh grader. To help guide your students, we've developed approaches for conducting investigations at two different developmental ranges. Suggestions for using each approach are presented on the following pages. Each process is also outlined for your students in a student reproducible. Through repeated exposure and use, we hope these approaches to problem solving become second nature for you and your students.

   The **Plant a Question** process, described on page 9, will help guide primary-level students as they ask questions and then set up explorations to discover answers. Writers can use the "Plant a Question" reproducible, page 282, to record their investigations. You can use it yourself to help guide pre-writers.

   The **Problem Solving for Growing Minds** process, described on page 10, should be followed by students ready to conduct more controlled investigations. It uses garden metaphors in place of the traditional steps of the scientific method. Students should record their investigations on the corresponding "Problem Solving for Growing Minds" reproducible, page 283.

Plant a Question, Watch it Grow

Your indoor garden will continually spark students' curiosity and questions. Keep a running class list of questions that emerge about plants, science, and the indoor garden. A question for exploration may come from you (*What do you think seeds need to sprout?*) or from your students (*How can we wake the seed up?*)

As questions arise, it's important that students have the opportunity to express their own ideas. Facilitate class discussions in which all students can share their thoughts on the question. Encourage students to share what they've experienced or observed to support their beliefs. It can be useful to have materials (seeds, plants, etc.) for students to observe and handle while they consider questions. Disagreements are bound to emerge and some ideas will be incorrect. This offers the opportunity to ask further questions, gather more information, and conduct investigations.

(see page 282)

What will happen if...
Help students frame some of their own thoughts into "What will happen if" questions that can lead to hands-on investigations. For example, "What will happen if we leave some seeds on a wet sponge and some seeds on a dry sponge?"

I predict...
Have students draw on previous experiences, observations, and knowledge to predict what they think the results will be. They can dictate their predictions for a class chart or write or draw them in individual journals.

This is what happened...
Communicating observations and findings is an important part of science. Students should regularly record observations verbally, in writing, and/or through drawings. At the end of the investigation, have students compare results with their predictions. Help them summarize their exploration using such tools as experience charts or sequence charts or by verbally sharing results with others. If results contradict what you think they should be (for example, if the plants in the dark grew better), brainstorm what other factors might have affected the exploration.

Now I want to find out...
Generating a list of new questions about the topic is a good way to wrap up an investigation. Some questions may provoke new investigations. Others may lead to research or interviews with experts. Students will also discover that many questions must go unanswered, since there is much we do not yet understand. This step can help your students appreciate that in science, as our understanding increases, so do our questions.

Problem Solving for Growing Minds

Plant a Question

Your indoor garden will no doubt stimulate your students' curiosity and elicit constant questions. Although some questions will be answered best by research or interviews, and others perhaps cannot be answered (there are many of these), many questions can become the basis for a scientific exploration. Asking and encouraging open-ended questions is central to learning more about the world. Facilitate a brainstorm of questions on a particular topic (e.g., light and plants – I wonder what would happen if...). Then identify, as a class, those you'd like to explore further. Consider making a class chart with the following headings: "What I Believe About _____"; "Questions I Have About _____." Encourage each student to keep an ongoing list of questions on different topics.

Sprout a Hypothesis

Encourage students to draw on their experiences, to reflect on what they already know (or think they know), and to speculate on answers to their questions. Students may choose to do preliminary research to gather information to help them frame a hypothesis.

Describe Your Growing Exploration

Students should consider how they'll systematically explore their ideas. Explorations could entail open-ended observations, or setting up a controlled "fair test". Important elements to consider when designing a fair test are:

• **Choose one experimental variable.** *What one factor or variable (e.g., water temperature) will you look at or change during the investigation? How will it vary from group to group? Why?*

• **Keep all other variables constant.** *Other than the experimental variable, what factors (e.g., light, fertilizer, or time) can influence the answer to your question? How will you keep these constant for each group?*

• **Have a control group.** *Which group will be the "normal" condition (e.g., the group that's given water at the recommended temperature) to which we can compare the other groups?*

• **Repeat experiment.** *How can we be sure our results were due to the experimental treatment, and not to another factor (e.g., a bad seed)?* To have more confidence in the validity of your results, have at least two pots/plants/ seeds in each group.

• **Decide what to observe.** *What observations will you make? How often will you record observations/measurements? Why do you want to gather that data?* When doing experiments with plants, consider looking at changes in size, shape, color, weight, smell, growth rate, etc., of leaves, fruit, roots, stem, and flowers. Remind students that, although they may choose certain criteria, it is important to keep an open mind and look for the unexpected. Many important discoveries (such as penicillin) have been "accidental".

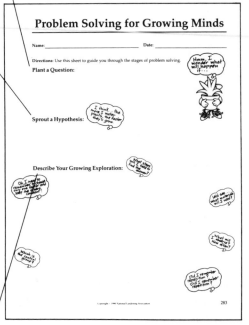

(see page 283)

Record Fruitful Observations

Help students decide how to keep track of their observations, ideas, and newly generated questions. Charts, graphs, and journals all offer different ways of organizing data. We've included reproducible record-keeping sheets for many investigations. Students should record raw data and not what they believe they should be finding. Records of these observations and data will be important as students try to derive meaning from their explorations. Always attach separate record-keeping sheets to this worksheet.

Harvest Your Findings

Help students organize the data and describe connections that exist. Ask: *Based on what you've observed, what's your explanation of what happened? After drawing your conclusion, what other questions do you have?*

Remind students not to overgeneralize their conclusions. Ask: *Based on your findings, can we assume that all plants will respond the same way?* Encourage small group discussion as students try to make sense of their exploration. Sharing between groups will also enhance communication skills and reinforce the fact that there are always multiple ways of looking at the same thing.

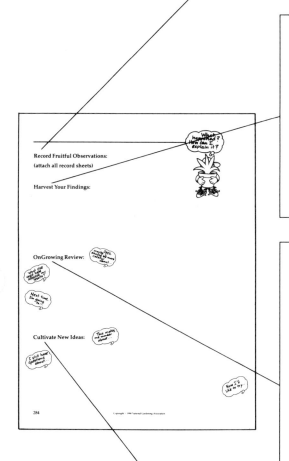

OnGrowing Review

An important element of true scientific exploration is reflection on and healthy skepticism of our process. *How effective were the procedures we used to answer the question?* Throughout investigations, encourage students to reflect on their process, either individually or with a peer review. They will hopefully learn to view feedback as an important part of the learning process.

Ask: *How do the results compare to your predictions? Why do you think they do or do not compare?* If you have conflicting data, or results that contradict conventional scientific knowledge, brainstorm a list of other factors that might have affected your results. Also consider questions such as: *What were some of the weaknesses of the experiment? How might other factors have influenced the results* (e.g., human error—They really didn't all get the same amount of water because when Blair had the flu we forgot to water her pot)? *How and why might you design the experiment differently if you were to repeat it?*

Cultivate New Ideas

Exploring the natural world inevitably leads students to extend their thinking into other related areas. Encourage students to continue to ask more questions and transfer the classroom experience to a broader setting. Let students know that these new ideas and questions are integral to the science process. Questions might dig deeper into relevant scientific topics or extend into other disciplines. Ask: *What else would you like to know about...? How do you think you could find out?* Allow students to brainstorm "I wonder what would happen if...", and the cycle continues.

What if.....?

To provide a structure for students to consider the multiple, long-range effects of a particular event or occurrence, use the "Futures Wheel" reproducible, page 292. For instance, *What would happen if all pollinators were destroyed by insecticides?* Many questions found in the "Making Connections" sections can be examined with the help of this worksheet.

The Art of Science

"Anyone can look for fashion in a boutique or history in a museum. The creative explorer looks for history in a hardware store and fashion in an airport."
—Robert Weider, Journalist

An entire generation is growing up without needing to learn to tie their shoes! The reason: When one man returned from a walk in the woods, he became fascinated rather than annoyed by the burrs attached to his clothing. It spurred his imaginative mind to develop the product, Velcro. Heightened imaginations permitted two men named Watson and Crick to envision the invisible structure of a molecule of DNA. Encourage your students to look at the familiar in unfamiliar ways. Inspire them to look at the unfamiliar in familiar ways. Your students come to school with incredible abilities and desires to imagine, play, pretend, and create. Let them know how essential these abilities are to the nature of science.

Science Teaching Tips

How can you turn your students' innate curiosity about the natural world into a love of science? The suggestions in this section are based on current research and test classroom feedback.

Effective Questioning

Your questions to the class are fundamental to an inquiry-based approach. Different types of questions will:

• find out how students already perceive things
• encourage them to articulate their observations
• help them connect explorations to other experiences
• stimulate them to share different perspectives
• enhance communication skills
• provide a model to help students shape their own questions
• encourage reasoning

Each type of question has its place. By asking open-ended questions, such as: *Why do you think trees in a forest might grow taller than those in an open field?* instead of *What is the definition of phototropism?*, you encourage your students to explore, reflect on observations, and question further. Questions such as *What did you observe that leads you to believe that?* require students to reflect and provide evidence to support their inferences and conclusions. Students' answers and ideas can then become starting points for further reasoning and inquiry. Suggested teacher questions to students appear in *italics* in each activity.

"Wait time." Educational researchers recommend pausing, for a minimum of a few seconds, after asking a question. This "wait time" allows for reflective thought and seems significantly to increase the number of students responding and the quality of their responses. Rushing students' answers can conflict with the purpose of asking questions: to enhance communication, to stimulate unmotivated students, and to promote more complex thinking.

Facilitating class discussions. Class and small-group discussions help students process questions, make connections, and derive meaning from explorations. Establishing that all contributions are valid and important encourages open dialogue among the entire group. Because science is tentative, there are not always right and wrong answers. We can only be as right as our observations, past experience, and reasoning power allow. Encouraging students to explain what they saw or experienced that led to their claims helps them clarify their own ideas and provides a model for challenging others. It can also provide new material for investigations.

Fostering Healthy Attitudes

As your students learn concepts and practice science skills, they are gradually shaping their attitudes toward science and the natural world. These become more stable as experiences reinforce them. Although such change is long term and difficult to assess, it's important to be aware of the attitudes your science instruction promotes. The activities in this guide help support the development of the following attitudes:

Attitudes about the nature of science. By providing opportunities for planning investigations, peer review, reflecting on discrepant results, and collaborative group work, the activities promote the following goals:

• confidence in one's ability to "do science"

• appreciation for the value of cooperation in solving problems and respect for others' contributions

• enjoyment and enthusiasm for working with living and non-living materials

• regard for creative thinking as part of the scientific process

• appreciation of the need for flexibility and open-mindedness in the science process

• respect for science as dynamic and tentative — recognizing that new explorations continually yield new information, understanding, and questions

• regard for the role of skepticism; always raising new questions

• respect for the necessity for careful, systematic investigation

Attitudes about the environment. A significant goal of NGA's GrowLab Program is for students to develop an awareness of and sensitivity to the natural environment. Attitudes cultivated by GrowLab experiences include:

• curiosity about the natural world

• respect for nature's complexity, diversity, and consistency

• respect and appreciation for the environment

• concern about human impact on the environment

• appreciation of the need to consider long-term consequences of short-term actions

Student Grouping

Most GrowLab activities recommend small student groups. Small group efforts can address some of the logistical problems of individual hands-on explorations. Strategies such as assigning different group roles (data recorder, timekeeper, materials manager, etc.) or asking for a random reporter from each group will encourage full group participation.

Group collaboration can improve cooperative skills and communication skills. It also reflects the way scientists actually work, drawing from different perspectives to solve problems. Many teachers agree that when students work in groups, they

Three Heads Are Better Than One

When Alexander Fleming investigated an unexpected mold that was capable of killing bacteria, it was found to produce penicillin. Since he was a bacteriologist, Fleming was not able to go any further researching the properties of penicillin. It was not until ten years later that a biochemist, Ernst Chain, and a pathologist, Howard Florey, read Fleming's report and became interested in his earlier work. With their combined skills, they were able to research the antibacterial role of penicillin. Without communication and collaboration, we might never have benefited from one of the greatest "discoveries" in the history of modern medicine.

tend to concentrate more on what they're doing than on other distractions. Students often challenge each other differently than teachers do, by insisting on clarity or comparing results.

Assessing Students' Learning

It takes more than a paper and pencil test to assess changes resulting from a hands-on, inquiry-based approach to science. You will need to employ a variety of assessment methods, including some that are more informal and qualitative.

Before initiating a GrowLab activity or unit, decide in which areas you'd like to assess student progress. These might include comprehension, creative thinking, behaviors, attitudes, or use of process skills. Make and keep available a simple self-designed checklist or file cards to document changes in student performance. Keep your system simple so you're not trying to document too many things or too many students at one time. You might systematically observe just a few students or one or two small groups during a given class period.

Use the "Making Connections" section of each activity to help students derive meaning from their explorations and to help you assess gains in content understanding, skill use, and attitudes. It will help you determine what students have gained beyond mere recall. Be sure to leave adequate time in your lesson plan for this important step.

Student portfolios can be a useful tool to assess gains over time. Portfolios might include students' documentation from their science experiences (e.g., journal entries, activity reports, graphs, visual aids used in oral presentations, illustrations). Your anecdotes, quotes, and records can also be incorporated.

Other assessment suggestions:

• Have students keep science journals or notebooks to record observations, report on investigations, and keep ongoing lists of questions, drawings, ideas, or feelings. Record-keeping sheets included in this guide should be integrated into the students' journals.

• Incorporate questioning that requires students to use such skills as observing, measuring, and finding patterns. Also employ "What would happen if..." questions, requiring students to apply their understanding to new situations. For example: *What do you think would happen if pollution blocked out half the light that plants received? Why?* Avoid relying on recall questions (such as definitions), which challenge memory more than higher-order thinking.

• Describe poorly-designed experiments, and ask students to find errors or to critique the setup.

• Develop class science "experience charts." Encourage broad participation before and after the investigation and note changes in students' responses.

• Using video- or audiotape, record students working together in order to assess changes in their cooperative behaviors.

OnGrowing Ideas

You may be wondering, "How can I hold my students' attention during the eight long weeks when plants are maturing??" See "OnGrowing Ideas," Appendix C, for interdisciplinary ideas that can be implemented while any plants are maturing in the GrowLab.

• Observe student role playing and peer teaching and then record your impressions of students' grasp of content, use of process skills, or behavior.

• Challenge students to answer a question by designing a fair test. Have them describe, draw, and label the setup they'd use, and explain how they would gather data.

• Use a science process skills checklist during explorations and group activities, or when checking notebooks. Have students use a similar checklist for self-assessment.

• Record your impressions of a peer review of an experimental setup. Note students' ability to reflect on their own process.

"Imagination is more important than knowledge. For knowledge is limited, whereas imagination embraces the entire world, stimulating progress, giving birth to evolution. It is, strictly speaking, a real factor in scientific research."

—Albert Einstein

Classroom and Materials Organization

Does the idea of thirty exuberant students, up to their elbows in potting soil in an eight-square-foot garden, make you nervous? This active approach to science, which may be new for you and your students, requires additional planning and structuring. You'll need to help students develop skills to handle materials properly, work both cooperatively and independently, and share a variety of responsibilities.

The following suggestions for organizing an indoor gardening effort have been made by teachers field-testing the GrowLab program.

GrowLab can be a lively centerpiece around which to weave activities from all subject areas. Taking measurements, gathering data, displaying data, describing observations, and communicating results are all key elements of science. Plants and gardens can also be a focus for studying nutrition, food systems, cultures, and histories of plants and foods. The "Branching Out" section of each activity includes suggestions for extending your Grow-Lab lessons in these subject areas as well as in the arts. "OnGrowing Ideas," Appendix C, offers a list of teacher-suggested activities that can be done while plants are maturing in the GrowLab.

Read 'Em and Reap!

The indoor garden can provide fruitful themes for a Whole Language approach. The teachers' resource section in Appendix E lists many children's fiction and nonfiction books that can be used to support a plant/gardening theme.

• Refer to *GrowLab: A Complete Guide to Gardening in the Classroom* for basic planting and plant care information. Locate supplementary resources, listed in the back of both that book and this one.

• Before initiating your indoor classroom garden, have students take home a letter that introduces the garden project and asks parents for donations of milk cartons, plastic soda bottles, plant markers, and other indoor gardening materials. Contact, or have students or volunteers contact, local garden supply businesses for donations of materials.

• Depending on the age or experience of students, prepare and/or distribute materials in advance, or when students are out of the room. Initially involve one or a few students in the materials setup. As students become familiar with the procedures, gradually involve more of them.

• Involve assistants such as parents, master gardeners, or older students with activities. Plan to spend time preliminary to the activity preparing your helpers. You may have to remind them to allow students to do the work themselves!

• Some teachers like to confine the mess to one area of the room, so that one group at a time can plant. Others transform the entire class into a planting area and do all work at once.

• Use cafeteria trays or cardboard boxes (e.g., shoeboxes) to transport materials to desks.

• With younger students, use the largest possible seeds suggested for a given activity.

• If students are working in small groups, each can select a "materials manager" to collect and return GrowLab planting and activity materials.

• Consider rotating plant care tasks. Assigning plant care tasks can stem the problem of too many caretakers (a big problem in classroom gardens can be overwatering), and can offer individual students the opportunity to take on new responsibilities.

• Allow one small group to work in the GrowLab while others are doing other tasks.

Planning a Yearly Calendar

How you incorporate the GrowLab activities throughout your year will depend on your own interests, your curriculum goals, and your students, as well as on your time and space limitations. Some activities can provide a theme for a long-term unit. Others can be done concurrently or sequentially as part of a larger framework. Some possible frameworks include:

• horticultural theme (salad garden, houseplant cuttings, etc.)
• conceptual theme (changes, cycles, adaptations, diversity, etc.)
• topical theme (seeds, roots, etc.)

The activity summary on page 22 lists activities, topics covered, grade ranges, process skills used, and the duration from start to completion. This should help you identify which activities are appropriate to your needs.

Sample Horticultural Themes

Many teachers choose to have a garden theme, which can become a springboard for science investigations and studies in other areas. The following descriptions highlight possibilities for horticultural theme projects.

Salad garden. Plant salad vegetables and flowers at staggered intervals to culminate in a salad feast. Encourage students to use "days to maturity" information on seed packets to calculate when to plant different ingredients. As the salad garden grows, explore such areas as germination and growth needs, life cycles, and histories of plants. Plants to include: tomatoes, lettuce, beans, radishes, nasturtiums, carrots, beet greens, sprouts, and cucumbers. Plan 12 weeks to complete harvest if using long-season crops such as tomatoes or peppers. An example of a 12-week salad garden unit for grades K-2 follows:

Salad Garden Unit   Grade K–2

Week 1
Review seed options
Choose plants for salad
Plant tomatoes and peppers

Week 2
Develop salad survey questions—
   Celebrating Salad
Plant carrots

Week 3
Conduct salad surveys and graph
   results—**Celebrating Salad**
Plant cucumbers and beans

Week 4
Salad nutrition chart—
   Celebrating Salad

Week 5
Groundwork and exploration—
   Lettuce Be Different

Week 6
Supermarket survey and ongoing
   observations—**Lettuce Be Different**

Week 7
Groundwork and exploration—
   Make Room for Raddy
Ongoing **Lettuce Be Different**
observations

Week 8
Groundwork and week 1 exploration—**Yo Seeds, Wake Up!**
Ongoing observations—
   Lettuce Be Different and **Make Room For Raddy**

Week 9
Exploration, week 2—**Yo Seeds, Wake Up!**
Ongoing observations—
   Lettuce Be Different and **Make Room for Raddy**

Week 10
Exploration, week 3—
   Yo Seeds, Wake Up!
Ongoing observations—
   Lettuce Be Different and **Make Room for Raddy**

Week 11
Class chart of findings. Act out how it
   might feel to be a sprouting seed—
   Yo Seeds, Wake Up!
Ongoing observations—
   Lettuce Be Different and **Make Room for Raddy**

Week 12
Make more sprouts for salad, based on
   Yo Seeds, Wake Up! findings
Estimate weight of each radish and
   weigh to verify
Write invitations to salad party
Salad Party!!

Color garden. Particularly appealing to the primary grades, a colorful garden integrates well with art projects, language arts exercises, and studies of diversity, flower adaptations, and wildflowers. Crops to include: marigolds, zinnias, coleus, petunias, lettuces, impatiens, and nasturtiums.

Herb garden. A garden of annual and perennial herbs can be a delightful sensory addition to your classroom. In addition to studying basic plant needs, growth, or adaptations, consider integrating activities on the following: cultural differences in herb use, culinary and medicinal uses for herbs, sensory communications, sorting and classifying smells and flavors, and explorations of leaf adaptations. Plants to include: basil, dill, parsley, thyme, oregano, and chives.

Ethnic/cultural food garden. Tie your GrowLab garden into a social studies unit about a different geographic region by planting some indigenous crops. Two such gardens that have been created in GrowLab classrooms are: crops of the South (peanuts, cotton, collards) and a Japanese garden (including Japanese greens).

"Garbage" garden. In support of the "Generation to Generation" chapter, this project allows students to explore how otherwise discarded plant parts can be propagated to produce new plants. Include potato pieces, avocado pits, carrot and beet tops, ginger root, orange seeds, kiwi seeds and other leftovers from students' home kitchen sinks or the school lunchroom.

Houseplant cuttings. Learning about asexual propagation of different types of houseplants might culminate in gifts to take home or a student-organized plant sale. Since most houseplants come from tropical habitats, this might be tied into studies of adaptations to specific habitats. In four-plus weeks, you can get good results with ivy, spider plants, wandering Jews, aloe, snake-plants, impatiens, and jade plants. One class grew cuttings to sell, calculated the financial projections, designed and produced fliers, enlisted community volunteers, and used the money raised to finance a class field trip.

Wildflowers/native plants. Growing native wildflowers from seed in the GrowLab can lead to explorations of basic plant needs, reproduction, and adaptations. It can be a springboard for students to consider our actions' effects on the diversity of species and the implications of endangered and extinct species. An exciting and meaningful class project can be to raise regionally appropriate wildflowers from seeds or plants and replant them in appropriate habitats in the community. Black-eyed Susans (*Rudbeckia hirta*) grow particularly well in the GrowLab and can grow outside in most parts of the country. Contact your local Cooperative Extension office for other ideas.

More Horticultural Theme Project Ideas

- a garden of weeds
- a plant families garden
- a wild-to-cultivated comparison garden
- a pizza topping garden
- a children's literature garden
- a bulb garden

- a historical garden
- an alphabet garden

Sample Conceptual Themes

Many teachers choose broader conceptual themes around which to weave GrowLab studies. GrowLab activities might be used to supplement an existing conceptual unit or, with suggested "Branching Out" activities, as the basis for an entire unit. Some examples:

Form and Function. In a unit on form and function students can explore plant structures and how they enable plants to meet their basic needs. **Why Root for Roots?**, for instance, examines how root structure contributes to roots' ability to take in necessary water. **Look Out for Leaves** and **Puzzled by Photosynthesis** enable students to examine how leaves are designed to function as food factories. **Petal Attraction** investigates how flowers are exquisitely adapted to attract pollinators necessary for reproduction. **What's in a Name?** can be used as a culminating activity, encouraging students to use their understanding of form and function to invent new plant names. An example of an 11-week form and function unit for grades 6–8, follows:

Form and Function Unit   Grades 6–8

Week 1 - Seeds

Plant grass—**Earthgrippers**; plant beans and marigolds—**Why Root for Roots?**
Observe, draw, describe and classify seeds; begin exploration—**Journey to the Center of a Seed**
Try germinating seeds with and without cotyledons

Week 2 - Roots

Complete observations of germinating beans
Transplant beans into soil for root experiments
Begin **Why Root for Roots?**

Week 3 - Roots

Introduce erosion
Design **Earthgrippers** experiment

Week 4 - Roots

Complete observations, graphs, charts and prepare class presentations—**Earthgrippers**
Presentations and critique of experimental design and findings
Plant Fast Plants seeds—**Plant Parenthood**

Week 5 - Stems and Leaves

Plan and conduct experiments to test inferences about plants' responses to broken stems—**What a Sy-Stem!**
Explore leaf adaptations—**Turning Over a New Leaf**

Week 6 - Leaves

Puzzled by Photosynthesis
Thin Fast Plants

Week 7 - Flowers

Flowers: Up Close

Week 8 - Pollen

Complete pollination observations
Compare and discuss results—**Plant Parenthood**

Week 9 - Reproduction without Pollen

Snips, Slips, and Growing Tips
Design experiments for growing plants asexually

Week 10 - Petals

Ongoing record keeping for plant cutting experiments
Petal Attraction

Week 11 - Fruits and Seeds

Modify **Fruit for Thought**
Fruit-tasting party
Go Seeds Go!

Cycles. A unit on cycles in nature can integrate the GrowLab in a number of ways. For example, a unit on plant life cycles might begin with seed and germination observations (e.g., **Journey to the Center of a Seed, Yo Seeds, Wake Up!** and/or **Diverseedy**), and continue with plant growth, including such activities as **Root Watch, What a Sy-Stem!**, and **Magic Beans and Giant Plants**. The activity **Plant Cycles** can set the stage for a primary group to study plant cycles. A cycles unit might culminate by focusing on the reproductive, flower, fruit, and seed production stages (e.g., **Flowers: Up Close** and **Fruit for Thought**). "OnGrowing Ideas," Appendix C, suggests activities that can be done concurrently with long-term life cycle explorations.

Nutrient cycles could be another focus. Activities exploring plants' ability to produce food (e.g., **Puzzled by Photosynthesis**) can be sequenced with those that look at decomposition, another aspect of the nutrient cycle. A classroom worm center, as described in **Getting Hooked on Worms**, could be supplemented by studies of decomposition as suggested in **FungusAmongUs**.

Adaptations. In the indoor garden, students can examine some adaptations that allow plants to survive in different environmental conditions. This could include an exploration of seed coats in **Seed Busters** or an examination of leaf adaptations in **Turning Over a New Leaf. To Weed or Not to Weed?** suggests that some plants are particularly well adapted to compete for resources with other plants. An exciting aspect of an adaptation unit would be the exploration of flowers' adaptations for reproduction, as suggested in **Petal Attraction**. The activity **Rainforest Stories** is an example of a long-term project requiring research and observation of plants that are adapted to live in a special type of environment.

Sample Topical Themes

You may choose to organize your GrowLab units around specific botanical topics. As with other types of units, the GrowLab activities used could be interspersed with a wide variety of extension activities across the disciplines.

Leaves. A unit on leaves might begin by examining leaf variation and structure, as suggested in **Look Out for Leaves**. The role of leaves in the process of photosynthesis is explored in **Puzzled by Photosynthesis. Turning Over a New Leaf** directs students' attention to a variety of special leaf adaptations that enable leaves to survive in different environments. **Rainforest Stories** encourages students to explore some of the aspects of leaves adapted to a specific type of habitat. **Plants 'R' Us** can spark interest in exploring human uses of plant leaves.

Soils. Although your plants may be growing in a soilless potting mix, soil can still be the focus of a unit. The indoor garden offers opportunities to explore this precious resource. The activities in "The Soil Connection" section of Chapter One can be supplemented with explorations about the root/soil relationship, as suggested in **Earthgrippers. Getting Hooked on Worms** and **FungusAmongUs** naturally complement a soils unit.

Seeds. Activities from a number of chapters could support a unit on seeds. Seed structure and germination needs are highlighted in **Journey to the Center of a Seed** and **Yo Seeds, Wake Up!** **Plant Parenthood** launches an exploration to confirm that seeds are produced only after flowers have been pollinated. Seeds have unique adaptations for dispersing to new locations, as students will discover in **Go Seeds Go!**. **Seed Busters** examines the ability of seeds to survive a range of natural forces. Consider extending a seeds unit by researching and growing some unusual seeds that play important roles in our lives. **Plants 'R' Us** suggests long-term projects with such seeds as rice, wheat, and peanuts. An example of an 11-week seeds unit for grades 3–5, follows:

Seeds Unit Grades 3–5

Week 1
Sort and classify seeds; observe
    germinating beans—
Journey to the Center of a Seed

Week 2
Brainstorm what seeds need to
    sprout; begin moisture experi-
    ment on Monday—
Yo Seeds, Wake Up!
Complete observations and
    discussion—
Journey to the Center of a Seed
Ongoing **Yo Seeds, Wake Up!**
    record keeping

Week 3
Begin light experiment on Mon-
    day; ongoing observations and
    record keeping—
Yo Seeds, Wake Up!
Discuss human and plant cycles—
Plant Cycles
Plant Fast Plants on Friday (for
    use Week 6) and set up Fast
    Plants Growth Journals

Week 4
Begin **Yo Seeds, Wake Up!** tem-
    perature experiment on Monday
Ongoing **Yo Seeds, Wake Up!** and
    Fast Plants observations and
    record keeping
Discuss **Yo Seeds, Wake Up!** results
    using large class chart

Week 5
Start **The Eyes Have It**

Week 6
What makes a fruit a fruit?—**Fruit
    for Thought**
Count and compare seeds inside
    different fruits—**Fruit for Thought**
Voidroid mystery—
Plant Parenthood
Fast Plants Growth Journals

Week 7
Begin Fast Plants pollination experi-
    ment on Monday—
Plant Parenthood
Ongoing Fast Plants Growth Journal
    "Branching Out" activities (make
    fruit prints, build "fabricated fruit,"
    have a fruit-tasting party)—
Fruit for Thought

Week 8
Fast Plants Growth Journals

Week 9
Brainstorm natural forces that could
    prevent seed germination and select
    seeds to simulate—**Seed Busters**

Week 10
Seed-collecting walk—**Go Seeds Go!**
Sort mechanisms for seed dispersal—
Go Seeds Go!
Discuss results—**Seed Busters**
Fast Plants Growth Journals

Week 11: Seed Feast Week!
Invention challenge—**Go Seeds Go!**
Harvest Fast Plants seed pods and
    graph results
Write seed poetry and prose
Eat seed snacks

Key Concepts:

- Plants have basic requirements for growth and survival including water, nutrients, and light.
- Plant health is affected by the quantity and quality of resources.
- Plants have structures, processes, and responses that help them meet their basic needs.
- Plants produce their own food.
- Soil helps most plants meet their basic needs.

Science Process Skills

Approximate grade ranges K–2 / 3–5 / 6–8	page	Activities	observing	raising questions	predicting/hypothesizing	finding patterns/relationships	designing/conducting investigations	inferring	communicating
Beginning with Seeds									
K–2, 3–5	30	Title: **Journey to the Center of a Seed*** Topic: Seed structure Duration: 1 week	•	•	•	•			•
K–2, 3–5	34	Title: **Yo Seeds, Wake Up!*** Topic: Germination requirements Duration: 2+ weeks	•	•	•	•	•	•	•
Basic Needs									
3–5, 6–8	41	Title: **Magic Beans and Giant Plants**** Topic: Plant growth needs Duration: 4 weeks	•	•	•	•	•	•	•
3–5, 6–8	45	Title: **Make Room for Raddy**** Topic: Overcrowding/Limited resources Duration: 5+ weeks	•	•	•	•	•	•	•
3–5, 6–8	48	Title: **Enough is Enough**** Topic: Excess of basic necessities Duration: 4 weeks	•	•	•	•	•	•	•
Transport and Support									
K–2	56	Title: **Root Watch*** Topic: Root structure and growth Duration: 2-3 weeks	•			•			•
3–5, 6–8	59	Title: **Why Root for Roots?**** Topic: Roots' role in water intake Duration: 4 weeks	•	•	•	•	•	•	•
K–2, 3–5, 6–8	63	Title: **Root Loops*** Topic: Geotropism Duration: 1 week	•		•		•	•	•

** = requires GrowLab use
* = does not require GrowLab use

Chapter 1, continued

Approximate grade ranges			page	Activities	observing	raising questions	predicting/hypothesizing	finding patterns/relationships	designing/conducting investigations	inferring	communicating
K–2	3–5	6–8									
	3–5	6–8	67	Title: **Earthgrippers**** Topic: Roots and soil erosion Duration: 2 weeks	•	•	•	•	•	•	•
K–2	3–5		70	Title: **What a Sy-Stem!***** Topic: Stem functions Duration: 2 days	•		•			•	•
Plants as Food Makers											
K–2	3–5		78	Title: **Look Out for Leaves***** Topic: Leaf structure Duration: 1 day	•			•		•	•
	3–5	6–8	81	Title: **Puzzled by Photosynthesis**** Topic: Photosynthesis/Food production Duration: 4 days	•	•	•	•	•	•	•
K–2	3–5	6–8	87	Title: **A-Maze-in Light***** Topic: Phototropism Duration: 2 weeks	•	•	•	•		•	•
	3–5	6–8	93	Title: **Lighten Up**** Topic: Plants and light Duration: variable	•	•		•		•	•
Wrap-up Activity											
	3–5	6–8	97	Title: **What's in a Name?***** Topic: Plant part structure and function Duration: 1-2 days	•			•			•
The Soil Connection											
K–2			104	Title: **A Soil-a-Bration!***** Topic: Soil exploration Duration: 2 weeks	•	•	•		•	•	•
	3–5	6–8	107	Title: **Soil Sort***** Topic: Soil components/properties Duration: 2-3 days	•	•	•	•	•	•	•
	3–5	6–8	112	Title: **MockSoil***** Topic: Soil formation/properties Duration: 2 days	•	•	•			•	•

** = requires GrowLab use
* = does not require GrowLab use

Chapter 2 - Generation to Generation

Key Concepts:
- Plants change throughout their life cycles.
- Plants can reproduce from seeds (sexually) or from parts (asexually).
- Plants have a variety of adaptations to facilitate reproduction.
- Pollination is essential for plants to produce seeds.
- Humans take advantage of plants' many methods of reproduction.

Approximate grade ranges	page	Activities	observing	raising questions	predicting/hypothesizing	finding patterns/relationships	designing/conducting investigations	inferring	communicating
Plants from Seeds									
K–2, 3–5	123	Title: **Plant Cycles**** Topic: Life cycles Duration: variable	●						●
3–5, 6–8	125	Title: **Flowers: Up Close*** Topic: Flower structure Duration: 1-2 days	●			●		●	●
3–5, 6–8	128	Title: **Petal Attraction*** Topic: Flower function Duration: 2 days	●						●
3–5, 6–8	132	Title: **Plant Parenthood**** Topic: Pollination/Seed production Duration: 5 weeks	●	●	●	●	●	●	●
K–2	136	Title: **Fruit for Thought*** Topic: Fruit structure/function Duration: 2 days	●			●		●	●
Plants from Parts									
K–2, 3–5	141	Title: **Plantenstein**** Topic: Propagation from plant parts Duration: 2 weeks	●	●	●		●	●	●
3–5, 6–8	144	Title: **Slips, Snips, and Growing Tips**** Topic: Propagation investigations Duration: 2-3 weeks	●	●	●	●	●	●	●
3–5, 6–8	148	Title: **The Eyes Have It**** Topic: Sexual vs. asexual reproduction Duration: 2-3 weeks	●	●	●			●	●

Science Process Skills

** = requires GrowLab use
* = does not require GrowLab use

Chapter 3 - Diversity of Life

Key Concepts:
- Variations exist among the offspring of a species.
- Plants have adaptations enabling them to survive in many different environmental conditions and habitats; this has resulted in the great diversity of life.
- Humans develop systems to make sense of diversity.
- Humans take advantage of naturally occurring plant variations and manipulate plant genetics to meet our needs and preferences.
- Human actions can negatively affect the diversity of life on Earth.

Science Process Skills

Approximate grade ranges (K–2, 3–5, 6–8)	page	Activities	observing	raising questions	predicting/hypothesizing	finding patterns/relationships	designing/conducting investigations	inferring	communicating
Diversity									
K–2, 3–5	157	Title: **Plant Private Eyes*** Topic: Plant variation observations Duration: 1-2 days	•			•			•
K–2, 3–5	160	Title: **Diverseedy**** Topic: Diversity among seeds Duration: 3 weeks	•	•	•	•	•		•
K–2, 3–5	163	Title: **Lettuce Be Different**** Topic: Diversity within species Duration: 4 weeks	•	•					•
3–5, 6–8	166	Title: **Mystery Family Ties**** Topic: Plant family classification Duration: 8-10 weeks	•		•	•			•
3–5, 6–8	169	Title: **Order in the Class*** Topic: Classification systems Duration: 2 days	•	•		•			•
6–8	173	Title: **Designer Crops**** Topic: Plant breeding Duration: 6-8 weeks	•	•	•				•
3–5, 6–8	183	Title: **Rainforest Stories**** Topic: Rainforest simulation Duration: variable	•	•	•			•	•
Adaptations									
3–5, 6–8	191	Title: **Go Seeds Go!*** Topic: Seed dispersal adaptations Duration: 2 days	•	•			•		•
3–5, 6–8	194	Title: **Seed Busters*** Topic: Seed coat adaptations Duration: 1-2 weeks	•	•	•	•	•	•	•
K–2, 3–5, 6–8	197	Title: **To Weed or Not to Weed?**** Topic: Adaptations for competition Duration: 2-3 weeks	•	•	•	•	•	•	•
K–2, 3–5, 6–8	201	Title: **Turning Over a New Leaf*** Topic: Leaf adaptations Duration: 2-3 days	•	•	•	•	•	•	•

** = requires GrowLab use
* = does not require GrowLab use

Chapter 4 - Sharing the Global Garden

Key Concepts:
- All living and non-living things are interdependent; a change in one element affects all.
- The recycling of all nutrients on earth depends largely on decomposers.
- People depend on plants to meet many of our basic needs.
- Human activities have an impact on all other parts of the ecosystem; there are long-term environmental consequences of our actions.

Science Process Skills

Approximate grade ranges			page	Activities	observing	raising questions	predicting/hypothesizing	finding patterns/relationships	designing/conducting investigations	inferring	communicating
K–2	3–5	6–8									
Interdependence											
●	●	●	210	Title: **FungusAmongUs*** Topic: Decomposition Duration: 3-4 weeks	●	●	●	●	●	●	●
●	●	●	214	Title: **Getting Hooked on Worms*** Topic: Worms, soil, and plants Duration: variable	●	●	●	●	●	●	●
	●	●	224	Title: **Aphid Pets*** Topic: Insects and plants Duration: variable	●	●	●	●	●	●	●
●	●		227	Title: **Celebrating Salad*** Topic: Human nutrition Duration: variable	●	●		●			●
	●	●	232	Title: **Plants 'R' Us**** Topic: Human uses of plants Duration: variable	●	●					●
Human Impact											
●	●		240	Title: **Grass Blast*** Topic: Human impact on plants Duration: 3 weeks	●	●	●	●	●	●	●
	●	●	243	Title: **Pollution Solutions**** Topic: Plant sensitivity to pollutants Duration: 2-3 weeks	●	●	●	●	●	●	●
	●	●	251	Title: **PlantAcid**** Topic: Plants and pH/Acid rain Duration: 3-4 weeks	●	●	●	●	●	●	●
	●	●	258	Title: **Global ReLeaf**** Topic: Tree planting/Global warming Duration: variable	●					●	●

** = requires GrowLab use
* = does not require GrowLab use

Chapter 1   Plants Alive!

What enables a tiny seed to sprout and grow into a bean plant, a marigold, or an oak tree? This chapter invites you and your students to witness the miracle of life.

All living organisms are designed to be able to meet their basic needs for life. We have specific structures (such as lungs, hearts, and noses), systems (such as the circulatory and nervous systems), and responses to our environment (such as raiding the refrigerator!) that help us obtain what we need to thrive and grow.

Plants too have structures, systems, and responses that enable them to survive and thrive. Roots, for instance, give support and take in water and dissolved nutrients necessary for life. Leaves are factories where green plants turn the sun's energy into food. A plant's response to gravity, in which shoots grow up and roots grow down, ensures that leaves receive light necessary for photosynthesis while roots get needed water and nutrients.

The activities in this chapter encourage you and your students to explore the development of a living, growing plant, beginning with a seed. Discover some of plants' basic growth needs, and investigate how different conditions affect plant health and growth. Examine how different plant structures (roots, stems, leaves) and responses help plants meet their needs. Explore some of the factors contributing to green plants' unique ability to make food. Finally, investigate the vital role of soil in enabling plants to meet their needs for support, nutrients, and water.

Beginning with Seeds

Y ou can hold 100 radishes in one hand, 1,000 carrots in the other, and a meadow in your front pocket - for within every seed lives a tiny plant or **embryo**, complete with leaf, stem, and root parts.

The **seed coat** protects the embryo while a temporary food supply nourishes it, either as an **endosperm** packed around the young plant or stored in special leaves called **cotyledons** (see illustration). Most seeds are either **monocots**, having one cotyledon, or **dicots**, with two. Seeds remain inactive until conditions are right for them to begin to grow, or **germinate.**

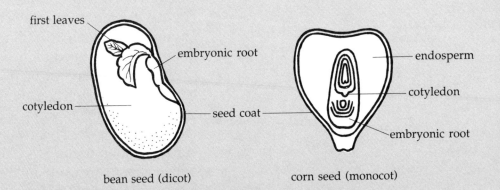

first leaves

embryonic root

cotyledon

seed coat

bean seed (dicot)

endosperm

cotyledon

embryonic root

corn seed (monocot)

All seeds require **oxygen, water,** and the proper **temperature range** in order to germinate. Oxygen and moisture, initially taken in through the seed coat and later by the root, help the seed get energy from its food supply. Different types of seeds have specific temperature requirements and/or preferences for germination. Some require warmer temperatures (70 to 75 degrees F is ideal for tomatoes), while others germinate better in cool temperatures (45 to 65 degrees F is ideal for lettuce).

Many seeds also require proper light conditions to germinate. Some require light to germinate and others are inhibited from germinating by light.

Seeds have their own source of nutrients (in the cotyledons

or endosperm) to sustain them through early life, so they do not require additional nutrients. The proteins, fats, and carbohydrates stored for the benefit of the young plant are what make seeds such a rich and vital food source for humans and other animals.

When a seed is exposed to proper conditions for germination, water is taken in through the seed coat. The embryo's cells begin to enlarge and the seed coat breaks open. The root emerges first, followed by the shoot, which contains the stem and leaves.

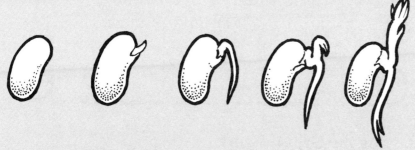

Our treatment of seeds during germination affects their chances of survival. If seeds (particularly small ones) are planted too deeply, the young plants can use up their food reserves before they ever reach light and begin to make their own food. If planted in soil that's too dry, seeds may not obtain the necessary moisture to germinate. Soaking-wet soil, on the other hand, may prevent seeds from getting oxygen, or may cause them to rot.

Your indoor garden provides an opportunity to consider different aspects of seed needs. The activity **Journey to the Center of a Seed** encourages exploration of seeds and an understanding that they are indeed living things, capable of growth. **Yo Seeds, Wake Up!** then examines what seeds require to begin to grow.

Special Seed Needs

Because some seeds have very hard seed coats, they will germinate more quickly after being soaked or scarred to allow water to penetrate. This adaptation helps prevent them from germinating until there's adequate moisture for survival. The seeds of many desert plants, for example, will grow only after exposure to large amounts of water.

Other seeds, like those of apples, require a period of chilling before they will germinate. This adaptation prevents some temperate-climate seeds from sprouting immediately after they drop from the plant in autumn and facing the winter as fragile seedlings. Activities in later chapters invite students to look more closely at some of the special adaptations that prevent seeds from germinating until conditions are right for their survival.

Overview: Students observe, sort, and classify a variety of seeds according to different properties, and then take a journey inside a bean seed to predict and observe changes that occur during seed germination.

Time:
Groundwork: 30 to 45 minutes
Exploration: 5 to 8 days, 10 to 15
  minutes per day
Making Connections: ongoing

Materials (per group):
• assorted seeds (see Advance Preparation and Laying the Groundwork)
• lima beans (one per student)
• cup of water
• hand lens
• glue
• toothpicks
• plastic bag
• paper towel
• "Bingo Seedso" reproducible, page 264 (optional)

Background: Page 28

Advance Preparation:
Prior to the activity, obtain a mixture of seeds of different colors, textures, and sizes. Large seeds like beans, corn, peas, and squash are easiest for young students to handle. Try to locate some fuzzy or fluffy seeds (tomato, dandelion, milkweed). Old seeds from outdated seed packets are ideal for the Groundwork activities. Old film canisters or small envelopes can be used to store seed mixtures for individual groups.

Journey to the Center of a Seed

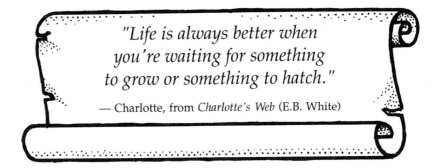

"Life is always better when you're waiting for something to grow or something to hatch."

— Charlotte, from *Charlotte's Web* (E.B. White)

Laying the Groundwork

Objective: To sort and classify seeds by external characteristics.

1. Give each pair or small group of students ten to fifteen assorted seeds. Ask each group to discuss how their seeds are alike and how they're different, and then to sort seeds into groups according to the way they look. Give some examples for grouping, such as: rough and smooth; dark colored and light colored; large and small.

As a class, discuss the different properties that the students used to sort the seeds. Put up a class chart with the headings: "Size," "Shape," "Color," and "Texture" (and any other properties, such as smell, that might have been suggested). Ask the class under which category each of their descriptive words belongs.

Size	Shape	Color	Texture
huge	oval	brownish	rough
tiny	round	tan	fuzzy
big	bumpy	spotted	smooth
	long	red	bumpy

2. Continue focusing on seed observations by conducting one or all of the following activities:

• Invite small groups to play "I'm thinking of..." with their pile of seeds. One student thinks of and describes a particular seed to the other students, who must carefully observe and guess which seed is being described. Or, have the audience ask "yes" or "no" questions about the description of each seed.

• Play Bingo Seedso, using the reproducible "Bingo Seedso" card or creating one from the descriptive seed word list generated by students. Give each pair a "Bingo Seedso" card, a new mixture of seeds, a hand lens, a cup of water (to float seeds), glue, and a toothpick to apply it.

Challenge each pair to fill its card by gluing a seed onto the matching description in each box. For non-readers, you can use the blank Bingo Seedso card and be the Bingo "master" by saying, for instance, "Find your fuzziest seed and put it...."

Every pair that fills its card is a winner at Bingo Seedso!

• Play a seed Memory Game. Have pairs of students carefully observe a mixture of seeds. Then have one student remove and hide just one of the seeds from the group. The other must describe the missing seed.

3. When the above activities are complete ask: *How do you think these seeds with different outsides look inside? What do you think you might find inside a seed? What have you ever observed to make you say that?* Give students each a lima bean seed. Ask them to draw a picture of what they predict it looks like inside.

Exploration

Objective: To discover what's inside a seed, to predict how seeds will change after sprouting, and to observe the sprouting (germination) process.

1. Give each pair of students two lima bean seeds (from Step 3 above), 1/2 cup of water, and a hand lens. Have them place their seeds in water for twenty-four hours and examine them regularly. Be sure to start some extra seeds, in case some don't germinate. Ask: *What do you predict will happen to the seeds while they are soaking?*

2. After twenty-four hours, ask: *How did your seeds change while they soaked in water? Did this match your prediction? What do you think was happening inside the seed?* Have students in each pair help one another carefully peel the outer coat from one of the seeds. Then guide them or help them to pull the coatless seed in half with a fingernail.

3. On the same drawing students made in Step 3 of Laying the Groundwork, ask students to draw a picture of the inside of one of the split seeds. Ask: *How does what you see inside the seed compare to your original prediction? Does any part of the inside of the seed look like a familiar plant part? Which? Do you think a seed is alive? Why or why not?*

4. Have students leave their seeds in a moist plastic bag, as illustrated on the next page, for a week. Ask: *What do you predict will happen to the seeds during the week?*

What's Alive?

If gum is dropped on the ground, will it grow into a gum-drop tree? To help your students distinguish between living and non-living things, pass around various small objects such as pebbles, marbles, coins, jelly beans, and seeds. Ask students which things they think are alive. *What makes something alive? How do you know if an object is alive or not?* Have students plant the different objects and see if they grow. Discuss whether growth is the only way to tell if something is alive or not.

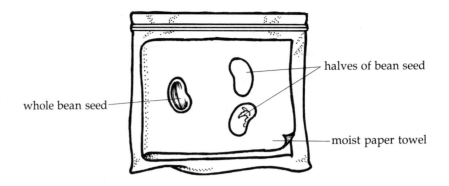

whole bean seed

halves of bean seed

moist paper towel

Fast Food

Explain to students that seeds contain starch and other nutrients. These get the young plant off to a good start and sustain it until it has true leaves and can make its own food. You can test cotyledons for starch using iodine (see page 84), after soaking them for twenty-four hours. Another investigation could include removing different parts (one or both cotyledons) of the seed or emerging plant to see how this affects plant growth. When both cotyledons are removed from a seed or young plant, the plant will lack adequate nutrients to continue growing properly.

5. At the end of the week, discuss findings. Ask: *How did different parts of the seeds change during the week? What happened first? Next? Did everyone's seeds change at the same speed? In the same order?*

6. Continue observing the seeds daily for a week. Students should record changes by making new drawings next to their originals. Consider having students make a growth chart to record changes during germination, by folding a long strip of paper like an accordion and clipping it with a paper clip. Draw on one section at a time as the seed grows. When complete, unfold to view the sequence.

 Just budding in: If you germinate one bean seed every day for the next seven days, you'll end up with all stages of germination at one glance!

Making Connections

Possible discussion questions:

• *Which different parts of the seeds turned into what you predicted? Did any surprise you? Which?*

• *Do you think seeds are living or non-living? What did you observe to make you believe that?*

• *After exploring seeds inside and out, why do you think seed coats are so hard?*

• *What new questions do you have about your seeds?*

Branching Out

• Plant your seeds and continue to observe and measure growth with Unifix Cubes or paper strips.

• Have students secretly line up assorted seeds in certain sequences (smallest to largest) or patterns (rough-smooth-rough). Challenge other students to guess the sequence or pattern.

• Investigate the power of a growing seed. Fill a plastic container (e.g., yogurt) with pea or bean seeds and add water. Seal the container and watch what happens once the seeds have expanded overnight.

• Find out about monocots (e.g., corn and other grasses) and dicots (e.g., bean, pea, tomato). Compare the insides of these seeds and observe differences in early growth.

• Design and construct a chamber, using recycled materials, to view seed growth.

• Generate a list of seeds eaten by humans. Consider those that are eaten whole (rice, peanuts) and those that are processed so they don't resemble seeds (flour).

• Make a list of questions you would ask a young plant as it grows from a seed.

• Act out the process of seeds growing.

• Create seed dolls by rolling up seeds such as grass seed in moist paper towels. Cut out holes for arms and legs. Seeds will sprout from these holes and from the top.

Who Eats Grass Seed for Breakfast?

Do any of you eat grass seed for breakfast? Of course, you or I don't eat grass seed ... or do we? Ask students to bring in empty boxes of their favorite breakfast cereals. Have them look for ingredients that might have originated with seeds. Share that some of our most important crops come from the seeds of grasses.

Such seeds are rich in nutrients since they must help the young plant through its early stages of growth. Many breakfast cereals contain wheat, rye, oats, corn, and barley, all produced from the seed of different types of grasses. If possible, have some seeds of these crops available for observations. Consider planting some of them to allow students to observe the early development of these grasses.

Can anyone think of a flavoring that comes from a seed? How about vanilla or chocolate?

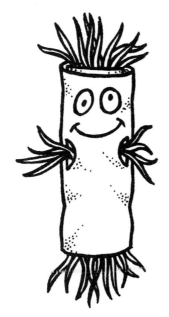

"seed doll"

Overview: Students examine ideas about what seeds need to sprout.

Time:
Groundwork: 30 minutes
Exploration: 40 minutes setup
(for each of 3 weeks);
ongoing observations
Making Connections: ongoing

Materials:
• seeds (suggested— beans, mung beans, sunflowers)
• plastic bags
• paper towels
• refrigerator
• "Yo Seeds, Wake Up!" reproducible, page 265

Background: Page 28

Advance Preparation:
If students are unfamiliar with seeds, conduct **Journey to the Center of a Seed** prior to this activity.

Yo Seeds, Wake Up!

Laying the Groundwork

Objective: To predict what factors will affect seeds' sprouting.

1. Pass some seeds around the classroom. Ask: *Do you think these seeds are alive? Why or why not? How could we find out if they're alive? If they are alive, or could be, what do you think will make them start to grow?* Explain that when seeds begin to grow, we call it "sprouting" or "germinating."

As a class, brainstorm a list of factors students think seeds need to sprout. List these on a class chart.

2. Read the story called "The Garden" in *Frog and Toad Together* (see Appendix E). After reading the story, add to the class chart Toad's ideas about how to "wake up" seeds. Discuss some of Toad's ideas. *Do you think yelling might wake seeds up? Were Toad's ideas the same as or different from yours?*

Exploration

Objective: To understand that certain factors affect seeds' sprouting.

1. Have the class test some of the ideas from the chart to find out what helps seeds sprout. Use large seeds such as beans or, if you want to have edible sprouts, try mung beans or sunflowers. (Alfalfa and radish seeds also make nice edible sprouts, but may be too small for young students to handle.)

Week 1 - Moisture

If water was one of the factors mentioned by students, ask: *Do you think seeds need to be moist or dry to sprout? What have you ever observed that makes you believe this?* List the headings "Moist" and "Dry" on the board, and have students suggest how we could try and sprout seeds in these different conditions (e.g., by using sponges, paper towels, or soil).

If none of the students' ideas resembles the setup below, suggest it as another option. As a class, choose several setups to test both moist and dry conditions.

Ask: *How will we decide when seeds have sprouted?* Tell students that they must decide together what constitutes "sprouting" in their experiments (e.g., when they first see the root or when it's 2 cm long).

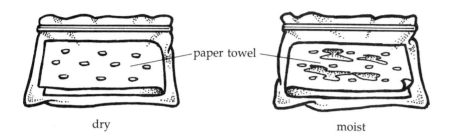

dry   moist

Using the "Yo Seeds, Wake Up!" reproducible, have students draw setups for both moist and dry conditions. Each day, students should fill in the total number of seeds that have sprouted to date.

At the end, have students chart on a bar graph the number of seeds that sprouted in each setup. Ask: *How did seeds seem to sprout best? How did you decide when they'd sprouted? Why do you think we tried sprouting seeds in different conditions? What factors, other than the amount of water, might have affected whether seeds sprouted* (e.g., some may have been in a warmer spot)?

What to expect: Within five days, most of the moist seeds should have sprouted, but not the dry seeds. If the students' setups included submerging the seeds in water, they may find that seeds fail to germinate when too wet.

Week 2 - Temperature

If students mentioned temperature as a factor to help seeds sprout, ask: *Do you think seeds might sprout better in warmer or cooler temperatures? What have you ever observed that makes you believe that? How do you think we should set up a test to see whether warm or cool conditions help seeds sprout?* List student suggestions for the setup under the headings "Warm Temperatures" and "Cool Temperatures."

Suggest the setup below as another option. As a class, use several of the suggested setups to test how temperature affects seed germination.

Ask: *From what we've already learned, do you think we should keep the seeds moist or dry for this experiment? If the cool-temperature seeds are in a dark refrigerator, where should we place the warm-temperature seeds?* Remind students that they must give both sets of seeds the same conditions, except for temperature, to have a fair test. Ask: *If we kept one set of seeds in cool, dark conditions and one in warm, light conditions, how would we know whether it was temperature or light that affected sprouting? The warm-temperature seeds, therefore, should also be in a dark place.*

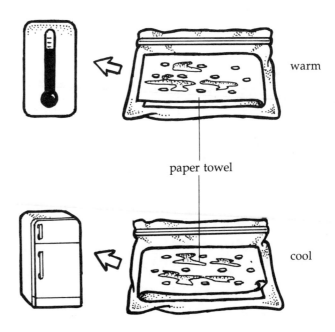

warm

paper towel

cool

Students can keep track of their investigations, as in Week 1, using the "Yo Seeds, Wake Up!" reproducible. Have students chart the number of seeds that sprouted after five days under both warm and cool conditions. Ask: *How did seeds seem to sprout best? What do you think would happen if we tried sprouting seeds in warm, dry conditions? In cool, moist conditions?*

What to expect: Within five days, you should find that seed sprouting is generally improved with moderate warmth and inhibited with cool temperatures. Temperatures at either extreme can inhibit sprouting. (See page 41 in *Grow-Lab: A Complete Guide to Gardening in the Classroom* for specific information on temperature and germination.)

Week 3 - Students' and/or Toad's Ideas!

Review the conditions suggested by the class and by Toad in Laying the Groundwork. Have the class vote on one condition, or have small groups each choose one condition to test. Set up investigations similar to Weeks 1 and 2 to determine what other conditions (e.g., light, yelling, fertilizing, singing) help seeds to sprout. Help students think about whether they're conducting fair tests.

2. When all experiments are complete, combine results on a class graph, as illustrated below. Ask: *What conditions seemed to be the best for sprouting seeds?*

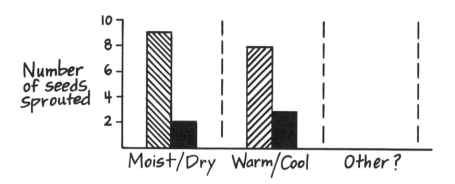

Making Connections

Possible discussion questions:

• *How did you decide when seeds had sprouted?*

• *Were you surprised by any of your findings? Which ones?*

• *If we knew that some seeds preferred warmth, could we assume that they preferred very hot temperatures? Why or why not? How could we find out?*

• *Would you plant bean seeds outside in early February? Why or why not?*

• *What other questions do you have about seed sprouting?*

Branching Out

• After reviewing findings, write a class recipe for making sprouts to eat. (See page 23 in *GrowLab: A Complete Guide to Gardening in the Classroom* for a sprout recipe.) Grow and taste different edible sprouts. Prepare different sprouted foods (e.g., salads, soups, "hairy" peanut butter sandwiches).

• Try removing parts of bean seeds to investigate which are not essential for germination.

• Try sprouting different types of seeds brought by kids from home and from the outdoors. (Some seeds will not germinate easily because they require a chilling period. See page 70 in *GrowLab: A Complete Guide to Gardening in the Classroom* for information on breaking seed dormancy.)

• For each investigation, figure out the fraction of the number of seeds that sprouted.

Seed Life Spans

Because they are living things, seeds require certain conditions in order to remain healthy. Generally cool, dry conditions (the opposite of what's needed for sprouting) are recommended for storing seeds. Even under good conditions, however, some types of seeds remain alive or "viable" for only a certain period of time. Others have been found to be viable for hundreds of years!

If you have old seed packets, students can determine what percentage of the seeds are viable and likely to sprout and grow. Gardeners frequently do this to determine whether or not to bother planting seeds from a particular packet. Do this by placing ten seeds from a packet on a moist paper towel, rolling it up, and sealing it in a plastic bag. After seven to ten days, open the towel and count the number of germinated seeds. Students can then calculate the germination percentage.

• Explore the effects of extreme conditions (boiling, freezing, etc.) on seed germination.

• Play Seedling Tic-Tac-Toe. Divide flat containers into nine squares. Plant one type of seed in each square. The first student to have three germinated seeds in a row wins.

• Plant seeds in a pot in the shape of students' initials. Watch initials come to life as the seeds germinate.

• Design experiments based on student-generated questions starting with: "I wonder what will happen to a seed if...."

• Describe, in drawings or words, how it might feel to be a sprouting seed.

Basic Needs

L ike all living things, green plants have basic needs. If light, water, air, nutrients, and an adequate temperature range are not available, plants cannot thrive and grow.

Light energy is required for **photosynthesis**, in which plants make sugars in the leaves. Light also triggers changes, particularly flowering, in certain plants.

Water is necessary to carry dissolved nutrients into the plant through the roots. It is one of the key ingredients in the process of photosynthesis, and helps the plant release energy from stored food when needed. Water pressure in plant cells, which are 65 to 95 percent water, supports stems and leaves. Water transports nutrients and gases into, around, and out of the plant. It is an important component in the cells of all living things.

Plants require two of the components of **air**. They use **carbon dioxide** to make food (photosynthesis), and they use **oxygen** —as do humans and other animals—to release the energy from that food (respiration).

Plants require **mineral nutrients** for growth, repair, and proper functioning. Mineral nutrients are formed by the breakdown of rocks and other materials in the earth. While humans obtain these minerals from plants, animals, or in the form of supplements, plants take these minerals from the soil (dissolved in water) or through fertilizers applied by humans. Although these minerals are important supplements for health and maintenance, they cannot replace the sugars produced in the leaves, which can also be stored as carbohydrates, fats, and proteins. Pages 48 to 50 in *GrowLab: A Complete Guide to Gardening in the Classroom* have more information on the role of specific mineral nutrients in plants.

Basic Needs Explorations

The activities in this section encourage students to investigate how variations in necessary resources can affect plants. The activity **Magic Beans and Giant Plants** provides an open-ended challenge to investigate how specific conditions affect plant growth. In **Make Room for Raddy** students recognize that over-crowding causes competition for limited resources and limits the ability of individual plants to meet basic needs.

Too much of a good thing can be as harmful as too little. An excess of fertilizer, for instance, can cause plant cells to grow too quickly, resulting in weak or dead plants. Too much water can prevent necessary oxygen from reaching roots. The activity **Enough is Enough** challenges students to investigate how an excess of a needed resource will affect plants.

Magic Beans and Giant Plants

Overview: After predicting what, other than magic, caused Jack's beanstalk to grow so tall, students design and conduct experiments to explore how different conditions affect plant growth.

This open-ended investigation of conditions for plant growth assumes some student knowledge of basic plant needs (light, water, etc.). It can be a springboard for more in-depth investigations of these factors.

Time:
Groundwork: 40 minutes
Exploration: 30 to 60 minutes setup;
  4-plus weeks of observations

Materials:
• beans (pole beans such as limas or scarlet runners are best)
• *Jack and the Beanstalk* (optional)
• potting mix
• 4- or 6-inch pots
• "Problem Solving for Growing Minds" reproducible, page 283
• "Observation Journal" reproducible, page 286

Background: Page 39

Laying The Groundwork

Objective: To consider which specific conditions might affect plant growth.

1. Tell your students a version of *Jack and the Beanstalk*. Hand out some "magic" beans (see materials) and ask: *What do you think is the secret to growing tall bean plants?*

2. Explain that although magic *may* have influenced the growth of Jack's plants, scientists do know that other important factors contribute to plant growth.

As a class, generate a list of general factors (light, temperature, water, etc.) that students think green plants need to stay alive. Label it "All Green Plants Need." Next to each factor, ask students to predict what specific conditions they think might result in the tallest bean plants. Be sure to accept all student suggestions whether or not you think they're correct. For example:

All green plants need	Predictions: Conditions for tallest bean plants
light	* Sunlight better than fluorescent light * 24 hours of light better than 14 hours
water	* cold water better than hot water * water every day better than once/week
soil	* sandy soil better than clay soil * real soil better than soilless mix
nutrients	* more fertilizer better than less
other	* rock music better than classical * magnetism better than none

3. Ask your students how they might explore which of these conditions would help grow the tallest bean plants.

Exploration

Objective: To design and conduct experiments using a problem-solving process. To understand that different types of conditions influence the health and growth of living things.

1. Challenge small groups of students to choose one of the predictions for growing the tallest bean plants generated in the Groundwork. To test predictions, have each group design an experiment, lasting up to four weeks. Use the Problem Solving for Growing Minds process, page 10, to help guide and later record investigations. A sample setup:

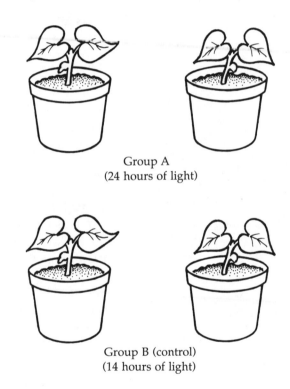

Group A
(24 hours of light)

Group B (control)
(14 hours of light)

2. Before groups set up experiments, have each present its design for review by the class. Have students explain why they predict their particular conditions will improve plant growth. For example, "We think twenty-four hours of light will make the beans grow taller in four weeks, because we know they need light to make food. So the more light, the more food, and the taller the plant."

3. Have each group decide how they'll gather their data. Suggest that at the end of each week students graph the daily growth rate of their plant and predict, based on the growth rate, how tall their plant will be by the end of the next week. On the graph, illustrate both predictions and actual growth rate results.

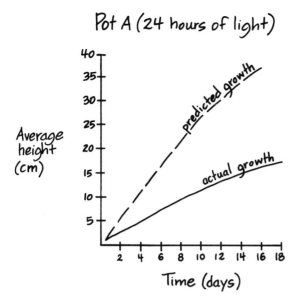

Pot A (24 hours of light)

Average height (cm) vs. Time (days), showing *predicted growth* and *actual growth* curves.

4. After four weeks of experimenting, have each group present a three-minute "news conference" to the class highlighting its findings. Suggest a title such as: "Grade ____ Scientists Find That _____ May Have Contributed to Jack's Mammoth Beanstalk." Have students use creative summary charts and graphs to present data. See "Create-a-Chart", page 287, for suggestions.

Encourage other class members to review the findings and ask questions about the nature of the experiment, conclusions, etc. For example: "Why did you plant X number of seeds in each pot? How did you treat each of your groups? What might you do differently if you were to repeat the experiment? How do you know it wasn't ____ that affected your plants?"

5. Combine results from different experiments on a class chart. Refer to the chart in discussing the questions in Making Connections, below.

	Group ___	Group ___	...
Question/Hypothesis			
Experimental findings			
Comments/New questions			

Making Connections

Possible discussion questions:

• *Were there growing conditions that the tallest plants seemed to have in common? What seemed to contribute most to the height of bean plants?*

• *Did any of your findings surprise you? Which ones?*

Although growing tall plants rapidly is an exciting focus, it's important to recognize that plant height does not necessarily reflect plant health. If lights are kept too high, for instance, or a plant is kept under warmer than optimal conditions, it may grow tall and spindly. A plant in this condition is actually less healthy than a shorter, stocky plant. Tall plants may have less leaf area and thus less food-making ability than smaller plants with more and/or larger leaves.

• *Did the tallest plants seem to be the healthiest plants? Explain your response. Do you think bigger is necessarily better? Why or why not? (See the sidebar, "Taller is Not Necessarily Better".)*

• *How did the data from the whole group help give us a better understanding of conditions for good bean plant growth?*

• *Do you think your findings about best conditions for growth can apply to all plants? Why or why not? Consider needs of a cactus, for example, compared with a lily pad.*

• *Although humans need food, are certain types or quantities better for our health and growth? How do you think this compares with plants?*

• *What other questions about conditions for plant growth do you have? Which could you set up an experiment to test?*

Branching Out

• Devise an experiment to grow the smallest bean plant that will produce flowers.

• Replant beans harvested from your stalks. (Wait to replant seeds until pods have dried, about four weeks after the beans are ripe.) Notice whether the seeds from the biggest plants produce bigger offspring.

• Create an instrument that will let a plant draw a record of its own growth.

• Calculate the average heights and total height of all plants used in the experiments.

• Prepare recipes using different types of beans.

• Rewrite or act out a new version of *Jack and the Beanstalk* using some of the new information gained from your exploration. Post these "techno-tales" around the room.

• Discuss how experiments like yours could contribute to addressing the world's food problems.

Make Room for Raddy

Overview: Students observe how plants—and people—respond when crowded and forced to share limited resources.

This activity will help students understand that even their precious garden plants must sometimes be thinned.

Time:
Groundwork: 40 minutes
Exploration: 30 minutes setup;
    5-plus weeks ongoing observations
Making Connections: ongoing

Materials:
• newsprint
• crayons
• masking tape
• raisins (optional)
• three 6-inch pots
• 30 radish seeds
• potting mix
• "Plant a Question" reproducible, page 282, or "Problem Solving for Growing Minds" reproducible, page 283
• "My Plant Journal" reproducible, page 285, or "Observation Journal" reproducible, page 286

Background: Page 39

Advance Preparation: Tape one or two 4-by-4-foot squares on the floor in the classroom (see Laying the Groundwork).

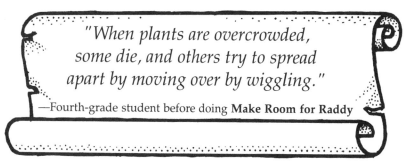

"When plants are overcrowded, some die, and others try to spread apart by moving over by wiggling."

—Fourth-grade student before doing **Make Room for Raddy**

Laying the Groundwork

Objective: To experience and reflect on the limitations of a crowded situation.

1. Divide your class into an even number of small groups, with a maximum of eight students per group. Ask each group to draw a mural showing plants growing in a garden. Give half of the groups the following resources:

• a long sheet of drawing paper
• enough crayons for each student
• a snack of raisins with plenty to go around (optional)
• a large area in which to draw
• five minutes time to complete the drawing

   Here is the twist—ask the remaining group(s) each to work in a 4-by-4-foot square taped on the floor, and give them a shortage of resources:

• one very small sheet of drawing paper
• a couple of small crayons
• a couple of raisins for snacking (optional)
• limited space
• three minutes time to complete the drawing

2. After the allotted time, ask members from each group to show and describe their drawings to the rest of the class. Ask each group: *How did you feel about your drawing experience? Did you have any problems? What were they? What do you think was different about the two groups' experiences?*

   Help the groups focus on the contrast between having limited resources and having plenty of resources. Ask: *Besides a lack of space, what else was in short supply? What might happen if you never got enough of what you needed? How do you think a lack of space might affect plants? Why?*

Exploration

Objective: To conduct an experiment to examine how radishes respond to crowding. To infer that overcrowding affects the ability of living things to meet basic needs.

1. As a class or in small groups, discuss how you might set up an investigation to test the effects of crowding on radish plants. Use the "Plant a Question" or "Problem Solving for Growing Minds" process, page 9 or 10, to guide the investigation. A sample setup follows.

Question: *What will happen if radishes are crowded in a pot?*

Pot A	Pot B	Pot C
3 seeds	6 seeds	18 seeds
(thinned to 1 seed)		

Just budding in: For good root development of radishes grown indoors, keep lights within 2 to 3 inches of the plants and have students pile more soil mix around the base of the plants as radishes grow.

2. Have students record predictions comparing the growth and appearance of radishes in the pots. As the experiment progresses, students should continue to record their observations in words and/or drawings on the "My Plant Journal" or "Observation Journal" reproducible. After four or five weeks, dig up radishes to compare and record root development.

What to expect: The crowded radishes may look stunted and pale from competing for necessary nutrients and water. Sometimes crowded plants will actually look taller ("leggier") as they compete for light. Radishes in a crowded situation, however, are less likely to develop the large food storage roots that we eat.

3. If different groups set up the experiment, make a class chart to compare observations. Review observations as a class. Ask: *What did you notice about the plants in each pot? Which pot seemed to have the healthiest plants? How did you decide if they were healthier? Which pot had the tallest plants? Did they look healthier? How did these compare to your predictions? What was the biggest difference between the radishes in the three pots?*

Making Connections

1. Use student findings to ask specific questions about the investigation. For instance, ask: *Why do you think...*

...the radishes were rounder in the less crowded pot?
...the leaves in the more crowded pot turned yellow?
...there wasn't much difference in the radishes in Pots A and B?

2. Possible discussion questions:

• *How was what happened in your "mural" challenge similar to what happened to the radishes in the crowded pot?*

• *Do you think you would have felt crowded if you had had enough paper and/or crayons?*

• *What are some other situations in which crowding can be a problem for people, animals, or plants?*

• *Would we have learned as much if we had planted only one pot of crowded radishes? Why or why not?*

• *What are some other ways we could set up an investigation to test the effects of crowding on plants?*

• *What do you think would happen if...*

...an entire pack of radish seeds were planted in one pot?
...we gave more water to the more crowded pot?
...carrots in a garden were not "thinned"? Consider introducing the concepts of thinning and/or transplanting. See pages 51 and 52 in *Growlab: A Complete Guide to Gardening in the Classroom* for information.

Branching Out

• Weigh your radish plants, without soil, to compute the average weight per pot.

• Plant the same number of seeds in different-sized pots.

• Try similar overcrowding experiments using other seeds such as grass. Examine how different plants respond to crowded conditions.

• Plant seeds in several pots. Place dividers between the seeds and give each section its own nutrients and water. Examine whether this can compensate for overcrowding.

• Develop a progressive story about an overcrowded situation involving people or plants. One student begins the story and passes it on for continuation to the next student, and so on.

• Write or tell stories and describe feelings based on students' own experiences with crowding or competition for resources.

Enough is Enough

Overview: Students conduct experiments to examine how excessive amounts of necessary resources affect plant growth.

Time:
Groundwork: 30 minutes
Exploration: 40 minutes setup; 4 weeks ongoing explorations
Making Connections: ongoing

Materials:
• fertilizer
• potting mix
• seeds (beans, marigolds, cucumbers, or radishes)
• 4- or 6-inch pots
• "Problem Solving for Growing Minds" reproducible, page 283
• "Observation Journal" reproducible, page 286

Background: Page 39

Laying the Groundwork

Objective: To consider how even healthy things, in excess, might be harmful to humans and plants.

1. Set the stage by asking students if they think one can have "too much of a good thing." Have small groups of students each generate a list of three things that are good for us in smaller doses, but harmful in larger amounts. To stimulate thinking, ask: *What do you think might happen if you breathed twice as much air, ate twelve meals a day, or played baseball for twelve hours?* Ask each group to share their ideas to be added to a class list.

2. As a class, consider how this concept might apply to plants. Make a list of things that are good for plants, but that students think might be harmful in excess.

Exploration

Objective: To conduct an investigation and recognize that excesses of certain necessary resources can be harmful.

1. As a class discuss which factors, generated in Step 2 of Laying the Groundwork, you'd like to test. Using the Problem Solving for Growing Minds process, page 10, decide how you'll set up a class investigation. Nutrients and water, given to plants in excess, will yield the most dramatic results in the GrowLab. The sample experiment described uses nutrients, in the form of fertilizer, as the experimental variable.

Question: *How will an excess of nutrients affect bean plants?*

Group A
No fertilizer

Group B (control)
Recommended dose of fertilizer

Group C
2x recommended dose

Group D
10x recommended dose

Just budding in: When doing this experiment, use whichever fertilizer you're already using in the GrowLab.
Although most fertilizer directions recommend a dose every two weeks, many classroom teachers find it easier to use the recommended amount every time they water. So, in this setup, the control group (B) would receive the recommended dosage, Group C, 2 x the recommended dosage, and Group D, 10 x the recommended dosage, every time the plants are watered.

2. As a class, brainstorm a list of observations you'll make and record on the "Observation Journal" reproducible - for example, average height of plants per pot, tallest plants per group, leaf color, number of leaves, and/or size of leaves.

Consider having students work in small groups, each taking responsibility for observing two factors. Remind groups they'll be responsible for collecting and presenting information to be used by other class members.

3. After four weeks, each group of record keepers should prepare and present their findings to the rest of the class. Encourage reporting that allows findings to be compared at a glance. See "Create-a-Chart," page 287, for suggestions. Display these results around the room. An example follows.

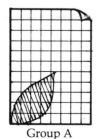
Group A

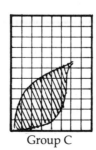
Group B

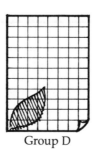
Group C

Group D

Average size of leaves

Don't Drown Me!

To teach younger students that too much of a good thing can be harmful, try an exploration using water. Since a big problem facing many classroom plants is overzealous waterers, this exploration will hopefully result in healthier GrowLab plants in the long run.

Engage students by asking them to consider their own water needs and how they've felt when they've had too much or too little to drink. Ask: *How would you feel if I gave you each a gallon of water and told you to drink it before you went home today, whether you were thirsty or not?*

Set up a simple experiment with three small plants (bean, cucumber, marigold, or tomato) as illustrated. Make daily observations for two weeks.

Pot A
1 T. water per week

Pot B
(control)
water as needed

Pot C
Leave pot in bowl of water

Discuss whether all plants need the same amount of water. Ask: *Have you observed some GrowLab plants that need more water than others? Can you name some types of plants that require very little water* (e.g., cactus)?

Too much water can be as harmful to plants as too little water. Overwatered plants may be yellow, stunted, and may die. Practice how to tell when plants need water, as described on page 47 of *GrowLab: A Complete Guide to Gardening in the Classroom.*

What to Expect: Plants receiving a shortage of nutrients, particularly nitrogen, tend to look pale, yellow, and/or stunted. An extreme excess of nutrients also has a number of observable effects, again primarily related to the excess of nitrogen. Too much nitrogen will result in a dark green leaf color and will promote unnaturally rapid, lush foliage growth at the expense of flower development. Because the plants grow so rapidly, they may appear leggy and develop thin, weak cell walls and stems. This encourages pest and disease problems (aphids love high nitrogen levels!). An extreme excess can kill the plant.

An excess of water is one of the most common causes of unhealthy plants in classroom gardens. Too much water can result in stunted, yellow plants, rotting roots, mold growth and, ultimately, the death of the plant.

Making Connections

1. As groups compare their data, ask:

• *How did an excess of this basic necessity seem to affect the plants?*

• *How did your results compare with your original predictions?*

• *What signs tell <u>you</u> when you're getting too much of a good thing?*

• *Has this activity given you ideas about how to be a better gardener? What are they?*

• *Human and animal wastes are high in nutrients, particularly nitrogen. Many people are concerned about runoff of human and farm animal wastes into streams and lakes. If your experiment focused on nutrients, what do you think might be the effect on the environment of these excess nutrients? (See "Dirty Waters" sidebar.)*

2. Have groups reflect on their experiment by making a list of all the things, other than the experimental factor, that might have affected their results (e.g., unequal watering or different distances from lights).

Branching Out

• Research and experiment with the effects of specific nutrient deficiencies. Use fertilizers with one major nutrient missing.

• Experiment by giving plants an excess of a different necessity (water, CO_2, fertilizer, light).

• Experiment to determine specifically how much fertilizer, beyond the recommended dose, will result in the death of bean plants.

• Research "organic" fertilizers and conduct experiments to compare them with synthetic fertilizers.

• Set up a series of jars containing pond water and different levels of fertilizers. Observe the differences in algae growth. Find out about eutrophication (see "Dirty Waters" sidebar).

• Given the recommended dose of fertilizer and your average rate of watering, calculate how much fertilizer you would need for a week, a month, and a year of indoor gardening.

• In small groups, create poems, songs, skits, or pictures expressing how you might feel if you experienced "too much of a good thing"—if you were set loose in a candy store, for example, or if you were a plant that had been overwatered. Or write about your own personal experiences of getting "too much."

Transport and Support

R oots and stems form a partnership, enabling most green plants to meet their basic needs for nutrients and water. This background section highlights the design and functions of these important structures.

Root Function

We might find thirteen million roots in 2 cubic feet of soil. Laid end to end, they could extend from where you sit to a town hundreds of miles away. (With a reach like that, it's no wonder weeding is so difficult!) Roots play a vital role in enabling plants to meet their basic needs, by providing support, anchoring the plant, and by absorbing necessary water and nutrients. Many roots are further specialized to store sugars and other carbohydrates that the plant can use to carry out other functions.

Root Structure

As a seed germinates, the first part to emerge is the primary root. It anchors the plant and begins to absorb water and minerals so the shoot can develop. From that point on, root development takes one of two directions, depending on the type of plant.

Some types of plants have a primary **tap root** with a few smaller, hairy branches. Reaching deep into the soil, these long, strong roots pull up nutrients and water from far below the surface. Dandelions are examples of tap roots. In some plants (e.g., carrots, sweet potatoes, beets, radishes, and turnips), tap roots expand in size and become storage sites for sugars and starches.

Other types of plants have a **fibrous root system**, a network of branching rootlets and root hairs appearing off the primary root. These networks can be extensive: a ryegrass plant, for instance, can have more than thirteen million branching roots, covered with billions of root hairs. Fibrous roots are thus particularly good at holding onto soil particles. Beans, tomatoes, and grasses are examples of fibrous root systems.

In both tap roots and fibrous root systems, tiny **root hairs** are the bridges between the root and the water and dissolved nutrients in the soil. These root hairs provide a huge surface area for absorbing water and nutrients. If these root hairs are broken or damaged, a plant will have difficulty meeting its water and nutrient needs. Some plant roots in the GrowLab (e.g., beans and cucumbers) are more fragile than others (e.g., tomatoes).

What a Reach!

One scientist measured a rye plant's roots and found them to total 387 miles in length. When he added the estimated length of root hairs, the total was 7,000 miles!

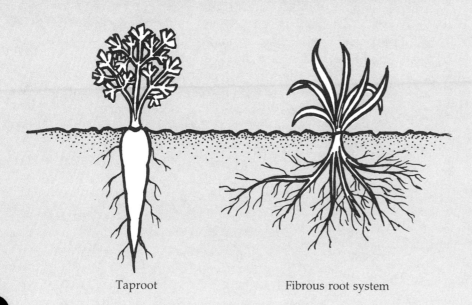

Taproot   Fibrous root system

The activity **Root Watch** has students examine and compare early roots from different types of plants. In the activity **Why Root for Roots?**, students investigate how roots take in water, focusing on the role of root hairs.

Roots in Motion

Roots must grow in an appropriate direction, normally downward, to meet the plant's nutrient and water needs. The force of gravity is the signal roots use to orient downward. Roots have a sophisticated gravity-sensing guidance system, as do stems and leaves. This results in the phenomenon called **geotropism** or **gravitropism**—root's ability to grow downward and shoots upward, regardless of their original position.

In the activity **Root Loops**, students explore this phenomenon as they try to influence the direction of root growth. A sidebar activity suggests investigating roots' tendency to grow toward water, called **hydrotropism**.

Although root hairs are quite fragile, **root tips** are protected by a cap of cells. Plant growth hormones called **auxins**, concentrated in root tips, cause these cells to divide and grow larger. Dead root cap cells are shed ahead of the root tip, making a pathway that allows the delicate root to work its way through the soil, around hard objects, and into tight places. As roots grow in size, they can exert a powerful force, capable of cracking concrete, pipes, and rocks.

Roots and Soil: A Partnership

As plant roots grow through cracks in rocks, breaking off tiny pieces of rock, they assist the long process of soil formation. Some roots even produce substances that help dissolve rocks. When living, roots aerate and loosen soil, and provide tunnels for burrowing insects and animals. When dead and decomposed, they contribute to the rich humus in the soil.

The billions of root hairs absorbing water and nutrients from the soil form a network with a tenacious hold on soil particles. This hold protects topsoil from **erosion** - the wearing away of soil by the action of ice, water, or wind. Water and soil can form a muddy soup that clogs the soil pores, allowing the water to run off and carry precious topsoil with it. While it might take nature 20,000 years to create an inch of topsoil, a good downpour on a bare slope can wash it away in a flash. In planted ground, however, roots not only absorb and recycle some of the water, but they also cling to the soil.

The activity **Earthgrippers** challenges students to look at the relationship between roots and soil erosion.

Roots We Use

Because roots store sugars and starches for plants, many are sweet and nutritious food sources for humans and other animals. Sweet potatoes, carrots, beets, turnips, and radishes are actually plant food storage roots. About two-fifths of the world's sugar comes from the roots of sugar beets. The root of the tropical plant cassava gives us the tapioca we use in desserts and is a food staple in many tropical countries. Root beer flavor comes from the bark of the roots of the sassafras tree. Some medicines (belladonna) and insecticides (rotenone) come from plant roots.

Stem Function

If a plant didn't have a transport system, all its parts would have to be close to the ground to have access to water and minerals in the soil. Plant stems, however, provide a vital link between plant leaves and roots, enabling all plant cells to be within reach of water and nutrients. Stems are conduits, through which water and minerals taken in by the roots can travel to the leaves, and food produced in the leaves can travel to other parts of the plant.

Above-ground stems also provide support to the plant, allowing leaves to reach the light necessary for food production. Below-ground stems typically serve as food storage sites.

Water and dissolved minerals actually move upward, against the force of gravity, through stems. This results from a combination of factors. Water moving into the roots pushes water upward into the stem. Water molecules **cohere** to one another, forcing the water column farther upward, and they **adhere** to the sides of the conducting stems. In addition, **transpiration**, evaporation of water through leaf openings, actually pulls the water column upward. In some plants, water can be pulled up stems as fast as 30 inches per minute!

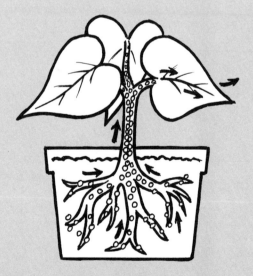

Water movement in plants

The activity **What a Sy-Stem!** highlights a simple exploration of the role of stems in transporting water.

Stem Structure

Stems come in a variety of shapes and sizes. Some are soft, like the stems of plants in your GrowLab (tomatoes, marigolds, beans, carrots, etc.). Larger, longer-lasting plants such as shrubs and trees generally have harder, woody stems. Although their structures vary somewhat, both soft and woody stems serve the same type of transport functions.

Not all stems grow high above the soil. Some plants, like dandelions, have very short stems. Others actually grow underground. A potato, for instance, is an underground stem that also stores food for the plant. Some plants, such as irises, have horizontal stems or **rhizomes**. These too are food storage organs.

Some structures that appear to be stems are actually leaf stalks or **petioles**, extensions of the leaf veins that attach the leaves to the stems. Rhubarb and celery are examples of leaf petioles that appear to be stems.

Stems in Motion

Like roots, stems respond to their environment to help the plant meets its needs. The most dramatic example is the way a plant responds to light by bending either toward or away from it, a phenomenon called **phototropism.** Like geotropism, this movement is triggered by concentration of **auxins.** As with roots, the higher the concentration of auxins, the faster the cells grow in that particular area. In most cases, where light hits a plant, the side of a stem away from light, it's believed, accumulates auxins. Cell growth on that side increases and the stem becomes longer, resulting in the plant stem bending toward the light. (See page 87 for an activity about phototropism.)

Cell growth increases on "dark" side

Auxins are also concentrated in the tip of the stem. When this growing point is cut (pinched off), the auxins, that had previously inhibited the lower branches, allow them to grow. We take advantage of this tendency in many plants (e.g. tomatoes) by pinching growing points to induce bushier growth.

How We Use Stems

Sugar in the stems of sugar cane provides much of the world's table sugar supply. One of the world's most important food crops, the white or Irish potato, is actually an underground stem. Maple syrup is produced by concentrating the dissolved sugar (sap) in the stems of maple trees. Linen and many types of rope are made from the materials inside plant stems. Paper and lumber come from tree stems. Rubber comes from latex removed from tree stems. Gum, dyes, turpentine, flavorings (cinnamon from bark), and many medicines hail from plant stems. Asparagus, broccoli, and bamboo shoots are examples of stems we eat.

Root Watch

Overview: After imagining a "worm's-eye view," students discover similarities and differences among the emerging roots of different plants.

Time:
Groundwork: 30 minutes
Exploration: 45 minutes setup; 2 to 3 weeks ongoing observations
Making Connections: ongoing

Materials:
• radish, corn, and/or pea seeds
• clear plastic cups
• brown paper towels
• plastic bags
• "My Plant Journal" reproducible, page 285

Background: Page 52

Laying the Groundwork

Objective: To examine students' ideas about what plant roots look like underground.

1. Take students through a guided imagery exercise in which they experience the soil from a "worm's-eye view."

You are an earthworm on a journey under the soil. Close your eyes and imagine you've turned on a light switch underground. What kinds of things do you see all around you? Watch out, you're heading right into a carrot bed! You are surrounded by huge plant roots. How does it make you feel to wiggle your way around these gigantic roots? What do they look like? It's hard moving in and out of all these giant carrots.

You tunnel down, down, down. As you go deeper in the soil, the tips of the carrots get smaller and smaller. Now you're underneath the carrot roots and you find it easier to move around. Because you are strong enough to move forty times your own weight, you push the smaller roots out of your way. Push, push ... there are lots of tiny roots to squeeze past.

Soon you find your way through the roots and pass out of the garden, underneath a sidewalk. What does it look like here? There's a patch of weeds between the cracks of the sidewalk. What do you see? What do the plant parts look like here? How does it feel underground? How does it smell?

2. When the guided imagery is complete, have students open their eyes and draw their underground visions. Have students exchange pictures with a partner. Ask: *How is your picture the same as your partner's? How is it different? What kind of plant roots did you draw?*

3. Hold up a couple of different GrowLab plants. Ask: *How do you think these plants look underground? What do you think their roots will look like? Will they all look the same? Since roots grow underground, can you think of a way we could watch roots grow?*

Exploration

Objective: To observe early root development in different garden plants.

1. Follow student-generated suggestions for observing root growth, or use one or all of the following setups to watch roots develop. Have students predict how they think the different roots will look in a couple of weeks.

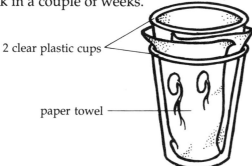

2 clear plastic cups

paper towel

Place four seeds (radish, peas, or corn) against the inside wall of a clear plastic pot or cup. Wrap a brown paper towel inside the seeds and fit another cup inside it to hold the seeds and towel in place. Keep towel moist. Keep in darkness until seeds have sprouted. Set up two more cups with other plant seeds.

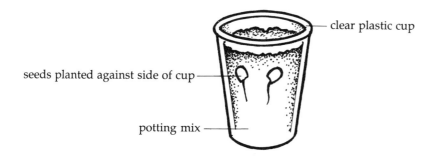

clear plastic cup

seeds planted against side of cup

potting mix

Plant four seeds against the sides of a cup filled with moist potting mix. Keep in darkness until they have germinated.

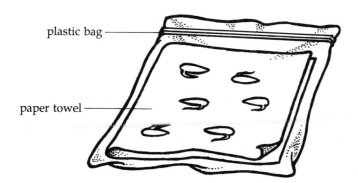

plastic bag

paper towel

Set seeds on a moist paper towel in a plastic bag. Again, keep in darkness until they have germinated.

2. During the next two to three weeks, have students observe root development and record drawings on the "My Plant Journal" reproducible.

3. Discuss findings. Ask: *How long did it take for the roots to sprout from the seeds? How did you know what was the root? In what ways were the roots of each plant the same? ... different? Which plants' roots were thicker, longer, or had more branches? In which direction did the roots grow? Was the direction always the same? Which roots grew faster than others? Did any reach the bottom of the container? What did they do then?*

Making Connections

Possible discussion questions:

• *How are the real roots like the ones you drew after pretending to be an earthworm?*

• *After observing different plant roots, what ideas do you have about how roots help plants?*

• *What kinds of roots do we eat? Can you think of other uses we have for roots?*

• *What types of patterns are made by the roots? What other things in nature have a pattern of smaller and smaller branches* (rivers, tree branches, human arteries)? *What seems to be special about branching patterns?*

Branching Out

• Try to find the root hairs, using hand lenses. Discuss how you think root hairs might help the roots do their job.

• Carefully dig up some plants outside, such as dandelions and grass. Compare their root systems. Discuss what you notice about how roots affect soil.

• Plant the top of a carrot, as illustrated, to discover whether a new plant can be started from a piece of root.

• Have a "root-tasting party." Include carrots, radishes, beets, parsnips, and turnips.

• Create a larger-than-life diorama of an underground scene, including worms, roots, soil, and seeds.

• Read stories or myths about life underground—for instance, the myth of Persephone, the Greek goddess of the underworld.

Plant carrot top with a 1"-2" piece of root in soilless mix.

Why Root for Roots?

Overview: Students confirm assumptions about the role of roots in water intake. They then explore the importance of rootlets and root hairs in this process.

Time:
Groundwork: 30 to 40 minutes
Exploration—Part 1: 45 minutes setup;
  2 weeks observations
Exploration—Part 2: 30 minutes setup;
  2 weeks observations

Materials:
• four potted plants, 2 to 3 weeks old (bean, tomato, marigold, etc.)
• pea, bean, or cucumber seeds
• three 4-inch pots
• potting mix
• hand lenses
• plastic bag
• "Problem Solving for Growing Minds" reproducible, page 283
• "Observation Journal" reproducible, page 286

Background: Page 52

Advance Preparation:
If students have not carefully examined roots, have them conduct **Root Watch** prior to this activity. Alternatively, start some tomato or pea seeds on a moist paper towel in a plastic bag seven to ten days prior to the activity.

Laying the Groundwork

Objective: To consider how plants take in water.

1. To stimulate thought about plants and water intake, either draw students' attention to plants outside in the rain, or simulate a rain shower with a watering can in your GrowLab. Ask: *How do you think plants take in the water they need to thrive and grow?* If students respond that plant roots take in water, ask: *What makes you so sure that it's roots that take in water and not some other part of the plant? After all, the rain falls directly on the leaves and stem also.*

2. Ask: *How many of you have actually seen roots take in water?* Discuss that we must often make assumptions and inferences about what is true based on things we observe, experience, read, or are told by others—for example, that unwatered houseplants wilt because they need water. Ask: *How might we design an investigation to test our assumption that roots, and not another plant part, take in water?*

Exploration—Part 1

Objective: To conduct an investigation to test assumptions about the role of roots in water intake.

1. Have small groups of students discuss how they might design an experiment, using the Problem Solving for Growing Minds process, page 10, to examine whether roots or other plant parts are more important for water intake. Ask a reporter from each group to describe their proposed exploration.

Have the class review the proposed experiments and choose one that is possible to do in the classroom, which would enable them to infer an answer to their question. Have students consider what type of observations will indicate whether or not the plants are taking in water.

Refine and choose an experiment to conduct. For example:

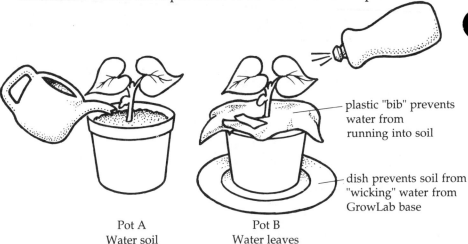

plastic "bib" prevents water from running into soil

dish prevents soil from "wicking" water from GrowLab base

Pot A
Water soil

Pot B
Water leaves

2. Keep records of daily observations on the "Observation Journal" reproducible.

3. After two weeks, review observations and discuss findings. For example, ask:

• *What did you observe? What can we infer about the role leaves and stems play in taking in water? ... about the role roots play in taking in water?*

• *How did your findings compare with your predictions? Did we actually see roots taking in water? Did the experiment help make you more confident about your assumption that roots take in water? How?*

• *What other factors might have affected what happened to the plants?* (For example, the leaves may have been damaged when they had water on them.)

Exploration—Part 2

Objective: To infer the importance of rootlets and root hairs in water intake by observing how plants respond when rootlets and root hairs are damaged.

1. Focus students' attention on observations of roots from **Root Watch** and/or have them use hand lenses to observe the emerging roots on the seeds started during the Advance Preparation. Ask: *What pattern do most roots seem to have in common? How might this design be useful for taking in water? Which size branches would be in closest contact with water? What do you think might happen if the smallest branches or root hairs were broken? Why?*

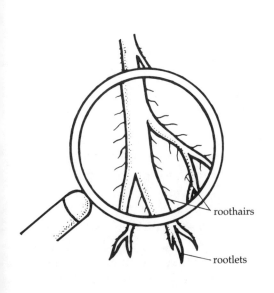

roothairs

rootlets

2. Challenge students to find out how plants respond when their rootlets and root hairs are broken. Use plants such as beans, peas, or cucumbers that have sensitive root systems. Other plants, such as tomatoes, peppers, or marigolds, have hardier root systems and will not show as dramatic results. A sample setup follows:

Plant three pea, bean, or cucumber seeds in each of three pots. Once the first true leaves have appeared (in seven to ten days) treat the plants as follows:

Pot A: Leave plants alone.

Pot B: Carefully remove all plants from the pot with a spoon, keeping soil as intact as possible. Examine rootlets with a hand lens (root hairs are difficult to see on these plants). Record observations. Carefully repot plants in same pot.

Pot C: Roughly yank all plants out, pulling from the base of the stem. Examine rootlets with a hand lens. Record observations. Repot plants in same pot.

Just budding in: Since most indoor potting mixes are very lightweight, your plants will likely suffer minimal root hair damage when they're pulled out. If possible, try this experiment with outdoor garden soil, which tends to be heavier. Results will be much more dramatic, and the plants in Pot C probably will not survive the treatment.

3. Ask: *How do you think the plants in each pot will look after a week? Why? What effect do you think our rough treatment of Pot C might have had on roots?* During the next seven to ten days, have students care for all plants equally and continue recording observations of heights, general health, and appearance in the "Observation Journal."

What to expect: When root hairs are damaged, plants cannot readily absorb necessary water and nutrients. After several days, plants in Pot A should be tall and healthy, while those in Pot C should show signs of wilting and stunted growth. Those in Pot B may exhibit some signs of stress, but should survive.

Making Connections

Possible discussion questions:

• *What did you observe about the smallest roots on the plants in each pot before transplanting? What differences did you observe during the week? What can you infer about why there are differences in appearance? What other factors might have affected what happened to the plants?*

• *What can you infer about how rootlets and root hairs help a plant meet its needs? Why can you make that inference?*

• *What other plant parts seem to be affected when roots are disturbed? Why do think that is? What can you infer from this about the movement of water in plants?*

• *If a plant looked unhealthy after transplanting, what might you infer about what happened to it during transplanting?*

• *Do you think all types of plants would respond the same way to transplanting? Why or why not? How could you find out?*

• *From what you've learned in this investigation, how would you transplant seedlings indoors or to an outdoor garden?*

• *How do you think networks of creeks, rivers, and streams are like roots?*

• *What parts of your own body do you think work like roots? Why?*

Branching Out

• Dig up a dandelion and a clump of grass. Compare root structures and write a description of each. Create a display that compares different types of roots.

• Build a root view box from a milk carton, as illustrated.

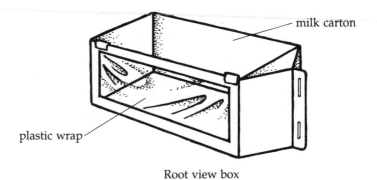

Root view box

• Measure and try to estimate the total length of the plant roots, including root hairs, in each pot.

• Try some root growth rate problems. For instance, roots of young seedlings can grow at .2mm to 1mm per hour. At the maximum rate, how long would it take a carrot root to reach the bottom of a 10-cm pot?

• Observe the ability of roots to grow around obstructions by placing a block of wood, a rock, or another barrier 2 inches beneath the soil in a pot. Plant bean seeds, and pull up plants to view root growth after four weeks.

• Make root soup!

Root Loops

Overview: Students explore how plants respond to gravity by trying to influence the direction in which roots grow.

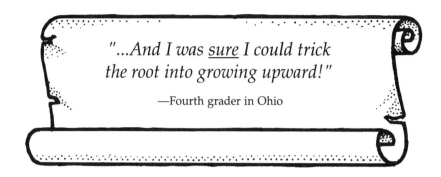

"...And I was <u>sure</u> I could trick the root into growing upward!"

—Fourth grader in Ohio

Time:
Groundwork: 30 minutes
Exploration: 30 minutes setup; 4 to 8 days ongoing observations
Making Connections: ongoing

Materials:
• any plant for demonstration
• bean seeds
• plastic bags
• paper towels
• plastic lids
• plastic cups or glass jars
• "Observation Journal" reproducible, page 286

Background: Page 52

Advance Preparation:
Two days prior to this activity, put a plant that's at least 4 to 5 inches tall on its side in a totally dark spot (e.g., a closet or a large box). Make sure the plant has been recently watered.

Laying the Groundwork

Objective: To appreciate the way objects and people respond to gravity.

1. Hold up any plant in front of the class and ask: *In what direction is this plant growing? In what direction have you seen most plants grow? Do different parts of the plant grow in different directions? Which ones? What do you think could be causing roots to grow down and leaves and stems to grow up?*

If students say that the leaves are reaching up for light, show them the plant that has been growing in the closet. Explain that even without light, the stem and leaves would not grow sideways; they were still growing straight up! Ask why the roots would still be growing down. Suggest that something else must be affecting the direction of root and shoot growth.

2. To explore that "something else," invite your students to play Gravity Says! Direct the class to follow your instructions, preceding each sentence with *Gravity says...*

> *...jump up!*
> *...jump up, and come back down again!*
> *...jump up and stay up!*
> *...hold a pencil above your desk and let it go!*
> *...hold a pencil above your desk, let it go, but don't let it drop!*
> *...reach for the ceiling!*
> *...touch the ceiling!*

3. Ask students: *What happens every time you jump up in the air? Why couldn't you follow my directions and stay up? Why can't your pencil float in the air? What would happen if you tried to walk on the ceiling?* If they are not already familiar with the concept of gravity, explain to students that gravity is a force belonging to massive objects. A gravitational force pulls us toward the earth.

4. Ask: *We've seen how people and objects respond to the force of gravity, and we've already described the direction plants grow. Do you think we could change the direction roots and shoots grow? How?*

Exploration

Objective: To understand that plants respond to gravity by attempting to change the direction of root and stem growth.

1. Challenge pairs of students to change the direction bean seed stems and roots grow so that roots grow up and stems grow down. Using common classroom or household materials, have students design and set up a system to influence the direction of root and stem growth. For best results, use seeds that have been soaked overnight and that have already begun to germinate. For example,

paper towel

jar

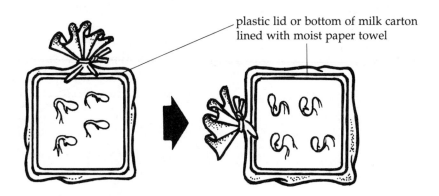

plastic lid or bottom of milk carton lined with moist paper towel

 Just budding in: To prevent mold growth on germinating seeds, soak them for a few hours in a mixture of 1 tablespoon of bleach in a quart of water.

2. Have students draw what they predict the seeds in their setup will look like in one week, and then record what the seeds look like each day using the "Observation Journal."

3. After four to eight days, discuss findings. Ask: *How did your results compare with your prediction pictures? What parts of the bean plants seem to respond to gravity? What parts don't?*

Making Connections

1. Set up the following "corn loops" challenge for your students:

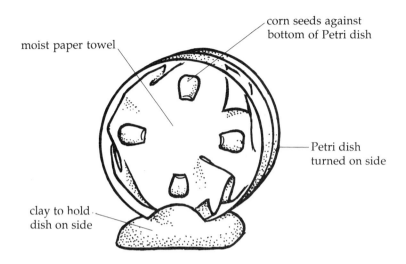

moist paper towel

corn seeds against bottom of Petri dish

Petri dish turned on side

clay to hold dish on side

Ask students to draw what they think the corn seeds will look like in a week. Let seeds germinate, and compare prediction pictures to germinated seeds.

2. Possible discussion questions:

• *From this exploration, would you infer that all plants respond to gravity the same way? Why or why not?* Share with students that what they have been trying to overcome—probably fruitlessly—is plants' natural response to gravity, called geotropism. (See background information, page 53.)

• *How do you think roots growing down and stems growing up help a plant meet its basic needs?*

• *Could you be as sure of your answer if only one group had set up a Root Loops experiment? Why or why not?*

• *From your setup, can you be sure the stems were growing up and the roots were growing down because of gravity? Why or why not?* (If this experiment were done in the light, the shoots may have been growing toward the light, exhibiting phototropism.)

• *How might you change your exploration to find out what else might have caused the stems to grow up or the roots to grow down?* (Try conducting it in the dark.)

• *Do you think farmers need to worry about whether seeds are planted in the "right" direction? Do we need to worry about the direction we plant our GrowLab seeds? Why or why not?*

• *How do you think raising food in space might be different from growing crops on Earth?*

Root Routes

Another way roots may help plants meet their needs is by growing toward moisture—a phenomenon called **hydrotropism.** Suggest that students set up an investigation, like the one illustrated below, to explore this controversial theory. After observing results, discuss the conditions in nature where such a response might be useful.

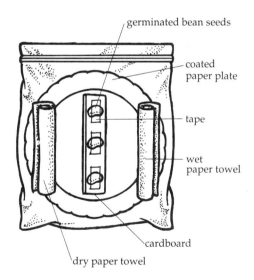

germinated bean seeds

coated paper plate

tape

wet paper towel

cardboard

dry paper towel

Branching Out

• Try to make a mature plant grow upside down. Calculate how long it takes different plants to respond to gravity.

• Experiment to see which way roots and stems grow when constantly revolving, e.g., on a turntable.

• Observe plants outside your home and school to find examples in nature that support what you learned about geotropism.

• Write to NASA for information on research about raising plants in space.

• Draw, write, or make a topsy-turvy diorama about what you imagine your surroundings would look like if there were no gravity.

Overview: Students consider the functions of roots, then simulate erosion in the classroom to examine the role played by roots in stabilizing precious topsoil.

Time:
Groundwork: 30 minutes
Exploration: 30 minutes setup;
 2 weeks ongoing observations
Making Connections: ongoing

Materials:
• one mature plant
• shallow growing containers (at least 5 x 7 inches)
• grass seed
• potting mix

Background: Page 52

Spanish Roots

If you have Spanish-speaking students, try the following sentences with the word root, or *raíz*:

"Tenemos que arrancar de raíz el problema de la droga."
"Aunque mi amigo ha vivido en los Estados Unidos por ocho años, tiene raíces en España."
"Aunque sólo llegó a está comunidad hace dos meses, Marcos ya está enchando raíces."

Earthgrippers

"Our homes have locks on the door, latches on the window, and insurance policies in the dresser drawer.... Meanwhile, outside our windows, every rainstorm carries away thousands of tons of valuable topsoil upon which we depend for our very survival."

— Malcolm Margolin, Naturalist

Laying the Groundwork

Objective: To examine how the use of the English word "root" gives us insight about the functions of plant roots. To consider the relationship between roots and soil.

1. Write the following sentences on the board and, as a class, discuss the meaning of the word "root" in each sentence. Ask students to come up with other sentences that include "root."

"Money is the root of all evil."
"The farmer's pigs rooted around in the mud."
"My ideas are finally taking root."
"I want to learn about my family's roots."
"The Cherokee people feel very rooted to the land."

2. Have pairs of students discuss how the word "root" in these sentences gives insight into the functions of plant roots. Have them share their ideas with the class. Ask: *Based on what we know about how roots help plants, can you think of anything else roots do? Do you think roots have any effect on soil? What have you observed in nature to support this?*

3. Choose any mature plant in moist soil. Pull it straight up from the pot and ask: *How would you describe the relationship between this plant's roots and the soil? If the plant were growing outside on a steep slope or on a windy prairie, how do you think it might affect the soil? How do you think the structure of roots would contribute to this effect?*

4. Share with students that the wearing away of the surface of the land—including soil—by water, wind, or ice is known as erosion. Although erosion is a natural force, constantly shaping the mountains, valleys, and other aspects of our landscape, it can also be a serious problem. Precious topsoil, which can take hundreds or thousands of years to create, can easily be blown or washed away. Ask: *How do you think plant roots might affect soil erosion?*

Exploration

Objective: To design an experiment to investigate whether and how plant roots affect soil erosion.

1. Have students work in small groups or as a class to investigate whether plant roots affect soil erosion. Have students follow the Problem Solving for Growing Minds process, page 10, to design an exploration such as:

No grass   Thinly sown grass   Thickly sown grass

Start the simulation once grass is 1 or 2 inches tall, to give roots time to develop. Continue the simulation daily for a week.

2. When designing an erosion exploration to be carried out in the classroom, have students consider such questions as: How to ...

... simulate a sloping field?
... simulate rain, wind, or ice? (Use watering can, fan, plant mister.)
... provide equal impact of water in each group? (Water with same amount, frequency, and from same height.)
... measure the amount of erosion that takes place? (Measure soil depth before and after treatment; filter water from "runoff" to determine amount of soil lost.)

Extra challenge: Have students test factors that might influence the rate of soil erosion such as degree of slope, heaviness of rainfall, type of plants, soil type, water temperature, or wind speed. Students can graph the rate of erosion under varying conditions.

3. Have students develop graphs and other displays to report findings to the class. See "Create-a-Chart," page 287, for ideas. Encourage peer review of the experimental design and the findings.

Making Connections

Possible discussion questions:

• *Why didn't we look only at the erosion from a non-planted slope? Was it helpful to compare erosion on planted and non-planted slopes? Why?*

• *What are some examples in which plants help prevent soil erosion*

"It's a landslide!"
"No, it's a mudslide!"

—First graders in Indiana conducting **Earthgrippers**

Reduced to Dust

When settlers began to farm on the great plains, the natural grass cover was plowed under and replaced with annual crops of corn and wheat. Drought and constant tilling left the soil with little cover, few plant roots to hold it together, and little cohesiveness. When repeated windstorms whipped through the prairies, more than 300 million tons of soil particles —enough to fill six million railroad cars—were lifted and blown away from the plains. Dust clouds during this Dustbowl Era dimmed the sun as far away as New York City!

outside (roadsides, farmers' fields)?

• *If you were planting a garden on the side of a hill, would you plant rows going up and down the hill or across the hill? Why?*

• *What characteristics of roots do you think help prevent soil erosion?*

• *Do you think fibrous or tap roots would more effectively prevent erosion? Defend your answer.*

• *Since precipitation can either evaporate, soak into the ground, or run off, what role(s) do you think roots play in the water cycle?*

• *Do you think gullies are the cause or the result of erosion? Why?* (A thought-provoking question with no right answer.)

• *In addition to roots, how else might a plant protect soil from erosion* (leaves/stems protecting from wind or rain impact, plant debris as mulch, etc.)?

Branching Out

• Research other methods that are used to prevent soil loss, e.g., mulching, contour plowing.

• Research what substances, other than soil, might be carried away by erosion, e.g., fertilizer or pesticides. Discuss how this might affect an ecosystem. (See "Dirty Waters" sidebar, page 50.)

• Interview a local farmer or Soil Conservation Service agent. Find out what farmers in your state do to prevent soil erosion.

• Examine your schoolgrounds to determine areas of erosion. Figure out if plantings can improve the situation, and plant accordingly.

• Estimate the number of raindrops that fall on a 1-square-meter area outside your school. Experiment to verify your estimate.

• Discuss the meaning of Malcolm Margolin's quote at the beginning of this activity.

Overview: Students consider how materials are transported through plants by examining how stems and other objects conduct water.

Time:
Groundwork: 30 minutes
Exploration: overnight; 30 minutes
Making Connections: ongoing

Materials:
• pictures of plants and trees
• assorted materials that might transport water, e.g.:
  plant stems
  wooden dowel
  strips of paper towels
  plastic straw
  celery stalks
• glass jar
• food coloring
• hand lenses
• colored pencils or crayons
• "Plant a Question" reproducible, page 282

Background: page 54

What a Sy-Stem!

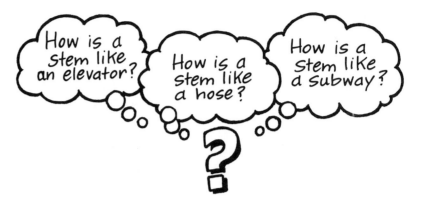

Laying the Groundwork

Objective: To consider the forms and functions of stems.

1. Show your students different GrowLab plants as well as pictures of plants, including trees, and have them point out the stem in each. Explain to students that just as they each have particular jobs to do at home and at school, each part of the plant has special jobs to do, too.

2. Have students generate a list of the possible jobs of stems. Accept all ideas. For example:

> **What jobs does a plant stem have?**
>
> Stems hold up the leaves.
> Stems carry water up the plant.
> Stems carry water down the plant.
> Stems shade the plant so it doesn't get too hot.

3. If students' ideas did not include that stems transport water, ask: *If you water the roots of a wilting plant, what happens to the plant? How do you think the water starts in the roots and ends up in the leaves?* Tell students that although plant stems have several different jobs, during this exploration you are going to focus on their water-carrying job.

Exploration

Objective: To observe and compare the transport action of plant stems and other objects.

1. Create a class list to answer the question: "What will happen if we leave a plant stem and other objects in colored water overnight?" Set up as follows:

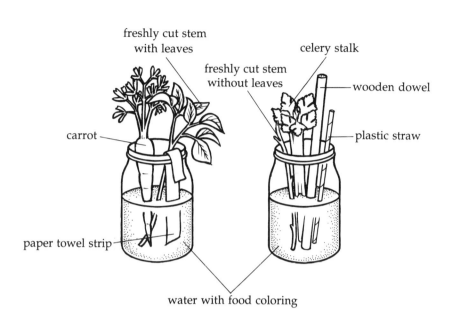

freshly cut stem with leaves

celery stalk

freshly cut stem without leaves

wooden dowel

carrot

plastic straw

paper towel strip

water with food coloring

Following the Plant a Question process, page 9, have students predict how the colored water will affect the different objects overnight. Have students make drawings of the setup and record their predictions.

2. The next day, rinse excess colored water from the objects. Give students hand lenses to observe how the colored water traveled into each object. Have students compare the heights the colored water reached in the different objects. Ask: *How does what happened compare with your predictions?*

3. Have students record results by using colored pencils or crayons on their original drawings to illustrate the height to which the colored water traveled in each object. Consider making a bar graph to compare water movement in different objects. Ask: *What direction does the water seem to travel in the stems?*

Making Connections

1. Possible discussion questions:

• *Why do you think the wooden dowel carried the colored water as it did? (Hint: Where does wood come from?)*

• *Why do you think the colored water did not rise in the plastic straw? What do you have to do to get your drink to rise in a plastic straw?*

• *In plants, where do you think the materials inside the stem are going? From where do you think the materials in the stem are coming?*

• What do you think would happen to a plant if its stem were broken? How could you set up a test to find out?

• How does the water you drink reach the rest of your body?

• Do you ever eat stems? If so, which ones? How else do people use stems?

2. Your students have been working as scientists; now is a good time to help them reflect on the processes they used to gather information. Go back over the students' original list of stem jobs and discuss what and how they found out about each of the jobs. For example:

The Jobs of Stems

What did we find out?	How did we find out?
Stems hold up the leaves.	We closely observed some plants.
Stems carry water up the plant.	By experimenting, we saw that stems do carry water up, so we think that's what happens in a plant too
Stems carry water down the plant.	We still don't know this. We could experiment or look in books.
Stems shade the plant so it doesn't get too hot.	We still don't know this either and are not sure how to find out.

This is a good opportunity to point out that scientists do not have all the answers either. Just like your students, scientists usually end up with more questions than answers! If appropriate, share some of the other jobs stems have besides transport (see background, page 54).

Branching Out

• Compare the rate food coloring travels up stems in light and dark conditions.

• Make tie-dyed flowers. Take a white flower, such as a carnation or a rose, and carefully slice the bottom of the stem lengthwise into two to four sections. Leave the top 3 to 5 inches of the stem attached to the flower head. Put each section in a jar with different-colored water. Place the entire setup in the GrowLab for one to two days. Have students predict what the flower will look like. Enjoy your rainbow flowers!

• Grow some underground stems such as tubers (white potatoes), corms (crocus), bulbs (tulips, daffodils), and rhizomes (iris).

• Grow a bean plant in a mini-terrarium, e.g., a gallon jug or 2-liter soda bottle, to promote rapid growth. With a marker, draw rings around the stem at 1-cm intervals. Measure the distance between the rings daily for one to two weeks to examine how stems grow.

• Prepare stem snacks including asparagus, broccoli, and bamboo shoots. Include celery and rhubarb for some petiole (leaf stalk) snacks, too!

Caution: While rhubarb petioles are delicious and nutritious, the leaves of the rhubarb plant are poisonous and should never be eaten.

• Grow new plants by taking stem cuttings from houseplants.

• Have a stem scavenger hunt outside. Search for stems with different characteristics such as rough, thorny, flexible, green, or large.

• Look carefully at pieces of logs, rough lumber, and finished wood. Try to figure out the orientation of the piece of wood in the original stem. (Hint: Trees grow in circumference by adding new rings each year.)

• Design original plants without stems. Consider what you might use to take over the jobs of the stem.

• Have a stem water-transport relay race outside! Draw two large plants on the pavement, with X's marking the roots, stems, and leaves. One student stands on each X, assuming the role of the plant part. At the teacher's signal, the student playing the root fills a paper cup with water from a bucket and passes it, bucket-brigade style, up the plant. The team that has the most water left in the least amount of time wins!

Plant This Ginger-ly

Plant some ginger "root"—actually, an underground stem. In a 4-inch pot place a 1-inch piece of ginger 3/4 inch below the surface of potting mix. Keep moist and wait patiently for the grass-like shoot to develop. Rub the leaves to find if they have the aroma of ginger. Have classroom guests rub and smell the leaves and try to guess this mystery plant!

Plants as Food Makers

How would you feed yourself if you were rooted to one spot for your entire life? Take-out food would get expensive. Would you stretch your tongue to catch a passing snack? Would you sink your toes deep in search of an underground diner? Perhaps you could capture the sun's energy and turn it into your food.

While all the energy our bodies use comes from the food we eat, green plants have the ability to make their own food and then use it for energy. All living things run on energy they obtain from food. Energy is needed for living cells to carry out all of the processes of life such as growing, disposing of wastes, making new cells, and using food. Green plants are food **producers**. Humans, other animals, and other living things such as fungi that do not make their own food are considered **consumers**.

How Do Plants Make Food?

Plants make their own food during the process of **photosynthesis.** Using light energy, plants can convert water and carbon dioxide into the energy-rich simple sugar, **glucose.** This sugar is the source of food used by most plants and, ultimately, by all other consumers.

The ongoing process of photosynthesis takes place in two phases, each phase consisting of many complicated steps that are not yet fully understood. The first phase of photosynthesis requires light. Light rays strike the plant and **chlorophyll**, a green pigment, traps the light energy. Water molecules, taken up by the roots and transported to the leaves, are split into hydrogen and oxygen, using the captured light energy. Carbon dioxide is meanwhile taken in from the air through openings in the leaf called **stomata**.

The next phase does not require light energy. During this phase, the hydrogen that's been split from the water molecules combines with the carbon dioxide to form glucose. The oxygen left over from the water molecules is released into the atmosphere

Plant Food?

"If plants are foodmakers, why do we give them 'plant food'?", we're often asked. Many of your students may have the same misconception. Actually, the nutrients taken in through plant roots are more analogous to the vitamins and minerals humans take to help in operation of body processes, growth, and repair.

through the stomata, where it's used by humans and other animals. As the stomata release oxygen, they also let in more carbon dioxide, so the process of photosynthesis can continue.

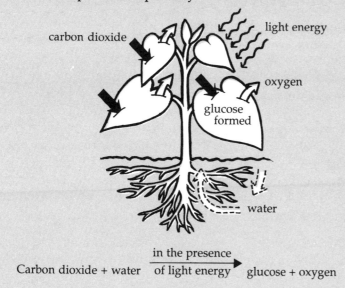

Carbon dioxide + water $\xrightarrow[\text{of light energy}]{\text{in the presence}}$ glucose + oxygen

How Do Plants Use Food?

When both phases of photosynthesis are complete, light energy has been converted to chemical energy in the form of glucose. The energy is locked up in the glucose and must be broken down into a form the plant can use. Plant cells release energy from glucose during a process called **respiration**—the same process used by humans and other animals.

Just like the process of photosynthesis, respiration is a series of many complicated chemical reactions. Plant leaves absorb oxygen from the air and combine it with glucose. Carbon dioxide and water are given off through the leaves, and the plant uses the energy released from the glucose.

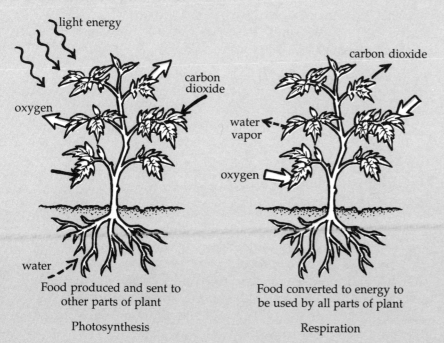

Food produced and sent to other parts of plant

Photosynthesis

Food converted to energy to be used by all parts of plant

Respiration

Although plants can immediately use the glucose as an energy source, glucose is usually changed and moved to other parts of the plant for use or storage through the following processes:

• Glucose molecules are combined to form larger, more complex carbohydrates such as sucrose, cellulose, or starch. **Sucrose**, commonly called table sugar, is the form in which carbohydrates are transported around the plant. It can be found stored in the roots of sugar beets and the stems of sugar cane. **Cellulose** makes up the walls of plant cells. **Starch** is stored in plant leaves, stems (white potatoes are underground stems), or roots (sweet potatoes) and can be broken down into simpler sugars for later use. For example, when a plant needs to use some of its stored energy, the starch can be changed back to glucose, so respiration can occur. Students can look at starch as a storage product of photosynthesis in the activity **Puzzled by Photosynthesis**.

• Plants also change glucose into the fats and proteins that make up the materials in plant cells, for example, in seeds (peanuts and soybeans).

• Glucose can also be combined with other materials to form vitamins, used by plant cells to carry on vital functions of growth and repair.

Let There Be Light

Without light, green plants couldn't make food. Because plants need light, they are affected by the quality and quantity of light received. In the activity **Lighten Up,** your students can examine the many ways light affects plant growth. Specific background information about light energy is found on page 90. Plants have adaptations that help them receive the light they need. For example, some plant stems grow toward a source of light; consequently leaves are well positioned to receive light energy. Your students can explore a plant stem's response to light in its environment, **phototropism**, in the activity **A-Maze-in Light**. For more information about how phototropism occurs, see page 55.

Leaves—Energy Factories

Leaves are sophisticated chemical factories. Using non-living raw materials in their environment, they convert energy from the sun to the energy green plants need to live.

Although leaves come in many different shapes and sizes, their general structure is well suited to the function of making food. For instance, most leaves, being relatively broad and flat, easily intercept light rays. In the activity **Look Out For Leaves** students look at the basic form of different leaves and consider how leaf structure helps a plant meet its basic needs.

The outer surface of most leaves contains many small pores, **stomata**, which open and close. CO_2 and O_2 enter and leave the plant through these pores. When open, stomata release excess water through a process known as **transpiration**. When closed, they limit water loss from the plant.

The Cycle of Light

Plants are not the only living things that depend on light. Light energy is transferred through plants, as producers, to other consumers. Animals eating plants or other animals utilize the food produced by plants in order to build up their bodies' materials and carry on life functions. When plants or animals die, their bodies decompose, releasing materials into the environment to be reused by other living things, and the cycle begins again. Activities in Chapter 4, "Sharing the Global Garden," explore some of these interdependencies.

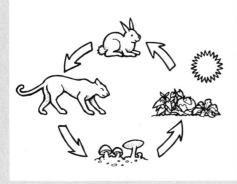

It is Easy Bein' Green

Green leaves are not the only plant parts that can photosynthesize. Examples of other plant parts that are green and photosynthesize include: stems (cacti), long aerial roots (epiphytes), sepals (flowers), and fruit pods (peas and beans).

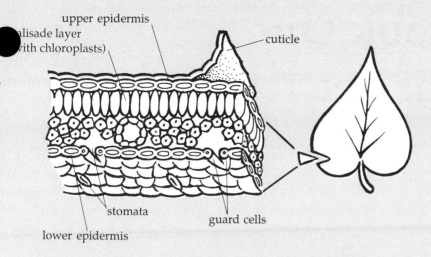

upper epidermis
palisade layer
(with chloroplasts)
cuticle
stomata
guard cells
lower epidermis

On either side of each stomate is a large kidney-shaped **guard cell**. When the weather is dry, guard cells quickly lose water pressure, the stomata close, and water loss is reduced. Temperature, pH, and light seem also to affect whether guard cells cause stomata to open or close.

The guard cells and the other cells on the surface of a leaf make up the **epidermis**, which, like our skin, protects the inside of the leaf. A waxy coating, the **cuticle**, waterproofs the leaf so that excess water does not enter and needed water does not transpire too rapidly. Some leaves have other adaptations to reduce the rate of water loss even further. See page 189 for a more in-depth discussion of these and other leaf adaptations.

A network of leaf **veins** carries water, nutrients, gases, and other materials to and from all parts of a leaf in order for food to be produced and energy to be used. Once food is made by the leaves, it travels through the veins to the stem and then to other parts of the plant for use and/or storage. Because the cell walls of leaf veins are usually thicker than other cell walls, veins have the additional function of providing support, helping position leaves to receive rays of light. Many leaves have a slender stalk, called a **petiole**, that attaches them to the stem.

Inside certain leaf cells are small structures called **chloroplasts** that contain a special green pigment called **chlorophyll**. Without chlorophyll, light energy could not be trapped and photosynthesis would not occur. **Puzzled by Photosynthesis** allows your students to discover the important role of chlorophyll and light in photosynthesis.

How We Use Leaves

Leaves are primary producers of our usable food energy. We also consume leaves such as lettuce, kale, cabbage, spinach, parsley, and onion (modified leaves) for vitamins, roughage, and flavor. Leaves from herbs and eucalyptus trees produce aromatic oils. Tobacco, teas, hair dyes, and fibers (e.g., sisal for rope) all originate with plant leaves. And we all appreciate the cool shade and autumn splendor of plant leaves.

Pigments of Your Imagination

Chlorophyll is usually found with one or more pigments that are not green, such as the yellowish-brown pigment carotene. Apparently, these other pigments absorb light in the green, yellow, and orange parts of the spectrum, and pass the light energy to the chlorophyll. This enables plants to use a wider range of light wavelengths than the chlorophyll can trap alone.

These pigments are also often masked by the more abundant chlorophyll, which is why leaves appear green. Leaves of many plant species change color in autumn, largely because chlorophyll is depleted and other pigments remain, no longer masked.

Other pigments seem to help attract pollinators. Found in various plant parts, these pigments range in color from blue-violet to purple-crimson or from pale yellow to orange-red. They are responsible for the colors of many flowers and other plant parts, e.g., coleus leaves.

Look Out for Leaves

Overview: Students look closely at similarities and differences among leaves and consider why leaves are important for most plants.

Time:
Groundwork: 40 minutes
Exploration: 40 minutes
Making Connections: ongoing

Materials:
• drawing paper
• crayons or markers
• assorted plant leaves
• assorted leafy plants
• hand lenses

Background: Page 76

Advance Preparation:
Have each student bring in two or three different kinds of plant leaves for observation. Have some extras on hand. If possible, bring in some leaves—blades of grass or lettuce—that students might not consider.

Laying the Groundwork

Objective: To observe similarities and differences among green plant leaves.

1. Without looking at their leaves, ask each student to imagine and then draw what a plant leaf looks like. Display pictures around the room. Ask: *How are all of these plant leaves the same? How are they different? How could we find out more about leaves?*

2. Collect all of the leaves that were brought in (see Advance Preparation) and have each student choose one to observe. To help students focus their observations, play a couple of rounds of Leaf Me Alone! as follows:

Leaf Me Alone!

Have all students stand in a circle, holding their leaves. Say: *Stay in the circle if you have a leaf that...*

...has green on it
...has veins
...is bigger than your thumbnail
...feels different on the top and the bottom
...has an unusual smell
...has smooth edges
...has two colors

Continue the game until only one student remains. Invite all students back for another round of Leaf Me Alone!

Exploration

Objective: To closely examine plant leaves and to consider their role as food makers.

1. Back at their seats, have students trace their leaves on paper and draw in veins. Let students use hand lenses to get a closer look at their leaves. Remind them to look at both the top and bottom sides of their leaves. Have several leafy plants also available for observation.

2. Ask each student to compare the new drawing with her/his original drawing of an "imagined" leaf. Draw students' attention to the fact that the second set of drawings have more detail because of the close observations they made. As a class, hang up the leaf pictures, grouping them according to shape, size, and/or any other category. Ask: *How are all of these leaves the same? How are they different?*

3. Before considering leaves' role as foodmakers, first consider how animals get food. Ask: *When you need food, what do you do?* List students responses on the board, for example:

"I get something from the refrigerator."
"I go to the store."
"I ask my mom."

Now ask: *How do other animals get their food?* Add responses to the list. For each response, ask if a plant can do those things. Ask: *How do you think a plant gets its food? Did you ever meet a tree at the supermarket?* Explain that plants are different from people and other animals because they make their own food, using energy from light. Leaves are the food factories for most green plants. Three of the things they need to make food are water, light, and a gas in the air called carbon dioxide.

Making Connections

Possible discussion questions:

• *Did all of your leaves have veins? What do you think leaf veins do for the plant?*

• *Why do you think leaves usually grow at the top of a plant? Why don't we find most leaves underground?*

• *Why do you think many leaves are big and flat?*

• *What happens to many leaves in the fall? Do you think plants need their leaves as much in the fall or winter? Why or why not?*

• *What do you think would happen to a plant if you took off all of its leaves? Why?*

• *Do you ever eat plant leaves? Which ones? How else do you use plant leaves?*

Finding Food

To help students consider how plants and animals get their food in different ways, have half the class make collages of different plants and the other half make collages of different animals, using pictures they cut out from old magazines. Display collages around the room. Ask students to think about what makes an animal an animal and what makes a plant a plant. *How did you know what pictures to cut out and put in your collage? What major differences are there between plants and animals?*

Let Off Some Steam!

To introduce the transpiration function of leaves, take one well-watered plant and cover its leaves with a plastic bag, as illustrated. Have a similar, uncovered plant for comparison. Ask: *What do you think we'll find in the bags covering the leaves if we leave them in the GrowLab overnight? Why?*

The next day, ask: *What appeared in the plastic bag covering the leaf? Did you expect to find water there? Besides making food for the plant, do you have any other ideas about what leaves do for plants?* Share with students that extra water passes out through very small openings in the leaves in a process called transpiration.

• What else would you like to find out about plant leaves? How do you think you could find out?

Branching Out

• On graph paper, draw outlines of leaves of different plants. Calculate and compare total surface area of leaves. Don't forget to multiply by two.

• Put some celery—actually a leaf stalk (petiole)—in a glass of colored water and watch what happens overnight. Discuss how the result might help a plant.

• Start a leaf collection. See the "Classroom Herbarium" sidebar, page 158, for directions on pressing leaves.

• Examine an onion to see how the bulb is actually made of leaves that store food for the plant. Try to figure out which are the oldest onion leaves.

• Start new plants from leaf cuttings.

• Make leaf rubbings. Place leaves underside up. Lay a piece of paper on top of the leaf and gently rub with a crayon.

• Make "leaf skeletons." Place several leaves at the bottom of a bowl or other container, cover with old newspapers, and fill with water. After six to eight weeks, gently rub away the leaf "skins" while holding them under water. Dry leaves between paper towels. Paint the "skeletons" and mount with glue.

Mounted leaf skeletons

• Have the class act out "the life of a leaf," with a leaf coming out of its bud, growing, taking in what it needs to make food for the plant, falling off, and rotting in the ground.

• Write descriptive poems about leaves starting with the letters L, E, A, and F.

Puzzled by Photosynthesis

Overview: Students compare green and non-green parts of leaves for starch production and explore the key roles light and chlorophyll play in photosynthesis.

Time:
Groundwork: 30 to 40 minutes
Exploration: Part 1—45 minutes
   Part 2—40 minutes setup; 4 days later, 40 to 60 minutes
Making Connections: ongoing

Materials:
• iodine solution
(see Advance Preparation)
• laundry or corn starch
• plastic straw
• assorted foods (see Exploration)
• four mature plants—two with a green and white pattern (e.g., variegated spider plant, silver-leaf geranium, or variegated Swedish ivy) and two solid green plants, (e.g., geranium, tomato, or bean plant)
• rubbing (ethyl) alcohol
• hot plate
• double boiler
• tweezers
• scissors
• "Puzzled by Photosynthesis" reproducible, page 267

Background: Page 74

Advance Preparation:
Make iodine solution for starch test by adding approximately 40 drops of iodine to 1/2 cup (approximately 125 ml) of water.

Caution: Iodine is toxic. Store away from heat and direct light. For long-term storage, place bottle in a plastic bag, close with twist tie, and place in empty paint can. Fill can with cat litter. Follow proper disposal procedures. Iodine will stain skin and clothing.

Laying the Groundwork

Objective: To consider how green plants are able to use elements from their environment to make their own food.

1. Facilitate a class discussion about how plants are different from animals. Ask questions such as: *What do you think animals and plants need in order to live and grow? What have you observed about animals that you think helps them meet their food needs? What have you observed about plants that you think helps them meet their food needs? You can go to the cafeteria or the refrigerator to get food, but how do you think plants get the nourishment they need for growth and energy?* Ask students to describe what they know about how green plants use the environment to make their own food.

2. Hand out the "Puzzled by Photosynthesis" reproducible. Help students fill in the blank puzzle using their own ideas as well as background information from page 74. (Also see sidebar, page 82.)

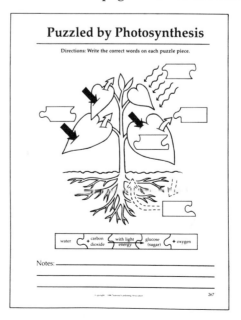

3. Tell students that a brownish yellow iodine solution turns blue-black when it touches starch. Demonstrate by dropping several drops of the iodine solution (prepared during Advance Preparation) onto some laundry or corn starch mixed with water. Also add some iodine to plain water as a control. Remember to use caution.

4. Ask students if they think they could produce starch in the classroom using the ingredients a plant uses: light, carbon dioxide, and water. Under the GrowLab lights, use a straw to exhale some carbon dioxide into a jar of water. Add a few drops of iodine solution. Ask: *What does the color change (or lack of change) tell you about the ability of carbon dioxide, water, and light to produce starch? If we cannot produce starch from these three ingredients, how do you think leaves of green plants are able to do so?*

If students have not yet discussed the role of chlorophyll in photosynthesis, hold up a few solid green plants and ask: *What do the leaves on all of these green plants have in common?* Students should realize that all the plants are green! Explain that the green in leaves is caused by a pigment, chlorophyll, that colors the leaves, just as a pigment in people's bodies gives color to our eyes, skin, or hair. Chlorophyll has a key role in trapping the light energy that green plants use to make their own food. Add chlorophyll to the "Photosynthesis Puzzle".

Exploration—Part 1

Objective: To demonstrate that plants store starch.

1. Hand out several plant-originated foods, e.g., table sugar, cooked pasta, crackers, potato chips, and raw or cooked starchy fruits or vegetables like corn, beets, or sweet potatoes. Have pairs of students taste the items, describe the tastes to each other, and record their observations. Ask: *How are all of these things alike? Before they arrived at the grocery store, where did the items come from?*

2. Ask: *Has anyone tasted starch stored by plants?* Have pairs of students choose several of the items they tasted, test them for starch, as you did with the laundry or corn starch, and record their results. After students have compared results, ask: *How do you think the starch got into the plant-originated items?*

Exploration—Part 2

Objective: To discover that light is necessary for starch production in leaves. To infer that something in the green parts of plants is needed for starch production.

1. Hold up some plants with variegated leaves (see Materials) and ask: *Do you think the leaves on these plants can make food? Why or why not? How do you think we could confirm that the green parts of*

Food Making at a Glance

All living things need food to give them energy and help them grow. Lacking legs, wings, or fins to carry them in pursuit of food, plants make their own food from raw materials in their immediate environment. Leaves are the main food-making factories in green plants. They have a special ability to trap light energy and use it to change carbon dioxide (taken in through the leaves) and water (taken in through the roots) to food, a sugar called glucose. During this process, called photosynthesis, plants give off oxygen, which humans and other animals need to live.

If the plant needs food right away, it uses the glucose. Since plants don't usually need all of the glucose right away, they change it to sucrose (table sugar), starch, and/or other materials (such as the oils or proteins in seeds), and store it for later use. Starch and/or other sugars are found stored in plant leaves as well as in roots (carrots) and stems (potatoes).

plants are needed to produce starch? How do you think we could con-firm that light is needed to produce starch?

2. Have students follow the Problem Solving for Growing Minds process, page 10, to conduct an investigation based on their own ideas, or use the following as a model:

Group A
One variegated plant and one
solid green plant in GrowLab

Group B
One variegated plant and one
solid green plant in closet

Make sure that the same type of plant in each group (e.g., both variegated plants) are of similar size, health, and age. Care for all plants equally. Have students predict what they think will happen when the leaves of the plants are tested for starch.

3. After four days, remove plants from the closet and GrowLab and have small groups of students remove one leaf from each of the plants. They should cut a notch in the leaves that were in the closet, to distinguish them from those that were in the light and to identify them after they're tested for starch. Have students sketch the leaves, outlining and shading the coloration. For example:

Leaves from Group A (GrowLab) plants

Leaves from Group B (closet) plants

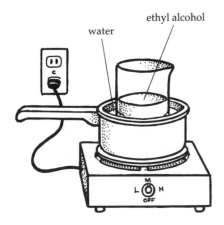

water

ethyl alcohol

4. Help students test for starch production in the leaves, carefully following these directions.

Test for Starch in Leaves

In a well-ventilated area, pour approximately 200 ml of rubbing alcohol (ethyl) into a small pot (or beaker or metal cup). Make a double boiler with a larger pot. Heat leaves in the alcohol in the double boiler for at least twenty minutes to remove chlorophyll.

 Caution: Alcohol boils at a lower temperature than water does and ignites easily. Never heat alcohol directly. Do not breathe fumes from the alcohol.

When the leaves become pale and flimsy, remove them with tweezers, rinse them with water, and place them in a shallow container, e.g., a Petri dish. Cover with iodine solution.

5. Compare actual leaves with leaf sketches. Ask: *What color change(s) took place in the treated leaves? How do the green parts of the leaves react with iodine differently than the non-green parts of the leaves do? How did the plants in the light react differently from those in the dark? What does the color change tell you about what is present or absent in the leaves?*

> **What to expect:** After four days, the plants in Group B will have used up any starch they had stored. Since they were not in the light, they were unable to photosynthesize and produce new starch. The plants in Group A, having received light energy, will have turned blue-black from the iodine because starch was being produced in these leaves. Any parts of the leaves that are not green (do not contain chlorophyll) cannot produce starch and, therefore, will not have turned blue-black from the iodine.

Making Connections

Possible discussion questions:

• *What factors do you infer caused the differences in the plants you tested for starch? How can you explain why starch is found only in some of the leaves or portions of the leaves? What else could have caused the differences?*

• *Besides water and carbon dioxide, what can you infer about what else a plant needs to photosynthesize?*

• *Why do you think carbon dioxide, water, and light alone could not produce starch?*

• *What evidence do you have at this point to support the claim that the leaf is the food factory of a green plant? Discuss why you can or cannot draw that conclusion from this activity. (See "Question Your Answer" sidebar.)*

Question Your Answer

Students should realize that this experiment did not prove that the starch in the leaves was produced as a result of photosynthesis. Couldn't the starch have been made in another part of the plant and transported to the leaf for storage? Also, students tested only leaves for starch, not roots or any other part of the plant, and thus they cannot conclude that the leaf alone is the food factory. Caution students to be aware of the limitations of their conclusions.

Based on prior knowledge and observations, however, students should feel confident to infer that photosynthesis occurred in the green parts of the leaves. Encourage students to think about other ways to substantiate their claims, for example, by asking: *What would happen to starch production if we removed all of the leaves?*

• *If we had watered one group of plants and not the other, could you be as sure of your explanation? Why or why not?*

• *Does anything still puzzle you about photosynthesis? How might you go about finding the solution to your puzzle?* (Remind students that there is a lot about the process of photosynthesis that still puzzles scientists!)

• Use the "Futures Wheel," page 292, to address the following question: *What do you think the world would be like if there were no green plants?* Have students consider questions such as: *What do plants require that humans give off? What do humans require that plants give off? Where do plants fit in food chains?*

Branching Out

• Try testing young sprouts for the presence of starch. Try testing mushrooms and other fungi for starch. Find out where fungi get their food if they can't photosynthesize. (Fungi do not contain chlorophyll and, therefore, are not considered food producers; they are food absorbers.)

• Clip a film negative to a leaf (see illustration below), leave plant in GrowLab for about four days, and see what "develops"!!!

• A serious environmental problem is the global warming resulting from excess carbon dioxide produced by the burning of fossil fuels. This carbon dioxide traps heat, much as heat is trapped in a glass greenhouse (for more information, see Global ReLeaf background, page 255). Considering how green plants photosynthesize, discuss how plants might be used to lessen the negative effects of global warming.

• Using a microscope, look for green chloroplasts. Elodea is a plant with large and very visible chloroplasts.

• Use water plants such as elodea (easily obtained from local aquarium/pet stores) to see evidence of photosynthesis by observing and measuring oxygen bubble production.

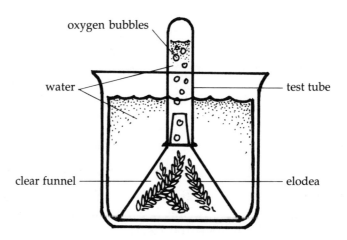

Photophictionary

Use a list of words relating to the process of photosynthesis to play a few rounds of Photophictionary. For each round, ask students to write a creative definition of one of the words. The goal is to make each pseudo-definition sound like the real thing in order to convince classmates that it is, indeed, the actual dictionary definition. For example,

Glucose - (n.) A type of paste that comes only from trees in Costa Rica.

   Read each of the fake definitions to the class along with the actual definitions supplied (see background information, page 74). Have the class vote for the definition they think is the real one. Read and discuss the actual meaning of each of these terms as they relate to the process of photosynthesis.

Figure labels: oxygen bubbles, water, clear funnel, test tube, elodea

• Read *Top Secret* by John Reynolds Gardiner, a novel about a boy who becomes the first human photosynthesizer (see Appendix E). Discuss the implications of the possiblity of "human photosynthesis"—e.g., economic impact and environmental effects.

• Write and perform creative skits to teach younger students about the process of photosynthesis.

A-Maze-in Light

Overview: Students create plant mazes to observe how plants respond to their environment in meeting their basic need for light.

Time:
Groundwork: 40 minutes
Exploration: 40 minutes setup;
   2 weeks ongoing
Making Connections: ongoing

Materials (per setup):
• cardboard box with cover
• cardboard scraps
• masking tape
• scissors
• colored pencils
• one 2-week-old pole bean plant or a sprouting potato
• "Problem Solving for Growing Minds" reproducible, page 283, or "Plant a Question" reproducible, page 282

Background: Page 55 and page 76

Advance Preparation:
Two weeks prior to this activity: Read through the Exploration to decide how many mazes you'd like your students to create. Plant enough pole bean plants—two seeds in a milk carton or other small growing container, thinning to one plant per pot—for each maze. You can use sprouting potatoes instead of bean plants.
At least four days prior to this activity: Place a plant (e.g., bean, tomato, or Swedish ivy) on the windowsill or to one side of a light source.

Laying the Groundwork

Objective: To observe and consider how plants respond to the direction of light in their environment.

1. Show students the plant you placed to one side of a light source (see Advance Preparation). Ask: *How do you think this plant is responding to its environment? Where have you seen plants outdoors showing this same type of response? How do you think this response helps a plant meet its needs?*

2. Ask: *In order to give this plant the best lighting for growth, do you think it matters where we place it? How do you think the plant would respond if we put it in the middle of the GrowLab? ...on a desk next to the GrowLab? ...if we rotated it every day? ...if we left it on a windowsill and never rotated it? How do you think a plant would respond if we grew it in a box and the only light came through a hole on one side of the box?*

Exploration

Objective: To understand that plants respond to the direction of light.

1. Challenge your students to use mazes to find out how their bean plants or sprouted potato (see Advance Preparation) will grow when the light source is not directly available. Have students use cardboard scraps, boxes, and other classroom materials to build their mazes. Suggest simpler or more sophisticated designs, depending on the level of your students. Include a control, e.g., one plant out of the maze, as well as experimental setups. Some sample maze designs are on the next page.

Sample 1.

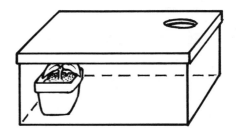

Sample 2.

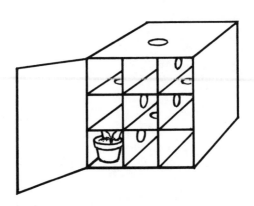

Sample 3.

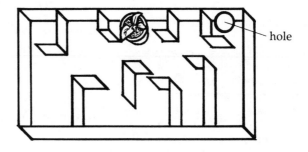

hole

2. As students design their setups, have them follow the Plant a Question process, page 9, or Problem Solving for Growing Minds process, page 10. When "sprouting a prediction," have students sketch their mazes, illustrating how they predict their plants will look after two weeks.

3. Have students measure their plants regularly and indicate how much they grow on their journey to become "enlightened." Students can update their prediction pictures, using a different colored pencil to show how the plants actually grew.

4. At the end of two weeks, have an A-Maze-ing Plants display. Have students orally describe their plants' adventures as they "cleverly" wove through the maze.

Making Connections

Possible discussion questions:

• *How did the a-maze-ing bean plants compare with the control plant that was not put in a maze? Why do you think they grew differently?*

• *What part of the plant seems to be responding to the light? How do you think this response helps a plant?* If appropriate, share the background information about phototropism, page 55, discussing how plant stems are adapted to grow towards the light.

• *Can we conclude that all green plants would have the same response to light? Why can we or can't we draw that conclusion?* (Remind students to be wary of drawing generalized conclusions based on the results of one experiment.)

• *How do you think the plants might have grown if there were no holes in the box? Why?*

• *What do you imagine the world would be like if plant stems didn't grow toward light?*

• Without warning, shut off the light for a few seconds. Ask: *How do you think your body responded to the change in light? In what other ways do humans respond to changes in their environment?* (Our pupils dilate when the lights go off, our eyes blink when we look towards a bright light, we shiver when it's cold.) *How do our responses help us survive?*

Branching Out

• Try to make a tomato plant grow upside down, using light as a stimulus.

• Find out how plants respond to different light wavelengths (colors).

• Research how animals such as earthworms and planaria respond to light as a stimulus.

• Calculate the growth rate of the a-maze-ing beans. Determine how long it would take the plants to wind through a larger or smaller maze.

• Make flip books showing the path of the bean plants.

• Make drawings depicting what the world might look like if plants could not bend toward light.

• Imagine being trapped in a cave with only some seeds, soil, and water. Write a creative story about how you might get out, given what you've learned in this activity.

Lighten Up

Light, the transfer of energy in the form of radiation, is one of the most important factors affecting plant growth and development. In natural ecosystems, sunlight provides the energy necessary for plants to produce food through photosynthesis. Without it, plants could not make food, and life on Earth as we know it would cease to exist.

Although you won't depend on sunlight in your indoor garden, the fluorescent lights in your GrowLab enable your students to explore some aspects of the relationship between plants and light. The quality and quantity of light available influence plant growth and development. The three key aspects of light affecting plant growth and development are color, duration, and intensity.

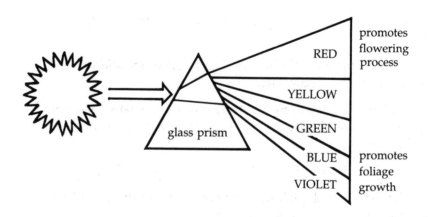

Light Color

Sunlight is actually a blend of all the colors in the spectrum. At one end of the visible spectrum are blue and violet light rays (shorter wavelengths); at the other end are red rays (longer wavelengths). If an object absorbs all wavelengths, we see the color black. If none are absorbed, and all wavelengths are reflected back to our eyes, we see the color white. If an object absorbs all but the red wavelengths, we see red. Leaves' green color indicates that they are reflecting more and absorbing less energy from the green part of the spectrum. If we put a translucent blue filter over a plant, the filter passes mainly blue light through to the plant.

Different types of lights emit different-colored light rays. Standard cool white fluorescent tubes tend to be strong on the blue end of the spectrum, while warm white tubes have more light rays in the red end, and incandescent bulbs have even more light rays in the red end. Special "grow lights" have been developed to match the sun's color spectrum more closely. See pages 44 to 46 in *GrowLab: A Complete Guide to Gardening in the Classroom* for more on light in the GrowLab.

The various colors have different effects on plants growth. Light rays in the blue part of the spectrum are important to photosynthesis. They also induce phototropism—the natural tendency of plants to respond to light. Red waves, at the other end of the spectrum, have more effect on flowering and growth. Although these interactions are quite complex and not thoroughly understood, you can still conduct interesting classroom investigations with light spectrums. For example: *How will the same type of plant respond when grown under red, green, or blue filters? What will happen if we grow plants under "grow lights" and regular fluorescent tubes?*

Light Duration

Plants growing outdoors are exposed to as many hours of light as there are hours of available sunlight. This varies according to time of year and latitude. Generally, the plants in your GrowLab will do well with fourteen to sixteen hours of light a day.

Flowering is particularly sensitive to another important factor—**photoperiodism**, or the plant's response to the proportion of light and dark in a twenty-four-hour period. Some plants require specific daylengths (actually, periods of darkness) in order to bloom, while others are neutral to daylength. Greenhouse growers take advantage of this habit by controlling hours of light to induce flowering, in chrysanthemums, for example. Outdoors, seasonal daylength signals changes that affect flowering in many plants.

Most of your GrowLab plants are neutral to daylength. Radishes and lettuce, however, are long-day plants, flowering when days are long and nights are short. This is why midsummer lettuce easily goes to seed.

Questions regarding light duration for GrowLab investigations might include: *What happens when plants receive fewer than the recommended hours of light? What about giving plants light when it's normally dark and vice versa? Will twenty-four hours of light help them grow faster?*

Head Lights

Certain crops, like cabbage, are not recommended for the GrowLab. This is due, in part, to their preference for a particular quality of light. Crops like cabbage, cauliflower, and head lettuce would not form heads under the color spectrum available in your fluorescent lights.

Light Intensity

The amount or intensity of light plants receive depends largely on the type of light used and its distance from plants. Not all plants have the same light requirements—shade-loving ferns, for instance, require less intense light than sunflowers do.

Light intensity is sometimes measured in terms of footcandles. The intensity of sunlight striking a plant at noon on a sunny day might be 10,000 footcandles, while office light might only be 500. Most of your GrowLab plants do well with the 1,000 to 1,500 footcandles provided by GrowLab. See page 46 in *GrowLab: A Complete Guide to Gardening in the Classroom* for more information on footcandles and measuring intensity.

The closer fluorescent lights are to the plants, the greater is the intensity of light that reaches them. If lights are raised from 2 inches above the plants to 12 inches above, there's a dramatic drop in light intensity. Diminished intensity will promote leggy, weak growth and slow down flowering. Although some plants may look tall when under inadequate light, this spindly growth is not healthy.

Questions regarding light intensity that students might explore include: *What happens if we decrease the number of light tubes, or surround the GrowLab with foil to increase light intensity to plants? How will lights at different heights affect plant growth?*

Now that you've read some of the serious nitty-gritty, it's time to **Lighten Up!**

Lighten Up

Overview: Students design and conduct investigations to explore the effect of light on plants.

Time:
Groundwork: 30 minutes
Exploration: variable; 45 minutes setup
Making Connections: ongoing

Materials:
• variable
• "Problem Solving for Growing Minds" reproducible, page 283
• "Observation Journal" reproducible, page 286

Background: Page 90

Advance Preparation:
One week prior to this activity: Place one plant in a closet, and leave an identical kind of plant in the GrowLab. Be sure to water both.

Laying the Groundwork

Objective: To stimulate curiosity and questioning about the relationship between plants and light.

1. Display plants (see Advance Preparation) for students to observe. Ask: *What factors do you think might have caused the difference in appearance between the two plants?* Explain that the only difference in treatment between the two plants was that one was exposed to light and the other was not.

2. Ask: *Based on your own experiences and observations, and on this demonstration, what can you infer about plants' needs for light?* You may want to share some of the background information on light with your students. Ask: *Assuming we agree that plants need light, what different characteristics of light do you think might affect plant growth and health?*

3. As a class, brainstorm a list of "What will happen if..." questions regarding plants and light. Encourage students to think about many different facets of light—for example, intensity, color, distance from plants, type of light, duration. Some examples:

"What will happen if plants...

...are grown under continuous dim light?
...receive more dark than light?
...receive only certain colors of light?
...are grown at different distances from light?
...are exposed to light when it's dark out, and vice versa?
...receive reflected light (from foil) in addition to GrowLab light?
...are raised under 'grow lights'?
...receive different amounts of light?"

Exploration

Objective: To design and conduct experiments to examine how different light conditions affect plant growth.

1. As a class, choose several of the "What will happen if..." questions from the Groundwork that can be tested in the classroom. If several questions can be investigated simultaneously, divide the class into small groups to do so; otherwise have the class vote on a question to tackle together. Have students use the Problem Solving for Growing Minds process, page 10, to plan the investigation(s).

Two sample setups, which could run concurrently, follow:

Question: *How do plants respond to different light intensities?*

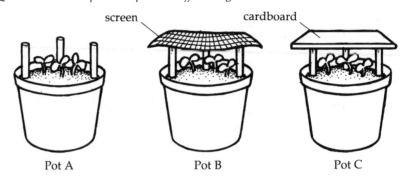

Pot A   Pot B   Pot C

Question: *How do plants respond to different light wavelengths (colors)?*

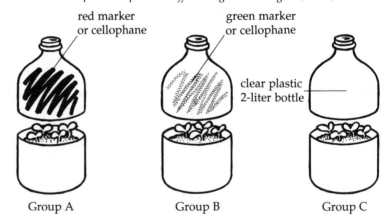

Group A   Group B   Group C

2. Have each group describe their proposed exploration to a "Light-Minded Jury" of their peers—the rest of the class. They should also describe how they'll record their observations. Encourage the "jury" to ask questions about the setup. For example, "How can you be sure the light intensity will be the same for all plants? How did you ensure repetition? What do you predict your findings will be? Why?"

3. Discuss findings. If more than one investigation is conducted, have groups design a way to combine class findings for review as they discuss and make connections.

> **What to expect:** There are many possible outcomes of these types of light explorations. If you're using colored filters, for instance, students may find the most dramatic effects under a green filter, which allows mainly green light to be transmitted to the plant. Since plants require less green light than red or blue, plants grown under green light may appear less healthy. Sometimes differences in light will result in subtle differences in plant growth. Draw students' attention to such variables as the distance between leaves on the stem, size of leaves, color of leaves, time of flowering, etc. These may change under different light conditions.

Making Connections

1. Possible discussion questions:

• *How do variations in light qualities or quantities seem to affect plant growth?*

• *Did your findings support what you have observed outdoors or in other settings? How? If not, why do you think you think there might be differences?*

• *Did any of the information collected by different groups seem contradictory? If so, why do you think that might have happened?*

• *How did the work of any other group shed any "light" on your own exploration?*

• *Do you think any of your results could have been caused by anything other than the light factor? Which? How would you set up this experiment if you were to do it again?*

• *Can you assume that all green plants are affected by light in the same ways as those in your investigation? Why or why not?*

• *Did your explorations give you any new ideas about how to be a better indoor or outdoor gardener? What are they?*

2. Have students make a list of findings that they feel were "enlightening," a list of conclusions that they question or feel would need more research or testing, and a list of new questions they have about plants and light. Keep these lists available to fuel new project ideas.

Branching Out

• Measure the hours of daylight received by a plant near your school during different times of the year. Correlate this with the plant's growth rate.

Turn Out the Lights!

Certain plants are very responsive to the length of light and dark periods. Spinach and lettuce, for instance, will flower when nights are short and days are long. They're such sensitive crops that people living in a city that's well-lit at night sometimes have problems growing spinach, lettuce, and other light-sensitive crops. The lights of the city essentially shorten the dark period and induce the plants to flower. Cabbages, on the other hand, grow to enormous sizes during the long summer days and short nights of far-northern latitudes. At the Alaska State Fair, prize-winning cabbages have a diameter of 3 feet across.

• Use a camera or light meter (see page 46 in *GrowLab: A Complete Guide to Gardening in the Classroom*) to determine the number of footcandles available in different spots in the GrowLab, a forest, a garden, the classroom, etc.

• Visit a commercial or university greenhouse. Find out how light is controlled to induce plants to flower at particular times.

• Compare plants grown under special "grow light" tubes with those grown under other types of light tubes.

• Explore differences in plant responses to artificial light and sunlight.

• Investigate whether different types of air pollution might affect the quality or quantity of light reaching plants.

• Propagate Christmas cacti or poinsettia by cuttings. Explore how daylength induces plants to flower or form red bracts.

• Research the concept of "health lighting" claiming to counteract the "winter blahs" or SAD (Seasonal Adjustment Disorder) experienced by people during periods of reduced sunlight.

What's in a Name?

Overview: Students invent new names for human and plant structures, based on how those structures help living things meet their needs.

*Use **What's in a Name?** as a culminating activity after students have learned about the form and function of different plant parts.*

Time:
Groundwork: 30 minutes
Exploration: 30 minutes
Making Connections: ongoing

Materials:
• newsprint or other drawing paper
• colored markers
• assorted plants
• "Plant Parts Chart," page 100

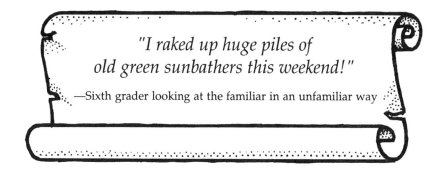

"I raked up huge piles of old green sunbathers this weekend!"

—Sixth grader looking at the familiar in an unfamiliar way

Laying the Groundwork

Objective: To create new names for body parts that reflect their form and function.

1. As a class, compile a list of human body parts. Then brainstorm lists of key words to describe what the body parts look like and what their jobs are. In both cases, encourage students to think creatively, using analogies whenever possible. For example:

Body part	What does it look like? (form)	What is its job? (function)
arm	pole long bent	reaching grabbing puller

2. Have students choose one word from each column to create a new, descriptive name for the body part. The new name doesn't have to refer to all of the part's functions. For instance:

Old name: arm
New name: grabbing pole

3. Have students use the new names to modify the jingle...

The grabbing pole is connected to the rotating cliff
The rotating cliff is connected to the ...

Exploration

Objective: To review plant part functions and create new names for the parts. To appreciate that the structures of plant parts help them function to meet plants' basic needs.

1. Have pairs of students repeat the above exercise using plant parts instead of body parts. Depending on your students' familiarity with plant parts, you may want to precede this exploration by reviewing plant part functions. See the "Plant Parts Chart," page 100. Place several GrowLab plants around the room for student reference. An example follows.

Plant part	What does it look like?	What is its job?
root	hairy branching underground string	soaks up water anchor stores food

2. Have students invent new names for plant parts using a word from each column. Then have each student pair team up with another pair to figure out which plant part is described by the other pair's invented name.

Old name: root
New name: underground string anchor

Making Connections

1. Challenge students to draw pictures illustrating their newly invented names. Compile the class drawings into a flip book that will enable students to mix and match their respective drawings and create new and unusual plants!

2. Possible discussion questions:

• *Why do you think...*

... your hand is not shaped like your ear?
... many leaves are broad?
... roots are hairy?
... flowers are brightly colored?
... roots spread out like a fan?

• *What do you think would happen if...*

... all of a plant's leaves were cut off?
... a plant's roots were pulled out of the soil?
... a plant's stem was bent over and broken?
... you picked all of the flowers off of plants?
... your lungs were made of bone and your bones were as elastic as muscles?

• *How do you think the structures of plant parts help plants meet their basic needs?*

Branching Out

• "Dissect" scientific names for plants to see if they describe plant parts. (For example, *grandiflora* means "large flower"; *Eriophyllum confertiflorum* (golden yarrow) means "wooly leaf crowded flower.")

• Have a Plant Part Scavenger Hunt outside. Some ideas:

- Locate parts with specific shapes or textures (e.g., six different-shaped leaves, two fuzzy stems).
- Use your invented words to find plant parts (e.g., four underneath stringanchors).
- Sort common garden vegetables into plant part categories and graph results.

• Estimate and verify the weights of different parts of a particular plant.

• Visit a grocery store and make lists of the plant parts found in various items.

• Identify the plant parts that different foods come from, using school lunches as a springboard—e.g., bread comes from seeds, pizza sauce comes from fruit. Calculate the percentages of different plant parts represented in a typical school lunch.

• Find out how diverse cultures use different parts of plants.

• Write stories that have creative analogies, like the ones students developed in this activity, in place of most common nouns.

Plant Parts Chart

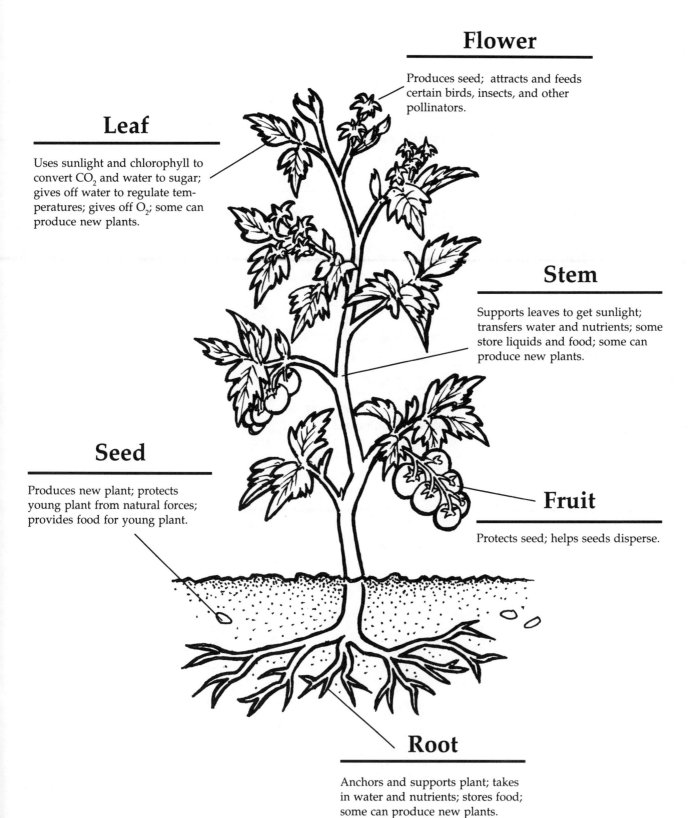

Flower

Produces seed; attracts and feeds certain birds, insects, and other pollinators.

Leaf

Uses sunlight and chlorophyll to convert CO_2 and water to sugar; gives off water to regulate temperatures; gives off O_2; some can produce new plants.

Stem

Supports leaves to get sunlight; transfers water and nutrients; some store liquids and food; some can produce new plants.

Seed

Produces new plant; protects young plant from natural forces; provides food for young plant.

Fruit

Protects seed; helps seeds disperse.

Root

Anchors and supports plant; takes in water and nutrients; stores food; some can produce new plants.

BACKGROUND
The Soil Connection

A Dirty Riddle

I am light and I am heavy.
I am strong enough to hold up a sky-
scraper.
I am fragile enough to be blown away
in the wind.
I am an anchor. I am a home. I am a
sponge.
I am one substance made of many
different things.
I am loose enough to flow like a river.
I am as solid as a mountain.
I can be fertile. I can be barren.
I am living and I am dead.

What am I?

Soil is a complex living system, composed of living and non-living materials, comprising a very thin layer on Earth. It helps provide plants with the support, nutrients, water, and air necessary for life. Living and non-living components interact, change, and combine over thousands of years to create soil. Time is an essential factor in soil formation. It can take up to 20,000 years to make 2.5 cm (one inch) of topsoil!

Although you may be using a soilless potting mix in your indoor garden, no garden experience would be complete without exploring soil.

Minerals: Non-living Components

For millions of years wind, rain, ice, intense heat, gravity, and chemicals have carved away at the Earth's crust. As water in and around rocks repeatedly freezes and thaws, the rocks are broken down into smaller and smaller particles. As rivers and streams rush downhill, they carry away these bits and pieces of the Earth's rocky surface. During the Ice Age, heavy glaciers crushed rocks and other materials such as shells into fine particles, carried them thousands of miles, and then deposited them as the glaciers melted.

The particles of rock present in soil range in size from large, coarse **sand** particles to fine **clay** particles. The proportion of these different-sized particles affects the amount of air, water, and nutrients available in a soil, and how the soil "behaves". The mineral particles in soil are described below.

Sand. These are the largest, coarsest soil particles. The **pore spaces** between sand particles are large, allowing water and nutrients to drain through very quickly. Soil with a high proportion of sand feels gritty and crumbles easily.

Clay. Clay particles are extremely fine and cling together. Because there is relatively little pore space, water moves through very slowly. Because of the many small particles, there is a great deal of surface area to which nutrients can adhere. Soil with a high proportion of clay feels heavy, slippery when wet, and will compact into a tight ball.

Silt. Silt particles are in between the sizes of sand and clay particles. Their other properties also lie somewhere between the previous two.

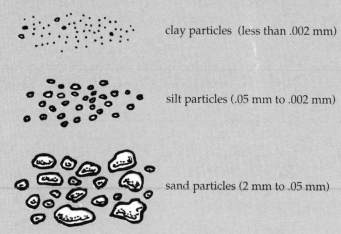

clay particles (less than .002 mm)

silt particles (.05 mm to .002 mm)

sand particles (2 mm to .05 mm)

Collecting Soil

When collecting soil for class explorations, with or without your students, consider such locations as school grounds, garden sites, stream banks, or parks, to get a variety of soil types. Dig down at least six inches with a spade to get a good sampling. If the ground freezes in your area, you can collect soil samples in warmer weather and keep them in plastic bags in the refrigerator until ready to use them.

Organic Matter: The Life of the Soil

The non-living mineral particles that result from the physical and chemical breakdown of rocks constitute only part of what we call soil. The other important component is **organic matter**, which includes the remains and waste products of living things. Plants and animals are continually being decomposed by bacteria, fungi, and other **decomposers** in the soil. In just one teaspoon of soil, billions of microscopic organisms exist. Without them, once-living materials could never decompose and be returned to the earth to provide nutrients for new life.

When remains of plants and animals have completely decomposed in the soil they form **humus**. Dark, crumbly, and spongy-textured, humus typically provides the majority of nutrients used by plants, helps retain soil moisture, and provides good aeration, drainage, and a loose crumbly structure for plants to grow in.

Plant roots also contribute to soil by exchanging nutrients, slowing down water loss, and aerating soil particles. Many animals, from ants to earthworms to rodents, also play important roles in the soil ecosystem, adding nutrients and loosening and mixing the soil.

A Good Balance

An ideal soil for growing most plants is one with a balance of different-sized particles (sand, silt, and clay) and a high proportion of organic matter. **Loam** is a term used by gardeners and farmers to describe these soils.

Not all soils are so ideal. A soil with an abundance of clay will tend to cling together in a solid mass, with individual particles indistinguishable. Problems with soils high in clay can include: slow warming in the spring; poor drainage, resulting in water-filled pores and lack of air for plant roots; and a texture too heavy for seed germination and root penetration. A soil with too much sand, on the other hand, can drain water too quickly and be low in nutrients. Adding organic matter can offset many of the problems associated with either extreme.

Your indoor garden can provide a springboard for exploring this vital resource. In the activity **A Soil-a-bration!** students use their senses to explore soil, and compare plants grown with and without soil. The activity **Soil Sort** challenges students to examine the different components of soil and how they affect it. In **MockSoil,** students try to create soil and recognize how complex and long term the natural process actually is.

Do Plants Need Soil?

Some plants, including certain aquatic and parasitic plants, have particular adaptations that allow them to meet their basic needs without soil. However, because of the role soil plays for most plants, it is often considered a basic need. **Hydroponics** is raising plants in a solution of water and nutrients, without soil. Hydroponic growers must continually supply nutrients and oxygen to the root system, and provide some way to hold the plant up.

The **soilless potting mix** used in many GrowLab classrooms serves some of the functions of soil. It is often recommended for indoor growing because it provides many of the advantages of soil without some of the drawbacks. Most soilless mixes consist of peat moss, perlite and/or vermiculite, and some nutrients. The spongy peat moss holds onto moisture, while the perlite and/or vermiculite provides good drainage and a texture lighter than most soils. This is particularly important for young seedlings. While potting mixes contain some nutrients, these normally have to be supplemented with fertilizer.

Garden soil typically contains more nutrients than does soilless mix, as well as the microorganisms capable of releasing additional nutrients as they decompose organic matter. It also, however, can contain disease organisms, which can thrive in a warm, moist indoor environment. One of the biggest advantages of potting mixes is that they are sterile, containing no living organisms. For more information on potting mixes, see page 32 in *GrowLab: A Complete Guide to Gardening in the Classroom.*

A simple soil key

Moisten your soil sample and rub it between your thumb and forefinger.

Does it feel gritty?

yes → sandy soil

no → Does it stick together and make a long ribbon?

yes → clayey soil

no → loamy soil

A Soil-a-bration!

Overview: Students use their senses to explore soil. They then grow seeds with and without soil to explore whether plants need soil.

Time:
Groundwork: 30 minutes
Exploration: Part 1—45 minutes
  Part 2—30 minutes setup;
  2 weeks ongoing observations
Making Connections: ongoing

Materials:
• 1/2 to 1 cup of "natural" soil per student (see Advance Preparation)
• blindfolds or brown paper bags
• water
• old newspaper, cardboard box tops, or cafeteria trays
• eyedroppers (optional)
• rapid-germinating seeds (e.g., lettuce, radish, or sunflower)
• pots
• sponges
• cardboard
• potting mix or soil
"Plant a Question" reproducible, page 282
"My Plant Journal" reproducible, page 285

Background: Page 101

Advance Preparation:
Carefully collect soils from at least two different outdoor locations. See the "Collecting Soil" sidebar on page 102 for suggestions.

Laying the Groundwork

Objective: To use senses to explore soil.

1. Give each pair of students 1 to 2 cups of "natural" soil (see Advance Preparation), a small amount of water, and several sheets of old newspaper, tops of cardboard boxes, or cafeteria trays to use as work surfaces.

Before they touch the soil, have one student describe the soil to a blindfolded partner, then switch roles. Have students then use their other senses to explore the soil. Allow them to "play" with their soil sample, working it through their fingers. Ask: *Can you think of three words to describe how the soil feels? When you touch it, what else does it remind you of? How does it smell? How does it sound when you drop it on the newspaper? Without actually tasting it, describe how you think the soil might taste.*

2. Have each pair of students join with another pair whose soil sample looks different from their own. Have new groups of four compare the feel, smell, look, and sound of the two soils.

3. Using eyedroppers, if available, have students slowly add water to their soil. Encourage students to make mudpies and other creative sculptures out of their soil. Ask: *How does the water change your soil? How does it look now? ...feel? ...smell? ...sound? How is it the same as before? How is it different?*

Exploration

Objective: To examine the role soil plays in plant growth.

1. Facilitate a class discussion about whether and how soil is important for plants. Ask: *What do you think soil does for plants? Have you ever seen plants growing without soil? Where? Do you think plants need soil?*

2. Following the Plant a Question process, page 9, have small groups of students design explorations to find out "What will happen if we grow plants without soil?" or set up the following:

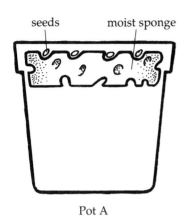

seeds   moist sponge

Pot A

potting mix   seeds

Pot B

Except for the presence or absence of soil, treat all plants the same. Students should record observations in the "My Plant Journal" reproducible for two weeks.

3. After two weeks discuss findings. Ask: *What differences do you observe in plants grown with and without soil? How are these plants the same? How did what happened compare with your predictions?*

> **What to expect:** As soon as the seeds germinate, students should notice differences. While seeds on the sponge might be able to anchor themselves at first, the lack of soil particles will make it difficult for roots to continue to grow well. Once seedlings exhaust their food supplies, plants grown without soil should be stunted due to lack of supplemental nutrients.

Making Connections

Possible discussion questions:

• *How do you think the soil is helping the plants? Why do you think there are differences in the plants grown with and without soil?* (The soil is helping plants meet their basic needs by giving them a place to anchor their roots and take in water and minerals as they grow.)

• *Imagine a tree growing without any soil. If it could talk, what do you think its complaints would be?*

• *Why do you think we planted more than one seed with and without soil?*

Plants Help Soil

As plants grow, how do you think they might help soil? As plant roots grow, they help break down rocks and other materials that make up soil. Roots also release acids and other substances that help break down materials to form soil. As plants die, decomposed organic matter adds nutrients and a spongy texture to soil.

Branching Out

• Design and conduct investigations to compare plants grown in different types of soils.

• Use microscopes to investigate the many parts of soil that can't be seen by the unaided eye. One teaspoon of natural soil can contain billions of living things!

• Explore earthworms and other animals that are interdependent with soil.

• Compare clays and other types of soil to find out how they "behave" when you try to make mudpies and soil sculptures.

• Grow "air plants" (epiphytes), plants that do not live in the soil. These are available in many nurseries and garden centers. Find out how these plants meet their basic needs without using soil.

• Find out how different human cultures depend on soil, e.g., as material to build shelter. Make some bricks by shaping wet, clayey soil in ice cube trays. After your bricks dry, use them to build a wall or a house!

• Imagine that you live under the soil. Write or tell a story about your adventures "down under."

• Have a Soil-a-bration! List what you think is special about soil and why it should be celebrated. Create names for soil holidays and figure out how to celebrate a party ...a parade ...making and sending greeting cards. Don't forget the mudpies!

Soil Sort

Overview: Students become "soil surgeons," dissecting soil and sorting its components, and begin to discover its unique properties.

Time:
Groundwork: 45 minutes
Exploration: two 45-minute sessions
Making Connections: ongoing

Materials (per pair of students):
• 1 to 2 cups "natural" soil
(see Advance Preparation)
• *optional:* clay, sand, humus
• butcher/freezer paper with shiny surface
• toothpicks or plastic spoons
• hand lens or magnifier
• clear liter (or quart) jars
• water
• paper and plastic cups
• rubber surgeon's gloves or masks (optional)
• "Soil Sort" reproducible, page 266

Background: Page 101

Advance Preparation:
Carefully collect soils from several different outdoor locations. See the "Collecting Soil" sidebar on page 102 for directions.

If your students haven't used their senses to explore natural soil, conduct the groundwork of **A Soil-a-bration!**

Laying the Groundwork

Objective: To understand that soil is composed of many living and non-living components.

1. Have your students imagine they are part of a medical practice called Soil Sort, Inc. These surgeons have a very special patient—soil! Give each pair of students 1 to 2 cups of soil. Have the surgeons use their senses to examine their patients. Then have them perform "surgery" to figure out what's "inside" their patients. In the "operating room," give each pair of surgeons:

• 1 to 2 cups of soil
• paper to work on (preferably butcher/freezer paper with a shiny surface)
• "dissecting tools" such as toothpicks or plastic spoons for moving particles
• a hand lens or magnifier
• rubber surgeon's gloves or masks—just for fun—if available

2. Challenge the surgeons to dissect their patients by separating the soil into rough piles of as many different types of soil components as possible. Suggest that they sort the soil into categories—e.g., different sizes, colors, shapes, materials. Have students use the "Soil Sort" reproducible to record their findings.

As they attempt to separate the different components, encourage students to try to figure out what different parts make up the whole. For example:

Pile #	Description (texture, color, etc.)	Where do you think it came from?
1	lots of rough, light brown pieces	big rocks
2	1 worm, 3 small red ants crawling around	other insects
3	lots of brown, soft, squishy stuff	lots of other things rotted together?

Just budding in: Since soil is made up of living and non-living substances that have gone through physical and chemical changes over a long period of time, it may be hard for students to identify all the individual components.

3. Have pairs of surgeons get a "second opinion" by teaming up with another pair. This new, four-person team should study one another's samples and compare observations. Ask the new teams to report to the rest of the class: *What types of piles did you all have in common? Why do you think you did not all have the same categories? What were some unusual findings?*

4. Once surgeons think they know what's "inside" their patients, have them run some tests (see Exploration) to find out how their patients "act."

Exploration—Part 1

Objective: To explore the drainage abilities of different soils.

1. Have pairs of students run a test called Dirty Drains to find out how quickly their soil drains water compared to other soils. Use the different soil samples and, if available, some clay, sand, and/or humus samples for comparison. Set up the following:

Based on their other observations, have students record predictions, on the "Soil Sort" reproducible, of which soils might drain fastest. Direct them to explain why they made each prediction.

2. Have surgeons pour 250 ml (approximately 1 cup) of water into their patient and have a race to see which soil drains most water in two minutes. Ask: *Think about what you observed when you touched and dissected your soil. Why do you think some soils drain better than others? What other materials can you think of that drain well* (coffee filters, sand, kitchen colanders, fish net)? *How are these other materials like soil?* (They all have pores or holes in them.)

3. Let the water drain out completely and tell surgeons to use the same soil as they conduct the next test, Settle Down, Please!, to help them figure out why the soils drained differently.

Exploration—Part 2

Objective: To understand that soils are made up of different-sized particles and that the proportion of these particles affects how water drains through different soils.

1. Have surgeons fill a clear liter or quart jar two-thirds full of water and add their soil until the jar is full. Making sure the jar lid is screwed on tightly, have students vigorously shake each jar, then place it upright and let it settle. Ask: *What do you think will happen to the soil in the jar? Why?*

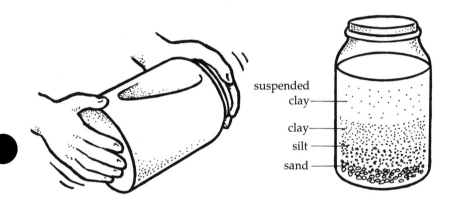

suspended clay
clay
silt
sand

2. Surgeons should continue to observe their patients (in the jar) when possible throughout the day. In twenty-four hours, have students observe, measure, and sketch the layers that settled out. Ask: *What happened to your patients? Why do you think there are different layers in the jar? Of what do you think the different layers are made? How do the layers of soils from different locations compare?* If they haven't already guessed, share background information with students about soil particles, their relative sizes, and their effect on soil characteristics.

What to expect: Most natural soils contain a mixture of different-sized particles. The largest and heaviest particles (sand) will settle out immediately and form the bottom layer. Silt particles take a little longer and will form the second layer. The extremely fine clay particles take a long time to settle, and some clay particles will remain in suspension indefinitely. Your students should have found that soils containing the largest proportion of sand particles drain water the most quickly. Soils that are primarily clay do not allow water to drain very easily.

Making Connections

1. Make a large, poster-sized class "Medical Journal," highlighting the findings about soil. Give each pair of surgeons one page where they can creatively write and/or illustrate what they found out about their patient. For instance,

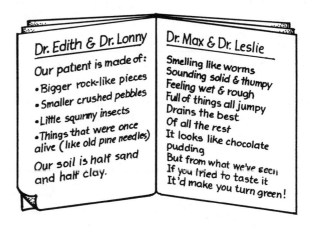

2. Possible discussion questions:

• *What general statements can you make about what makes up your patients? Do you think all soils are made of the same things? Why or why not?*

• *If the entire class had examined only one patient, do you think you would have understood as much about soil? Why?*

• *From where do you think the materials in each of your categories came? What do you think happens to the different components that makes them end up as one thing called "soil"? What other things that we didn't identify do you think might change over time to become part of soil (shells, rocks, plants, animals)?*

• *How old do you think your patients are? Why?* Share that because separate materials physically and chemically change and combine to become soil, it can take between 100 and 20,000 years to make 2.5 cm (1 inch) of topsoil!

• *Would you rather have sandy, silty, or clayey soil make up your sports/playing field? Why?*

• *What problems might you face if you had a garden with a lot of clay soil? ...with a lot of sandy soil?*

• *In what ways do you think plants depend on soil? Based on your observations, can you imagine how soil might depend on plants or animals? How do you think animals—including humans—depend on soil?*

• *What new questions do you have about soil? ...about plants and soil? How might we go about finding answers to your questions?*

Branching Out

• Design investigations to explore how each type of soil component contributes to its properties. For example, large particles allow better drainage, clay binds soil together, and organic matter increases its water-holding capacity.

• Compare soilless potting mix with a natural soil. Discuss how they are different and why people might want to use potting mix instead of natural soil.

• Identify and draw living things found in soil.

• Mix a small amount of water with some natural soil. Remove some of the water with an eye dropper and examine it with a microscope to find microorganisms. Debate whether soil is "alive."

• Acting as soil doctors, research and discuss ways humans affect soil composition. Some examples: we add compost, peat, or lime to soil; we drive on it; acid precipitation changes soil pH. Discuss how our treatment of soil affects plants and how negative impacts can be prevented and/or alleviated.

• Develop "jingles" for advertisements promoting the virtues of soil.

Overview: Students try to create soil that has many of the qualities of real soil.

Time:
Groundwork: 45 minutes
Exploration: 60 minutes
Making Connections: ongoing

Materials:
• "natural" soil samples (see Advance Preparation)
• *optional:* hot plate, small pan, limestone, glass jar, freezer, water, safety glasses, hammers
• student-generated materials for making MockSoil: e.g., rocks or shells, vegetable scraps, lawn clippings, leaves, sand or clay

Background: Page 101

Advance Preparation:
To compare making muffins to making soil, have each student bring in a muffin recipe. Have some extra muffin recipes available in case there aren't enough.
    Carefully collect soil from a couple of outdoor locations. See the "Collecting Soil" sidebar on page 102 for directions.

MockSoil

This one tastes more like fresh ground.

The "MockSoil" Challenge

Laying the Groundwork

Objective: To recognize that the nature of a final product is affected by its ingredients and how it was made.

1. In small groups, have students compare their muffin recipes (see Advance Preparation), making a list of ingredients they all have in common. Ask: *Why do you think there are so many similarities in the recipes? Why do you think there are differences? What do you think the flour contributes to the muffins? ...the eggs? ...the oil? What do you think the texture and flavor would be like if the recipe called for...*

...twice as much flour?
...half as many eggs?
...ten times as much honey?
...no baking soda?
...baking for only two minutes?
...no baking at all?

2. Facilitate a class discussion comparing muffin making to soil making. Ask questions such as: *Are there certain kinds of ingredients that need to be used in making muffins? ...in making soil? What role does time play in making muffins? ...in making soil?*

Just budding in: If time and resources permit, in class or as homework, have your students try some variations on a muffin recipe. Have them try using different ingredients, changing the oven temperature, or changing the procedure, e.g., mixing or baking for different amounts of time.

Whole Wheat Meadow Muffins

3 cups whole wheat flour
4 1/2 tsp. baking powder
1/3 cup melted butter
3/4 tsp. salt

2 eggs, beaten
1 1/3 cups milk
1/4 cup honey
raisins and/or chopped
nuts (optional)

Preheat oven to 375 degrees F. Sift whole wheat flour, baking powder and salt into a bowl. Combine the honey, eggs, milk, and melted butter. Stir into the dry ingredients until they are just moistened. Add optional ingredients. Fill oiled muffin tins 2/3 full and bake for 20 minutes.

Exploration

Objective: To understand that soil formation is a complex, long-term process, not easily duplicated in a short amount of time.

1. Give small groups of students some "natural soil" samples (see Advance Preparation). Let them explore (e.g., touch, observe through hand lenses, and smell) the soils. Have each group make a list of all of the ingredients that they know or have observed are part of natural soil.

2. As a class, discuss how soil relates to plants. Combine all input on a class chart. For example:

Relationship between Plants and Soil

Soil anchors roots.
Soil absorbs and holds water for plants.
It allows air to get to seeds.
Dead plants (and animals) rot in soil.
Roots can move through soil as they grow.
Strong roots break up rocks that make up soil.
Plants get minerals from the soil.

Discuss each item on the chart and circle those on which the class agrees.

3. Challenge small groups of students to use actual soil "ingredients" to write a recipe for making 2 cups of MockSoil that they think will support the growth of a plant. (Have them refer to the soil ingredients list and the class chart from steps 1 and 2 above.)

Students should include reasons they've chosen each ingredient. Ask, for example: *If you think soil soaks up water, which of your ingredients served that function? If you think plants depend on organic matter in soil, what did you add to your MockSoil?*

Have groups share recipes, explaining why they've chosen each component.

A sample student recipe:

Mama and Papa Nature's Best MockSoil
Ingredient — Function
¼ c. ground leaves — organic matter for plants
3 worms — mix soil and castings, make good fertilizer
1 c. crushed rocks — provides minerals, makes pores for air and water
¼ c. broken shells —
½ c. clay — support for anchoring plant roots
2 T. water — helps it all stick together
Mix all dry ingredients well. Add water and stir until moistened.

Soil Creation Simulations

Demonstrate some of the ways soils are created in nature (below). Students can recreate some of these processes themselves.

Caution: Students should always wear safety glasses and have adult supervision when working with sharp or caustic materials. When crushing rocks or shells, make sure materials are in a secure bag before banging them.

Freezing. Freeze water in a closed plastic container. The expansion of the freezing water breaks the container, just as freezing water trapped in rocks breaks the rocks into smaller and smaller pieces.

Heating. In a dry pan, heat some limestone. Drop the heated limestone in ice water. It will crack and break into smaller pieces as it contracts after expanding from the heat.

Abrasion. Simulate earth movements by rubbing together bricks, concrete, or limestone. Through friction, larger pieces will crumble into smaller pieces.

4. Have groups follow their recipes and make MockSoil. Using the natural soil samples for comparison, allow students to adjust recipes to make them more like real soil, as long as they can justify any adjustment. For example, they may find they need more coarse material to improve drainage.

5. When complete, have groups compare MockSoils. Have students brainstorm a list of what to compare, e.g., texture, drainage abilities, settling rate. Ask: *Why do you think they're similar or different? How does your MockSoil compare with the natural soil you explored earlier?*

6. Share with your students that the major differences between MockSoil and natural soil are:

• In real soil, there are lots of hidden ingredients. Just one teaspoon of soil can contain billions of microscopic organisms! This "invisible" life is responsible for releasing nutrients. Substances from microbial activity dissolve materials and decompose organic matter, which is essential to soil formation.

• Chemical and physical processes change and combine the separate components of soil (e.g., dead plant matter or crushed rocks) into the living soil system. Without changes due to such things as heat, frost, glaciers, wind, growth of large tree roots, acids from bacteria, or life processes of soil animals, natural soil would look very similar to MockSoil.

• Time is of the essence! No matter what the ingredients, if you don't bake muffins long enough, dough is all you'll get! It can take between 100 and 20,000 years for all the physical and chemical processes to change the ingredients of soil into 2.5 cm (1 inch) of topsoil. Perhaps students should add the following to their recipes: "Leave for 10,000 years in wind, rain, and an alternately warm and frozen environment!"

Making Connections

Possible discussion questions:

• *How was the process you used to form soil similar to the soil formation process that naturally occurs? How was it different? Why do you think your MockSoil is different from the natural soil? What do you think you could do to make your MockSoil more natural?*

• *How do you think a plant grown in MockSoil would compare to one grown in natural soil? Why?*

• *From your experiences with "soilless" potting mix in the GrowLab, how would you say natural soil compares with "soilless" potting mix? How does your MockSoil compare with "soilless" potting mix? (See background information on page 103.)*

• *It is estimated that the United States loses over one billion tons of topsoil (approximately half a million acres of crop-growing potential) every year. In light of what you've found out about making soils, discuss whether we should be concerned about this topsoil loss.*

• *How did it feel to try to play the role of nature?*

Branching Out

• Compare the growth and development of seeds planted in MockSoil with those planted in natural soil.

• Make compost (see page 213). Discuss how the process and outcome of composting compares with natural soil formation.

• Compare the types of soils found in different locations, ranging from a crack in a sidewalk to a garden.

• Examine how soil qualities change as you move from the top (ground level) down through a cross-section or **profile** of soil.

• Find out how natural gas and diamonds are formed.

• Write and perform original "rock" songs, with lyrics relating to soil formation.

• Draw a cartoon showing Mama and Papa Nature in their kitchen creating soil.

• Invite a food scientist, chef, or school cook to share the process he or she uses to create recipes. Try creating and eating some of your own original recipes.

Chapter 2 Generation to Generation

F lowers compete for pollinators' attention; potatoes sprout new shoots; spider plants send off young plantlets. What a variety of strategies exist in the plant world to guarantee that reproduction will occur! Life on Earth continues because individuals can stretch beyond their limited life cycles and produce offspring. While not a basic need for individual survival, reproduction is necessary for survival of species. Plant reproduction can be either sexual, combining the genes of two parents to produce seeds, or asexual, producing a new plant from parts of only one parent.

This chapter suggests activities to help you explore both types of plant reproduction in your classroom. Students will examine the relationships of seeds, flowers, and fruits. They'll recognize that flowers have an exciting array of strategies to ensure pollination. They'll explore various methods of creating new plants from parts of old ones.

Plants from Seeds

Over the course of 100 years an acorn matures into a great oak tree. In two months, a small seed becomes a 6-foot-tall sunflower, heavy with new seeds. Even the relatively small plants in your indoor garden undergo dramatic changes throughout their lives—beginning as seeds, maturing, flowering, fruiting, and producing seeds to start a new cycle. In the activity **Plant Cycles,** students observe the changes that occur during a plant's life cycle, from seed to seed.

The key agents in the process of seed production, complete with all of the necessary equipment, are flowers. Even though we humans enjoy their beauty, fragrance and, in some cases, nutrition, flowers are not here to please us. Their function is to produce seeds. The color, size, shape, smell, and other attributes of flowers are vital to this effort.

Flower Structure

Although flower structure can vary greatly, there are a number of basic parts. The female organ, the **pistil**, is generally in the center of the flower. The platform at the top of the pistil—often sticky to trap pollen—is the **stigma**, held up by the tubelike **style.** The style leads down to the **ovary**, inside of which are the **ovules**, containing female egg cells. The male parts, the **stamens**, typically surround the pistils. The **anther** on top of the stamen, held up by the stemlike **filament**, produces **pollen**, which contains male sperm cells.

Pollination is the transfer of pollen from male to female flower parts. When a grain of pollen lands on the stigma, a tiny tube grows from it and probes down the style into the ovary. Sperm cells then travel through this tube from the pollen grain to an ovule, and there join with an egg cell in the process called **fertilization.** The fertilized ovule will become a seed, and the ovary, a fruit. Without pollination and fertilization, fruit and seed production cannot occur in most plants. Your students will examine this concept in the activity **Plant Parenthood.**

Other important flower parts are the **petals** and **sepals.** Petals are often brightly colored to attract pollinators (birds, bees, and other insects), and broad and flat to provide good "landing pads." Wind-pollinated flowers, on the other hand, usually have inconspicuous petals, if any. Sepals are green leafy structures surrounding the petals, which initially protected the developing bud.

The activity **Flowers: Up Close** invites students to examine flowers closely in order to understand their function.

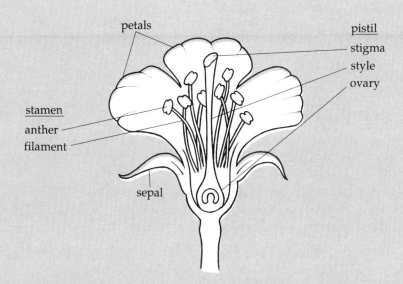

One Flower or Many?

Often, what appears to be one flower is actually a collection of hundreds. Sunflowers, daisies, dandelions, and all other members of the composite family are actually composed of hundreds of tiny flowers, many of which will produce seeds. Take a look inside a sunflower to find a host of seeds.

Male or Female?

Perfect flowers have both pistils and stamens. **Imperfect flowers** are either male or female, and pollen must somehow make its way from the male to the female flower. Even in many perfect flowers, however, the parts are arranged to keep pollen from easily reaching the ovary of the same flower. This prevents self-pollination, ensuring a mixture and diversity of genes and, therefore, increased health of the species. (Humans consciously apply the same principle by having taboos against reproduction between blood relatives.) In the GrowLab, peas and beans are examples of perfect flowers, while cucumbers are examples of imperfect flowers.

Flowers: Clever Advertisers

Since flowers can't move from place to place to find mates, they've evolved with an exciting range of strategies to ensure that pollination takes place. A flower's unsurpassed advertising can lure hungry bees, birds, moths, butterflies, and beetles into acting as pollen-carrying liaisons between flowers that might otherwise never touch. Flower adaptations that encourage pollination include:

• aromatic nectar (sweet fluid)
• bright colors
• shapes designed to accommodate specific pollinators
• designs or "tracks" to guide pollinators to pollen and/or nectar
• lightweight, petalless flowers for wind pollination
• structures that resemble other pollinators, evoking mating or aggressive responses

The activity **Petal Attraction** allows students to use their understanding of flower structure to "invent" flowers and consider how they are adapted to attract pollinators.

A Look at the Birds and Bees

Although bees are the best-known pollinators, many other animals visit flowers in search of nectar and inadvertently pollinate them. Pollen dusts these visitors' bodies and then brushes onto the female parts of the next flowers they investigate. Over hundreds and thousands of years, many flowers and pollinators have coevolved to develop special relationships. A pollinator capable of detecting certain colors or scents, or possessing structures that best fit certain flowers, passes these advantages on to its offspring. Over many generations these traits become well established. Flowers, meanwhile, also evolved with characteristics suiting particular pollinators.

Some pollinators and their preferences include:

Bees. They are attracted mainly to nectar and pollen, which they use for food. Although bees cannot perceive the color red, they are normally attracted to white, yellow, or blue flowers and can see special patterns that reflect ultraviolet light. Bees have a very well-developed sense of smell and are attracted to fragrant flowers. Many flowers attractive to bees, such as mints, violets, and snapdragons, have an irregular shape to provide convenient landing platforms.

Butterflies. Also attracted to nectar, butterflies often visit the same flowers that bees do.

Moths. Since moths are nocturnal, the flowers they pollinate tend to be pale or white, more visible at night, and very fragrant at dusk. The flowers are often tubular, so that their nectar is accessible to long moth tongues. Many orchids are pollinated by moths.

Flies. Many types of flies lay their eggs in decaying flesh. Some flowers have strong, unpleasant odors and maroon colors that attract flies. They lay eggs in the flowers, inadvertently pollinating them. Red trillium is an example.

Beetles. Beetles often eat flower parts. Flowers depending on them for pollination are often large, so that some will be left after beetles have dined. Magnolias are an example.

Birds. Most birds have a poor sense of smell, so flowers depending on them for pollination do not need to be fragrant. Red flowers, on the other hand, are attractive to hummingbirds. Since some birds can drink large quantities of nectar, certain flowers have evolved to be long and tubular, able to hold much nectar.

Hibiscus is an example.

Bats. Bats are often important pollinators in tropical areas. Flowers adapted to pollination by bats are often large, pale, and strongly odored, particularly at dusk when bats begin to fly.

Wind. Since flowers on wind-pollinated plants have no need to be bright, showy, or fragrant, most have no petals. Instead they have long stamens and long, feathery stigmas and styles exposed to wind currents. They produce large amounts of lightweight pollen that floats randomly on the breeze. Grasses and many trees are wind-pollinated.

From flower to fruit

Fruits

As ovules develop into seeds inside the ovary of a flower, the ovary swells and becomes fleshy or hardens to protect the developing seeds. This part of the plant containing the seeds is called the **fruit.** In addition to protecting the seeds, many fruits are designed to help seeds ultimately disperse, as described below. Many foods that we commonly call vegetables, such as tomatoes or cucumbers, are technically fruits since they contain the seeds. "Vegetable," a non-botanical term, refers to any edible part of a non-woody-stemmed plant. This includes leaves, roots, stems, flowers, or fruits. The activity **Fruit for Thought** enables students to examine a variety of fruits and discover what makes a fruit a fruit.

Fruits take many forms. The two general categories used to categorize fruits are fleshy and dry.

Fleshy Fruits. These fruits, including apples, oranges, plums, and berries, generally have sweet, fleshy ovaries surrounding the seeds. They are enticing food for animals who, in turn, scatter seeds away from the parent plant.

Dry Fruits. The ovaries of dry fruits also contain the seeds, but the ovary walls are thin and dry, rather than fleshy. With some dry fruits, such as corn, wheat, oats, and barley, each fruit is a single dry layer covering one seed. Each grain on an ear of corn, therefore, is a fruit. Many nuts, on the other hand, have double

Saving GrowLab Seeds

To explore life cycles, from seed to seed, consider collecting and replanting seeds to begin a new generation. Beans are the easiest seeds to replant in the classroom. When snap beans are ready for eating, they are still immature. To harvest them for replanting, let them grow for another four weeks or so, until the pods turn dry and brown. It's important to harvest seeds for replanting at the appropriate stage. Seeds that are picked too early, before the embryo is mature, won't have stored enough nourishment to get off to a good start and the seeds will have a poorer chance of germinating.

Collect the seeds and replant. If you're saving them to replant at another time, store the seeds in a cool, dry place, to protect the living embryos.

walls enclosing a single seed. Still other dry fruits, like beans, peas, and milkweed, have a non-fleshy pod containing a number of seeds. When dry, the pods split open, letting the seeds drop out. Some dry fruits have fluffy or feathery parts on their outer coats, which help the fruit float on the wind. Dandelions are an example of this type of fruit. Other dry fruits, like those of the maple tree, consist of stiff, winglike parts that allow the fruit to twist and flutter to the ground. For an activity on seed dispersal adaptations, see **Go Seeds Go!**, page 191.

When we eat fruits, we eat either the fruit (the ovary), the fruit and seeds, or just the seed. The table below gives examples for some common edible fruits.

Apple
(fleshy fruit)

Bean
(dry fruit)

Corn (kernels)
(dry fruit)

Fruit	Type	What we eat
apples	fleshy	fruit
oranges	fleshy	fruit
cucumbers	fleshy	fruit and seeds
tomatoes	fleshy	fruit and seeds
wheat	dry	seeds
beans	dry	fruit and seeds (if fresh) seeds (if dry)
corn	dry	fruit and seeds
peanuts	dry	seeds
wheat	dry	seeds
berries	fleshy	fruit and seeds
melons	fleshy	fruit and seeds
kumquat	fleshy	fruit and seeds

Plant Cycles

Overview: Students compare plant and human life cycles, and observe the life cycles of their GrowLab plants.

This is a good activity to do in conjunction with any long-term garden project. Whether students are growing a salad garden, have their own special pots, or are engaged in another project, they can observe and understand changes during plant life cycles. It's particularly valuable when flowering plants like beans or tomatoes are used.

Time:
Groundwork: 45 minutes
Exploration: 6-plus weeks ongoing observations
Making Connections: ongoing

Materials:
• GrowLab plants (plants that easily produce seeds such as tomatoes, beans or peas are preferable)
• "Garden Calendar" reproducible, page 288
• "My Plant Journal" reproducible, page 285

Background: Page 118

Laying the Groundwork

Objective: To consider how both plants and humans change throughout their life cycles.

1. Ask students to think about how humans change during their lifetimes. *How are you different now than you were as a baby? How are you the same? How do you expect to change when you're an adult?* Incorporate answers onto a class chart. Ask: *What similarities do you notice in the ways we all change over time?*

2. Having stimulated thinking about human life cycles, turn the discussion to plants. *In what ways do you think plants change throughout their lives? What have you observed to make you think this? How can you tell whether one plant is older or at a later life stage than another?*

Exploration

Objective: To observe and record how certain plants change throughout their life cycles.

1. Have students work in pairs to "adopt" a plant from the Grow-Lab to observe throughout its life cycle. (More than one group can use the same plant.) The activity should begin when seeds are planted, so students can observe the complete life cycle. Students can use personal journals, or the "My Plant Journal" reproducible to record regular observations of changes in their plants. Remind them to notice such things as changes in leaf number, leaf size, height, new parts, and the order in which changes occur.

2. While plants are maturing, refer to "OnGrowing Ideas," Appendix C, for suggestions for interdisciplinary activities to sustain students' interest and curiosity. Students can use the "Garden Calendar" reproducible to record events or changes during plant life cycles.

3. As plants mature, discuss student observations. Ask: *What tended to happen to leaves and plant height over time? Did the fruits always follow the flowers? What similarities are there in the ways different plants change throughout their life cycles? What happened to your plants after they produced seeds?* (You may want to follow this activity with **FungusAmongUs,** which illustrates how dead plant materials are also part of the cycle of life, decomposing and providing nutrients for new life.) *How were changes in your plants similar to changes in humans during our life cycles? How were they different? How does this compare with your predictions?*

Making Connections

1. Have pairs of students do a short class presentation about the life cycle of their adopted plant. Encourage them to prepare visual displays, short stories, poems, or skits.

2. Play Plant Cycles. Select six students to represent parts of a plant's life cycle: seed, sprout, mature plant, flowering plant, fruiting plant, another seed. Randomly position the students in a circle. Ask other students to rearrange the parts of the plant's life cycle into an order that shows a plant growing from a seed to the next generation of seeds.

3. Working from their observation journals, have pairs of students draw a number of the life cycle stages of their adopted plant. Mix up the drawings and share them with another pair. That pair must decide on the appropriate sequence for the drawings. Wrap this activity up by binding each set of drawings into a flip book.

Branching Out

• Save seeds from GrowLab plants for replanting (see sidebar, page 121.)

• Identify and explore other things in the enviroment (or in our lives) that follow cycles, such as water, seasons, or holidays.

• Take a walk outdoors and try to identify different life cycle stages of plants. Consider having a scavenger hunt for plants at different life cycle stages (e.g., flowering, sprouting, dying).

• Research differences between plants that complete their life cycles in one year (annuals) and those that take two (biennials) or many years (perennials) to complete life cycles (see sidebar.)

Life Cycles: From One Year to Many

Not all plants will complete their full life cycles during their time in your GrowLab. **Annuals** are plants that flower and complete a full life cycle, from seed to seed, in one year. Common GrowLab annuals are beans, cucumbers, lettuce, peas, peppers, potatoes, tomatoes, and annual flowers. (Some of these, like lettuce, probably will not flower in the short time they are in your GrowLab.) **Biennials** complete a full life cycle in two years. During the first year, the plant puts energy primarily into roots, and it flowers during the second year. Common GrowLab bienniels are beets, carrots, onions and parsley. **Perennials** continue to flower, produce seeds and grow for many years. They often have adaptations such as dormancy and dropping leaves to help them survive year-round in a changing environment. Perennials that you might raise in your GrowLab include tree seedlings and garden flowers like black-eyed Susans.

Flowers: Up Close

Overview: Students examine flowers inside and out and begin to understand how flowers are designed to promote pollination and fertilization.

Time:
Groundwork: 40 minutes
Exploration: 40 minutes
Making Connections: ongoing

Materials (per pair):
• assorted flowers (e.g., tulips, lilies, gladioli, daffodils, daisies, hibiscus, petunias, and GrowLab flowers)
• hand lenses
• "Flowers: Up Close—Part 1" reproducible, page 268
• "Flowers: Up Close—Part 2" reproducible, page 269

Background: Page 118

Advance Preparation:
Check with florists and funeral homes for donations of discarded flowers. Also ask students to bring some from home.

Laying the Groundwork

Objective: To observe and describe various flowers, and to begin to consider similarities among flowers.

1. Place each flower (see Materials) on a desk, counter, or in a circle on the floor, and tape a sheet of writing paper next to each one. Invite students to play Musical Flowers. Have each pair of students stand or sit by one flower while you play some appropriate music (e.g., "Waltz of the Flowers" from *The Nutcracker Suite* or "Honeysuckle Rose" by Fats Waller). Give pairs a minute or two to explore their flowers with their senses, and then have each member of the pair write one word or phrase, describing the flower, on the paper. Have the pair cover up their descriptions with a sheet of paper, to promote original ideas from the next group. Stop the music to signal time to move to the next flower. Repeat this until each pair has had a chance to add to each list.

2. Before collecting description sheets, number each one and keep a master list of flowers for yourself. Randomly pass one to each pair. Direct students, one at a time, to match the description with a flower. When each pair has done so, confirm their guesses using your numbered list. Ask: *Which types of descriptions were most useful? Were there certain words or types of words that showed up numerous times on different papers? What similarities were there among the flowers?*

3. Focus students' attention on their descriptions of colors, smells, and structures of flowers. Ask: *Can you guess what the function of flowers is? Why do you think many flowers look so pretty and smell so nice? What have you observed outdoors that might help answer this?*
   Share the information that flowers produce seeds for new plants. Pollen from one flower has to be transferred to another, so it can join with an egg cell and become a seed. Ask: *How do you think this pollen gets moved from one flower to another? What have you ever observed to make you believe this?* Discuss pollination.

Exploration

Objective: To examine, describe, and begin to understand the function of flower parts.

1. Give each pair of students one flower to examine closely with a hand lens. Have each pair sketch a cross-section of the flower and describe the separate parts.

1. eight long, skinny things with flat dark tops
2. six large, heart-shaped, sweet-smelling, soft petals around outside.

They can gently pull apart half the flower for a better view of its parts, saving the other half for the rest of the exploration. Ask pairs to discuss how they think the different parts might help in pollination. Share answers with the class.

2. Give each pair a copy of the "Flowers: Up Close—Part 1" reproducible, illustrating real parts from different types of flowers and describing what each part does. Tell students that not all flowers have all of these parts and that they don't look exactly the same on each flower. Ask each pair to try matching parts on their own flower with parts on the diagrams.

3. Give students time to rotate and observe others' flowers before having a class discussion. Ask: *Were some parts found on the diagram hard to locate on the flowers? Did everybody's flowers have the same parts?* This might be a good time to share some of the background information about flower structures with the class.

4. Hand out the "Flowers: Up Close—Part 2" reproducible with flower part names, so students can match names to the descriptions of the various parts. Discuss findings. Ask: *Did any of your flowers have all of the parts on the illustration? Which ones? Which parts were hardest to find or identify? Did the same parts look the same on all flowers? In what ways did they differ? How were they the same?*

Making Connections

1. Possible discussion questions:

• *Why do you think petals are often brightly colored?*

• *Why do you suppose flowers often smell sweet?*

• *Why might some stigmas be sticky?*

• *Can you guess why some petals have designs such as spots or stripes?*

• *If you were a pollinator, what type of flower would attract you? Why?*

2. As a class, generate one list headed "Things We Know About Flowers" and one headed "Questions We Have About Flowers."

Have students identify which could be answered through experimentation and which through books or interviews. As your studies of flowers progress, add to the lists and shift statements and questions from one column to the other.

Branching Out

• Soak a few whole cloves in water overnight. Try to identify the parts of these dried flower buds.

• Have an outdoor "flower hunt." Give pairs of students cards with directions such as "Find a flower that: has pistils and stamens that are hard to find; smells sweet; has loose pollen; has no petals; is on its way to becoming fruit."

• Have pairs of students group flowers in different categories, e.g., by color, smell, or shape. Challenge other students to guess what factor was used to distinguish each group.

• Compare some flowers that are wind-pollinated with those pollinated by birds or insects.

• Make models of flowers using classroom materials (such as clay, tissue paper, and pipe cleaners) to simulate different parts.

• Have a snack of flowers including cauliflower, nasturtium flowers, artichokes, and chive flowers.

• Collect poetry and music that refer to flowers. Identify which attributes are being described. Discuss how these flower characteristics please us and how they help the flower.

• Play flower charades, acting out flower part names.

• Press different types of flowers or parts between newspapers weighted with books. Mount on paper, tagboard, or index cards with clear contact paper. Use as wallhangings, placemats, or cards. (See the "Classroom Herbariums" sidebar, page 158.)

Petal Attraction

Overview: Students invent models of flowers and then create advertisements to illustrate how their invented flowers are adapted to attract pollinators.

Time:
Groundwork: 30 minutes
Exploration: Part 1—60 minutes
Exploration: Part 2—30 minutes
Making Connections: ongoing

Materials:
• magazine advertisements
• drawing paper and supplies
• miscellaneous classroom and natural materials (e.g., tissue paper, pebbles, sticks, pipe cleaners, foil, etc.)

Background: Page 118

Advance Preparation:
If your students are not already familiar with flower parts, functions, and pollination, they should first conduct **Flowers: Up Close**, page 125.

Laying the Groundwork

Objective: To understand that many flowers are adapted to "advertise" themselves to pollinators.

1. Display around your classroom some magazine advertisements with popular slogans—for example, "Pepsi, The New Generation"—and engaging photos. Have students work in pairs to discuss the following questions: *At what type of audience/person do you think each advertisement is aimed? What does the advertiser do to grab the reader's attention and interest* (e.g., claims to make them happier or healthier or uses colorful pictures.)? *How do television advertisements do similar things?*

2. As a class, discuss some of the students' ideas. Then ask: *What do you think this discussion has to do with our study of flowers? What do you think flowers and these advertisers have in common? Who are the flower's "audience"?*

Reveal that many flowers are really brilliant advertisers, luring pollinators who inadvertently transfer pollen from one flower to another. Referring to the background information, highlight that many flowers have specific colors, shapes, mechanisms, or smells to attract specific pollinators. Ask: *What types of "advertising" have you observed in flowers?*

Exploration—Part 1

Objective: To consider how every part of a flower is designed to help in pollination/reproduction.

1. Have students work in small groups to "invent" models of fictitious flowers. Give each group an assignment (see next page), which should be for their eyes only. Suggest that students in each group have specific roles, such as materials gatherers, reporters, and labelers.

All models must:

- consist of unique, labelled petals, pollen, pistils, and stamens;
- be made of recycled classroom or natural materials;
- be a minimum of 8–12 inches in diameter;
- function as specified in one of the descriptions below.

Suggested "wild"flower ideas:

- Invent a flower that might entice an unsuspecting human to pollinate it.

- Invent a flower that can pollinate itself with the help of gravity.

- Invent a flower that could easily be pollinated by the wind.

- Invent a flower that will make a pollinator think it's approaching a fellow insect.

- Invent a flower that would force bees to follow a particular route in and out, touching the anthers and stigma on its way.

- Invent a flower that would attract a pollinator with a long beak.

- Invent a flower with an anther that can easily be "tripped" and sprung by an insect, releasing pollen.

Extra challenge: Create models of specific pollinators that might be adapted to pollinating your particular flower.

> **Highway to Nectar**
>
> Flowers often have lines or honey guides that help lead bees and other pollinators to nectar. Some of these guides can be seen by bees but not by us—since bees can see ultraviolet light, a part of the spectrum not visible to humans.

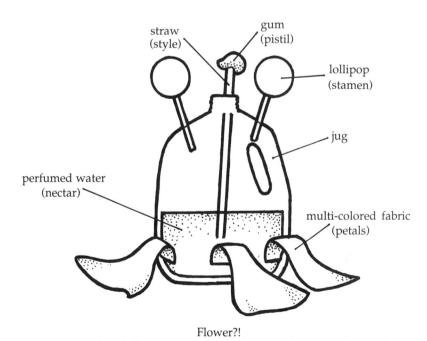

Flower?!

2. Have groups decide how to present their inventions to the class. They might choose a spokesperson or make a creative group presentation. Encourage the class to guess the purpose of the different structures of each invented flower.

Ingenious Adaptations

Flowers have some amazing adaptations for ensuring pollination. Many orchids have particularly sophisticated methods. One orchid flower mimics a female wasp. When the male wasp tries to mate with her, he inadvertently releases a spring-loaded lever that throws him headfirst into the flower, where he becomes covered with pollen.

Perhaps even more incredible is another type of orchid that secretes a pool of fluid in which it submerges the pollinator. The only escape is underwater, through a trapdoor. This route ensures that the pollinator transfers pollen to the stigma on the way out!

Exploration—Part 2

Objective: To demonstrate understanding of the relationship between flowers and pollinators by creating advertisements for fictional flowers.

1. Set the following scene for your students:

The place: Scentimental Advertising Agency
The plot: Groups of students are charged to design a full-page ad for their endangered, invented flower to run in National Pollinating magazine. The purpose is to convince pollinators of the need for their particular flower.

2. Encourage students to consider how they'll creatively highlight the traits that will attract pollinators to their flower. Suggest that students think about techniques used by human advertisers. To stimulate thinking, ask: *How can your ad...*

... make the nectar seem plentiful or nutritious?
... highlight easy access?
... make your flower more attractive to a specific type of pollinator?

3. Have the group or a spokesperson present the ad to the class. Display ads around the room.

Making Connections

Possible discussion questions:

• *What do you think would happen if...*

...bees and other insects couldn't detect color?
...motor oil were splashed on a flower's stigma?
...pesticides, toxic to bees, were sprayed on plants?

• *Although flowers have particular adaptations to attract pollinators, how do people take advantage of these traits (e.g., they use flowers' fragrance for soaps)?*

• *Do you think bees or plants benefit more during pollination? (This is a good question for debate, with no right answer!)*

• *Which parts would you not expect to find on flowers pollinated by the wind? Why?*

• *Why do you think flowers produce thousands of pollen grains, even if they have only a few eggs to be fertilized?*

Branching Out

• Research different types of pollinators (bats, moths, carrion flies, etc.) to find out their flower preferences.

• Try removing different parts of flowers while they're still on the plant. Notice how this affects the plant's development.

• Write and illustrate a description of a flower-of-the-future. Describe how this flower would be adapted to specific conditions and means of pollination.

• Research how different animals' adaptations, such as coloring and song, enable them to attract mates.

• Write an editorial for National Pollinating magazine from a pollinator concerned about pesticide use. First research how pesticides can affect pollinators.

• Research how different cultures use flowers (e.g., in their diets, for medicines, or for dyes).

• On an outdoor walk, try to identify different aspects of flowers' advertisements. Identify those flowers that are probably wind-pollinated.

• Find out about the origins of different flower names or about the historical significance of different flowers. Design cards using flower names and images.

Plant Parenthood

Overview: Students examine the role of pollination in plant reproduction by setting up an exploration to compare pollinated and unpollinated plants.

Time:
Groundwork: 30 minutes
Exploration: 40 minutes setup
  and 5 weeks ongoing observations
Making Connections: ongoing

Materials:
• 36 Fast Plants seeds, 12 growing containers, wicks, fertilizer (see Appendix D)
• small paintbrush
• potting mix
• "Observation Journal" reproducible, page 286

Background: Page 118

Advance Preparation:
Students should have some previous experience with the topics of pollination and fruits. Consider doing **Flowers: Up Close** and **Petal Attraction**, pages 125 and 128.

Laying the Groundwork

Objective: To consider what conditions might cause flowering plants to fail to produce fruits.

1. Read the following to your class or record and play it on tape (try using an "extraterrestrial voice"!). Tell them the letter is a plea for help from an alien with some gardening problems.

Dear Grade _____ Earthlings:

Last year, some of our scientists here on the planet Void took a trip to your planet in search of some new sources of food. (We've been living on dried carbon pellets for the last few million years, and our fellow Voidroids say the food is really BORING.) Our scientists were particularly overwhelmed by the totally awesome, ever-so-tasty fruits and vegetables they found in your Earthling gardens. After much tasting and testing, they brought back some seeds for us to try growing on the planet Void.

We started out growing cucumbers, melons, and a few other crops. We planted them carefully in our Voidian soil, watered them, gave them nutrition, and generally cared for them as I understand you Earthlings do. Well, we have beautiful plants, and lovely flowers, but not a cucumber, melon, or any other fruit. My fellow Voidroids are so eager to find an alternative to those tasteless carbon pellets, that I simply must find out what went wrong.

Other than this problem, we are without some of the problems plaguing you gardeners on Earth. We have no birds or insects on this planet, so we don't have to worry about garden pests. We have beautiful, sunny, completely windless days. So, as you can see, everything seems ideal for growing great gardens. Can you help us solve this mystery and show us how to reap the fruits of our labor?!

Fruitlessly yours,
I.M.A. Droid

2. On the board, make a class list of the things you know about the planet Void. Break students into small groups and give them five minutes to discuss the problems of the Voidroids. Ask them to consider what might help the Voidroids solve their problem.

3. Have each group share their thoughts with the class. If the discussion doesn't come around to the need for pollination (by insects, birds, wind, etc.) to produce fruit, ask: *What is missing on the planet Void that we have on Earth?* Once pollination is brought up, ask: *How could we set up an investigation to confirm your assumptions that pollination is necessary for fruit and seed production?*

Exploration

Objective: To understand that pollination is essential to the production of fruit and seeds.

1. Share with students the information in Appendix D about Fast Plants. Because they grow rapidly, cannot pollinate themselves, and can be easily pollinated by humans, they are ideal for this type of investigation. Solicit suggestions for how to set up an investigation, using Fast Plants, to examine how pollination affects fruit and seed production. Follow the Problem Solving for Growing Minds process, page 10.

2. The following setup should yield significant results:

• Plant twelve small growing containers with three Fast Plants seeds each, as described in Appendix D. Thin to one plant per pot once plants have germinated. Label four pots Group A, four pots Group B, and four pots Group C.

• As plants begin to flower, at about ten to fourteen days, treat the pots as follows:

Group A. Transfer pollen—Devise a way to transfer pollen grains (as described in Appendix D) from the flowers on one plant to the flowers of another plant.

Group B. Prevent pollination—Create a way to prevent pollination from occurring.

Group C. Bug Off—Your control pot. Let the plants do their own thing without intervening.

Group A

Group B

Group C

3. Have students keep records in the "Observation Journal" during the next several weeks. These will help later when they try to figure out when and where the three treatments started to show significant differences.

4. As a class, create a way to present results in a large chart for display. See "Create-a-Chart," page 287, for suggestions. Calculate the percentage of flowers in each pot that produced seeds.

What to expect: Within four days of inducing pollination, seed pods should begin to develop on some of the flowers in Group A. There might be some accidental pollination in Group C (e.g., from someone brushing against plants). Group B should not show signs of fruit development. When the plants are 26 to 28 days old, students should see clear differences in the seed pod development in the three pots. When the plants are about 40 days old, mature seeds should be ready to harvest from the pods (fruits) in Pot A.

Making Connections

Possible discussion questions:

• *What differences did you observe between the pollinated and non-pollinated plants? When did you first notice the differences?*

• *What factors, other than the pollination treatment, might have affected your results?*

• *What can you conclude from this investigation?*

• *Can you assume, based on your experiment, that all plants must be cross-pollinated?* (Share the information on perfect and imperfect flowers on page 119 with students.)

• *Why do you think we planted four pots for each treatment?*

• *Do you think seeds can be produced without flowers? Why or why not?*

• *How do you think Fast Plants would be pollinated outdoors?*

• *Bees, important plant pollinators, are sensitive to certain environmental toxins (including some pesticides). What long-term effects do you think the loss of large numbers of bees might have on our food system? On you?*

• *Why do you think picking wildflowers is discouraged?*

Branching Out

• Using a microscope to observe pollen, build a three-dimensional model of a pollen grain.

• Research how non-flowering plants reproduce and investigate whether they depend on pollination.

• Observe and, if possible, videotape bees at work on flowers outdoors.

• Visit or write to a commercial fruit grower. Find out how they ensure pollination in their orchards.

• Interview a local pesticide expert to find out which chemicals are harmful to bees and other pollinators.

• Find out what some of the disadvantages of self-pollination might be. Research some of the ways self-pollination is prevented in flowers. Consider how this might compare to people. Discuss why people from the same family shouldn't have children together.

• Write or tell a story as though you were a pollen grain. Describe a journey to pollinate a flower, and demonstrate an understanding of the process and parts you'd contact. You might find interesting ways to complicate the journey—for example, by getting lost and ending up in a sneeze!

Fruit for Thought

Overview: Students sort and closely examine a variety of fruits, and discover what makes a fruit a fruit.

Time:
Groundwork: 30 to 60 minutes
Exploration: 45 minutes
Making Connections: ongoing

Materials:
• assorted fruits

Background: Page 121

Advance Preparation: Have students bring in assorted "fruits" from home. Supplement student items with those less commonly considered fruits, such as tomatoes, beans, cucumbers, and peanuts.

Laying the Groundwork

Objective: To sort fruits and identify differences between them.

1. Display items you and the students have brought in (see Advance Preparation). Although students may have limited concepts of what a fruit is, don't discuss the broad meaning of the word at this time.

2. Play the game Line Up with the items on display. Give each small group of students an assortment of six different items. Have each group secretly choose a way to line up its fruit. If you cut the fruits open students can organize them by internal characteristics as well as external. For example:

• hardest to softest
• biggest to smallest
• most to least floatable
• heaviest to lightest
• wettest to driest flesh
• most to least seeds

Once each group has lined up its items, have students rotate to another group's area. Give them several minutes to examine the lineup and to guess what factor (size, weight, etc.) the original group used.

3. Ask: *Is anyone surprised that I called all of these items fruits? Which do you think are not fruits? Why do you think a tomato is considered a fruit like an apple or orange? What do you think makes a fruit a fruit?*

Exploration

Objective: To gather and compile observations to discover what all fruits have in common.

1. Give each small group of students halves of two different types of fruits (from Groundwork). Challenge each group to come up with four to six ways in which the two fruits are alike.

2. As a class, make a master chart, compiling the answers. Then ask students to find the words or descriptions that show up in the chart more than once. Circle them on the chart. Hopefully, your students will notice that all fruits have seeds, that they somehow surround or protect the seeds, and that they come from plants. If students have observed full life cycles or conducted flower activities, they may also realize that fruits always come from flowers. Caution students against assuming that all fruits are edible.

How Our Fruits Are Alike

Juan + Adriane	Simone + Bill	Xia + Cilla
Round	Soft	Hard
Bounces	Long	(Seeds inside)
(Seeds inside)	(Seeds inside)	Edible
Seeds sink	Skin	Red
(Comes from plant)	(From plant)	Seeds float
		(Comes from plant)

Making Connections

1. Possible discussion questions:

- *Based on our group effort, what do you think makes a fruit a fruit?*

- *Do you think a green pepper is a fruit? ... a carrot? Why?*

- *How did your classmates' observations help you better understand what a fruit is?*

- *What do you think fruits do for plants?*

- *What questions do you still have about fruits? How do you think we might find out some answers?*

Stem Shortcake?

Although fruits always contain the plant's seeds, not all fruits are easy to identify. For example, each juicy, sweet, red strawberry appears to be a fruit, but it is actually the stem. The fruits of the strawberry plant are actually the yellow specks dotting the outside!

2. Bring in an assortment of fruits (including some new ones) and vegetables (e.g., carrots, celery, radishes, lettuce). Have students individually sort them into a "fruit" and "not fruit" pile.

Extra challenge: Have students use intersecting sets to categorize the fruits and vegetables. One set should contain fruits, the other vegetables. The intersection should show those fruits that we commonly consider vegetables.

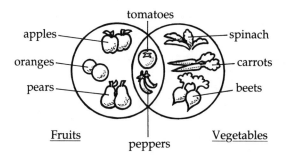

Branching Out

• Examine fruits for remnants of old flower parts.

• Find out how seedless fruits (watermelon, oranges, etc.) are produced.

• Count, compare, and graph the number of seeds inside different fruits.

• Make fruit flash cards or "Concentration" cards matching actual seeds on one card with pictures of mature fruit on another.

• Analyze what you eat for three days to determine how many different types of fruit items you consume. (Don't forget foods like grape jelly, ketchup, and orange juice!)

• Make a list of fruits in which we eat only the fruit (e.g., apples) and a list of fruits in which we eat the fruit and the seeds (e.g., tomatoes).

• Have a fruit-tasting party. Bring in a variety of fruits from different regions (e.g., pineapple, guava, pomegranate, kiwi). Try a new fruit creation like dried zucchini chips.

• Cut out magazine pictures and/or illustrate an AlFruitbet, from apples to zucchini. Research and/or imaginations may be required!

• Make fruit prints. Cut fruits in half, remove seeds, and use tempera paints to make prints. Try gluing the real seeds onto the prints as originally arranged.

BACKGROUND
Plants from Parts

Propagate-It

See *GrowLab: A Complete Guide to Gardening in the Classroom*, for specific information on taking and rooting houseplant cuttings (pages 66 and 67); raising bulbs (page 67); and starting white and sweet potatoes from parts (page 68). Many of the books in the resource section offer information and activity ideas on indoor vegetative propagation.

Plants and some simple animals such as sponges have an adaptation for survival that humans lack—the ability to regenerate an entire new organism from a piece of the original one. Although starfish can restore their missing legs, and even humans can regenerate skin cells to heal a wound, neither we nor most other animals can produce an entirely new organism from parts. Many plants, however, are capable of **vegetative propagation** or **asexual reproduction**, producing a new, complete individual from part of another one.

Unlike reproduction from seed, only one parent is involved in vegetative propagation. Rather than containing genetic material from two parents, the offspring produced asexually are the same genetically as the parent plant—that is, they are **clones**.

In nature, vegetative reproduction is quite common. Over millions of years, plants have developed adaptations to be able to reproduce in different ways. Most plants that naturally reproduce vegetatively will also reproduce from seeds. Some of the structures plants use to reproduce vegetatively include tubers (potatoes), bulbs (garlic, tulips), runners (strawberries), rhizomes (iris), and crowns (asparagus). Because every cell in a plant contains all of the genetic information for that plant, many plants can also be propagated from parts such as leaves, roots, and stems.

Rhizome (iris)   Bulb (tulip)   Bulb (garlic)   Tuber (potato)   Runners (strawberry)

Humans take advantage of these plants' reproductive abilities not only by planting the structures illustrated, but also by using artificial propagation techniques. For instance, we propagate houseplants by taking cuttings (or **slips**) from leaves, stems, or roots. With the proper warmth and moisture, plant growth hormones stimulate the production of roots, and sometimes leaves, at the cut surface. Another method, one of the most sophisticated vegetative propagation techniques used by humans, is "tissue culture," in which a new plant is produced from just a few cells of the parent.

The Advantages

The advantages of vegetative reproduction—some for humans and some for the plants—include the following:

• Offspring can be produced quickly;

• Offspring are exact replicas of parents (e.g., farmers can ensure passing along desirable traits such as disease resistance);

• The fragile seedling stage is avoided;

• Some plants (e.g., bananas) don't produce viable seeds;

• Seedless clones can be produced (e.g., trees can be grafted to reproduce seedless oranges);

• Propagation does not depend on pollinators or on the complicated cell fusion of sexual reproduction.

The Disadvantages

Among the disadvantages of vegetative reproduction are the following:

• Undesirable traits such as disease susceptibility will be passed on to the next generation;

• Plant parts are typically harder to store and heavier to ship than seeds are;

• Vegetative propagation does not allow new combinations of traits to be introduced into a population, with potentially successful adaptations to changing environments;

• Many plants reproducing vegetatively crowd one another and compete for nutrients, light, and water.

There are numerous opportunities in the GrowLab to explore vegetative propagation. **Plantenstein** helps students become aware of some of the different ways plants can reproduce asexually. **Slips, Snips, and Growing Tips** challenges students to survey houseplant growers and experiment with different methods of rooting houseplants. Finally, **The Eyes Have It** has students compare the same type of plant, potatoes, grown both sexually and asexually, and to consider some of the implications of each method of reproduction.

Celling Out

All cells in a plant contain the same exact genetic information. How then do some genetically identical cells in a germinating seed become shoots growing up and others roots growing down? When you make a cutting, how do some stem cells grow into roots and other stem cells into leaves? People as well as plants start off as a single cell which differentiates into many, many cells, each with different functions. The process of cell differentiation is very complex and not yet understood fully by scientists. One thing is clear: both genetic and environmental factors seem to influence how and when identical cells develop into different forms.

Bananas Split

Ask your students if they think a banana is a fruit. Challenge them to find the seeds. Your students may notice small black specks inside the banana—these are the seeds. But if you try to plant them, you'll find that they won't germinate. Banana trees reproduce asexually since their seeds are infertile.

Overview: Students examine some of the ways we propagate new plants from parts, by growing plant parts in the design of unusual faces.

Time:
Groundwork: 40 minutes setup;
  2 weeks observations
Exploration: 45 minutes setup;
  ongoing observations
Making Connections: ongoing

Materials (per student):
• one 6- or 5 X 7-inch pot
• potting mix
• assorted houseplants
• onion sets, garlic cloves, or potatoes
• seeds (optional)
• 1-gallon plastic bag
• twist ties
• "Plant a Question" reproducible,
page 282

Background: Page 139. Read about houseplant cuttings, potatoes, garlic, and bulbs on pages 66 to 68 in *GrowLab: A Complete Guide to Gardening in the Classroom.*

Plantenstein

Laying the Groundwork

Objective: To predict and examine what happens to houseplant leaves and stems when cut and placed in water.

1. Pass some seeds around your class and ask: *What do you think would happen if we planted these seeds? Besides planting seeds, how else could we get plants to produce more plants?*

   Hold up a houseplant (one that you know will root easily from cuttings, or one chosen from the list on page 66 of *GrowLab: A Complete Guide to Gardening in the Classroom*). Ask: *How do you think we could use this plant to create new plants without using seeds? Where have you seen this done before?* Tell the class that they can try growing houseplants from parts in the classroom.

2. Have several volunteers take cuttings from houseplants with suggestions from the class about where and how to cut. Place cuttings in jars of water. Ask: *What plant parts are missing from these cuttings? What do you think they need in order to become new plants? What do you predict will happen to these during the next two weeks?* Have students record their predictions and observations, following the Plant a Question process, page 9.

Just budding in: Parents and other teachers can be excellent sources of plants for propagation activities. Remind the donors that they won't be losing a prized plant, but gaining a few new cuttings in return.

3. At the end of two weeks, ask: *How did the plant parts in water change over time? Did they change as you predicted?*

Exploration

Objective: To practice and compare different types of plant propagation while creating "plant part faces."

1. Explain that cuttings can also be started right in potting mix. Demonstrate the methods for taking and starting cuttings described on pages 66 to 67 of *GrowLab: A Complete Guide to Gardening in the Classroom*. Show students which of your plants are best for stem, leaf, and plantlet cuttings.

Also show students some onion sets, garlic cloves, or potatoes and ask: *How do you think these can be used to start new plants? Where have you seen this done? How do you think we should plant them?* Using pages 66 to 68 in *GrowLab: A Complete Guide to Gardening in the Classroom* as a reference, demonstrate how to start some of these plants from parts.

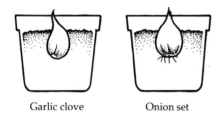

Garlic clove   Onion set

2. Invite students to use their new knowledge to create a "Plantenstein," a pot of plant parts designed to look like a face. Each piece of the face will illustrate a type of propagation. Suggest planting some seeds as well as starting plants from parts. This will allow students to compare differences in growth from seeds and from parts. Consider using the following for Plantenstein features:

- houseplant cuttings
- seeds (radishes, lettuce, ryegrass, beans, etc.)
- onion sets or garlic cloves
- potato pieces
- tissue paper, ribbons, etc. for embellishments

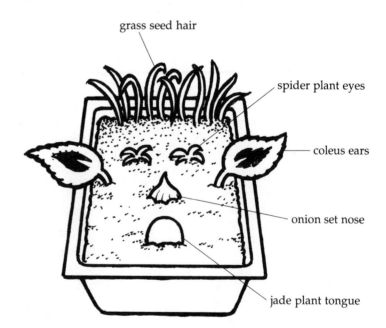

grass seed hair

spider plant eyes

coleus ears

onion set nose

jade plant tongue

When planting is complete, water well, cover each pot with a plastic bag to retain moisture, and leave in the GrowLab or other warm, well-lit spot. Over the next two weeks, students may need to check and water pots if they begin to dry out.

3. Have students draw and label pictures of their Plantensteins to post around the room. Have them predict, in words or drawings, how they think their faces will change over the next few weeks and make regular observations.

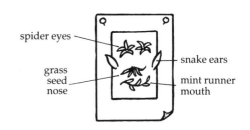

spider eyes
snake ears
grass seed nose
mint runner mouth

4. After a couple of weeks, students can gently tug on the plant parts to see if there is resistance from the newly formed roots. Ask: *What do you think we're trying to feel by gently tugging?* Remind them of their earlier observations of plant parts in water. *What changes do you notice in these plant parts above the ground? What do you think is happening under the soil? Does your Plantenstein look as you predicted? What's the same? Different? Did some parts grow more than others? Which were they?*

Making Connections

Possible discussion questions:

• *How do the face parts grown from seed differ from those grown from plant parts?*

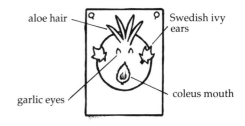

aloe hair
Swedish ivy ears
garlic eyes
coleus mouth

• *How do you think your Plantenstein might look in two more weeks?*

• *Do you think we could plant parts of ourselves and have them grow into new people?*

• *Which other plants would you like to try to grow from parts? How would you like to try and start them? Why?*

• *What new questions do you have about growing new plants from parts? How do you think we might answer them?*

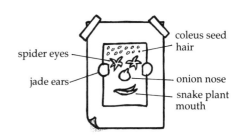

spider eyes
coleus seed hair
jade ears
onion nose
snake plant mouth

Branching Out

• Start new plants from parts of "kitchen scraps" such as onions, carrot tops, ginger, or potatoes.

• Experiment to see if a particular plant will root faster in water or in potting mix.

• Invite local greenhouse employees to class to discuss and demonstrate how they propagate plants commercially.

• Read *The Plant Sitter* (Appendix E) and discuss the creative problem solving that occurred.

• Organize a houseplant exchange. People who share parts of their houseplants receive back their original plant plus several newly rooted cuttings in exchange.

• Root houseplant cuttings and donate them to a person or group who could use some living beauty to brighten their lives. Or sell the plants and use the income for a class treat.

Overview: Students gather survey data and conduct investigations to determine the best methods for starting new plants from houseplant cuttings.

Time:
Groundwork: 4 days, 30 to 45
  minutes per day
Exploration: 45 minutes setup;
  2 to 3 weeks ongoing observations
Making Connections: ongoing

Materials:
• assorted houseplants (for recommendations see page 66 in *GrowLab: A Complete Guide to Gardening in the Classroom*)
• pots
• potting mix or perlite
• jars for water
• gallon plastic bags
• "Slips and Snips Survey Results" reproducible, page 270
• "Problem Solving for Growing Minds" reproducible, page 283
• "Observation Journal" reproducible, page 286

Background: Page 139

Advance Preparation:
If students are unfamiliar with plant cuttings, consider doing the Groundwork from **Plantenstein** preliminary to this activity. Refer to pages 66-67 of *GrowLab: A Complete Guide to Gardening in the Classroom* for information on houseplant cuttings.

Slips, Snips, and Growing Tips

The "empty pot" syndrome

SIGH!

Laying the Groundwork

Objective: To develop a survey to gather data on people's preferences for rooting houseplant cuttings.

1. Hold up a houseplant and ask: *If I wanted to grow another houseplant like this, and didn't have any seeds, what could I do?* Solicit suggestions on how to start a new plant from parts of an old one.

2. Share the following letter from the National Gardening Association with your students.

Dear GrowLab Classroom Members,

We've found that people who raise houseplants have different opinions about the best way to root cuttings to produce healthy new houseplants. We'd like you to be a part of a national study to examine the best way to create new plants from parts of others. Perhaps you could survey your families, teachers, and other people who make houseplant cuttings.

If classrooms across the country could experiment with different methods, we could share your results with houseplant growers. Some questions we have are: Do different types of plants root best with different methods (e.g., water vs. potting mix)? Do different plant parts grow better with different methods? Do some methods take longer to root, but produce healthier plants in the long run?

We appreciate your taking the time to read this, and look forward to receiving the results of your investigations.

Happy Gardening!

The National Gardening Association

---

3. Discuss NGA's letter and ask: *How might we set up a survey to find out more about people's preferences for creating new houseplants?* Make a class list of questions students want to ask indoor gardeners—parents, teachers, and others—about their houseplant cutting methods. Narrow down some of the questions to incorporate into a survey.

Things to consider when setting up your survey:

• Will you ask open-ended questions, or offer specific choices? (Open-ended responses could yield more information, but may be harder to tabulate. Consider a combination.)

• How do you want to present your final results—for example, as graphs, pie charts, narratives? (This will affect the type of questions you ask.)

• Would you like to find out specific details about people's methods for taking cuttings?

• Do you want to find out why people prefer certain methods?

A sample survey follows:

---

1. What is your favorite method for rooting houseplant cuttings?

    [ ] - Place them in jars of water and leave them there.
    [ ] - Place them in jars of water, then transplant them into potting mix.
    [ ] - Root them directly in potting mix.
    [ ] - Other (be specific)

_____

2. Why do you prefer this method? (Answer as many as apply.)

    [ ] - It's easier and takes less time.
    [ ] - It produces healthier plants.
    [ ] - It's prettier to look at.
    [ ] - I've never tried any other way.
    [ ] - Other (please explain)

_____

3. If you have more specific suggestions for successfully rooting houseplant cuttings, please describe them.

---

4. Conduct surveys and compile results. See "Create-a-Chart", page 287, for graph and chart ideas. Use survey feedback to guide the following exploration.

Exploration

Objective: To design and conduct experiments to compare different methods of rooting houseplant cuttings.

1. As a class, review the survey results. List all the suggested

---

Rooting Cuttings: Three Methods

• Place cuttings in jars of plain water. Transplant them into potting mix when roots have developed.
• Place cuttings in a well-drained potting mix and cover them with a plastic bag to hold moisture.
• Place cuttings in water, let roots develop, and leave them in water indefinitely.

Hints about Plant Cuttings

• The age of the leaves or stems used in cuttings can affect how well or how quickly they'll root.
• The length of a stem cutting and the number of leaves on it can affect how well or how quickly it will root.
• Different types of plants may root better using different methods.

methods of starting houseplants from cuttings, adding any of your own ideas from the original class list, and decide which you'd like to test in the classroom.

2. Use the Problem Solving for Growing Minds process, page 10, to plan and record the investigations. Consider having students work in small groups, with each group taking responsibility for trying a particular method (e.g., water only, water and later transplanting, potting mix). Alternatively, each group can take responsibility for rooting one type of plant by different methods.

Just budding in: In planning investigations, consider which factors, besides the specific rooting method, might affect results. For instance, if Group A proposes to root 7-inch pieces of ivy in water and Group B proposes to root 3-inch pieces of ivy in soil, we're not really conducting a fair test. It could be the length of the cutting, not the rooting method, that affects the results. Modify the plans until the class is satisfied that they'll be conducting fair tests.

Ivy

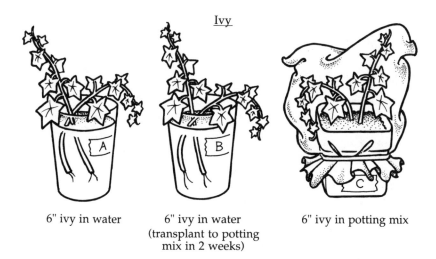

| 6" ivy in water | 6" ivy in water (transplant to potting mix in 2 weeks) | 6" ivy in potting mix |

Coleus

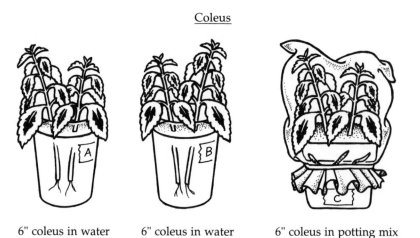

| 6" coleus in water | 6" coleus in water (transplant to potting mix in 2 weeks) | 6" coleus in potting mix |

3. Continue the investigations for two to three weeks, keeping records of observations on the "Observation Journal". At that point, compile data from different groups for discussion.

4. Send a summary of your survey and experiment results to the National Gardening Association, using the "Slips and Snips Survey Results" reproducible. We'll send your class a summary of findings from GrowLab classrooms across the country.

Making Connections

Possible discussion questions:

• *Did a particular method seem to produce the healthiest plants at the end of four weeks? Which? Could you conclude that all types of plants prefer a certain method? Why or why not?*

• *What factor(s) did you use to evaluate the "health" of cuttings* (e.g., number of roots, length of roots, growth of new leaves, general health of plant)?

• *How did the combined efforts of different groups help you better understand plants' responses to different rooting methods?*

• *Do you all agree on the best way to root cuttings? Did all of the people in your survey agree? Do you think scientists always agree on answers to problems? What do you think would be the implications if there were only one right way to do things and one answer to every problem?*

• *Why do you think different people prefer different methods for rooting cuttings? What kind of factors do you think affect different types of choices in our lives* (e.g., I use brand X because my family does; I eat bran because I read an article about fiber and health; etc.)?

• *Which other methods of starting plants from parts would you like to try? What new questions did the explorations spark? How might you go about answering them?*

Branching Out

• For an extra challenge, experiment with other factors that might affect the rooting success of cuttings, such as dipping them in rooting hormone, providing bottom heat, or making cuttings on a slant.

• Estimate the rate of root growth of a cutting started in water.

• Try propagating some GrowLab plants such as tomatoes using techniques you've discovered in this lesson.

• Research agricultural crops such as potatoes, fruit trees, and strawberries that are commonly propagated vegetatively.

• Explore more complex propagation techniques, such as rex begonia leaf wedges or fern divisions.

The Eyes Have It

Overview: Students learn some of the cultural and ecological history of potatoes. They then compare potato plants grown from seed (sexually) and from tubers (asexually) and consider the implications of both reproductive methods.

Time:
Groundwork: 30 minutes
Exploration: 30 minutes setup;
  2 to 3 weeks regular observations
Making Connections: ongoing

Materials:
• potato seeds (see Appendix F for sources)
• potatoes (with eyes)
• four 6-inch pots
• potting mix
• "Observation Journal" reproducible, page 286

Background: Page 139

Laying the Groundwork

Objective: To consider some of the cultural and ecological history of potatoes.

1. Read some or all of the following statements to your students, directing them to use these as clues to infer what food crop is being described:

• Pizarro, searching for gold and emeralds in the 1500s, found these underground stems in Ecuador and described them as tasty, mealy truffles.

• After receiving this strange new food as a gift from Sir Walter Raleigh, Queen Elizabeth's chefs threw away the nutritious underground tubers and cooked up the poisonous green stems and leaves. The queen's dinner guests soon became deathly ill.

• Many Europeans in the 1500s and 1600s were wary of eating this food, because it is related to deadly nightshade and other poisonous plants.

• In the late seventeenth century the Irish depended heavily on this crop as a food source, a typical family consuming more than 250 pounds each week. When a fungus disease hit this crop in the mid-1800s, 1 1/2 million Irish people starved, and another 1 1/2 million fled to the United States.

• The Irish referred to this food as the Apples of Life. The French still call it *pommes de terre*, or apples of the earth.

• As late as the mid-nineteenth century, many thought this food fit only for animals. Because of its appearance, many believed that it must cause leprosy in those who ate it.

• This food was accused of leading to the moral decay of house-wives in the late nineteenth century, since its preparation required little time and effort, leaving women too much idle time.

• This food might typically be eaten for breakfast, lunch, snack, or dinner.

• An average serving of this food contains half the adult recommended daily allowance of vitamin C.

• Seven pounds of this food and one pint of milk could meet all of your daily nutrition needs.

2. Ask: *To what food crop do you think these clues are referring?* When someone guesses "potatoes," find out which clues were most helpful and why. *Were any of the statistics surprising? Why?*

Exploration

Objective: To consider some of the differences between plants reproduced sexually and those reproduced asexually by comparing potato plants grown from seed and grown from tubers.

1. Pass around several potatoes and ask: *Where on the plant would you find a potato growing? What part do you think it is? How do you think a potato plant might reproduce?* Hold some potato seeds in your hand to show the class that 50,000 weigh only an ounce!

Explain that potatoes—underground stems (tubers) that store carbohydrates—can be grown either from seed or from pieces of potato. Each piece must contain an eye (an immature shoot) in order to sprout. Ask: *How do you think plants grown from seed might differ from those grown from a piece of potato? Why?*

2. Plant a potato piece in each of two pots. Make sure that each piece contains at least one eye. Plant potato seeds in each of another two pots. Press seeds lightly, with a firm object, into the top of the soil. Thin the seedlings to one plant per pot after germination.

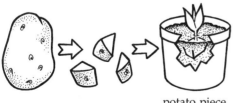

potato piece   potato seeds

3. For two to three weeks, have students make regular observations in the "Observation Journal" of the plants in each pot, comparing growth rates, height, color, and size and number of leaves. There should be obvious differences in the plants and an opportunity to discuss some of the Making Connections questions.

What to expect: Within a week of planting, the potato plants grown from pieces will be tall and sturdy while seeds will just be germinating. Since the potato pieces provide substantial nutrients for early growth, there will be a dramatic difference in growth rate.

Making Connections

Possible discussion questions:

• *What was the most obvious difference between the plants started from seed and those started from a piece of potato? How soon did you begin to notice a difference?*

• *Why do you imagine most farmers and gardeners might grow potatoes from pieces rather than from seeds?* (They produce sturdy plants more quickly. If your students understand the genetic differences between sexual and asexual reproduction, they might suggest that farmers plant pieces to get identical types of plants.)

• *What do you think might be the drawbacks for farmers and gardeners of starting potatoes from pieces rather than from seeds?* (Pieces are heavier and bulkier to transport and harder to store.)

• *The Irish potato famine resulted from a fungus that attacked the entire potato crop on which the Irish were dependent. Since the Irish planted largely the same type of potatoes (which all were sensitive to the fungus) the whole crop was destroyed. As a farmer or consumer what lessons might you learn from this event?* (Dependence on any one food crop can be risky. More diverse plantings and eating habits provide alternatives and safety nets.)

• *How healthy do you think you'd be if you ate only one type of food?*

• *Why do you think people's perspectives on potatoes might have changed so dramatically at different periods in history? What do you think influences our food attitudes and preferences?*

Branching Out

• Try growing other plants both from parts and from seeds. Carrots and beets can be started from both seeds and plant parts, as illustrated. Coleus is another good one to try using both methods.

Plant a 1"-2" piece of beet or carrot in potting mix. New leaves will sprout from the top.

carrot   beet

• Try growing potatoes to maturity in a 5-gallon bucket or other large container.

• Experiment to determine the smallest piece of potato that can produce a new plant. (It's rumored that poor farmers have started new plants from mere potato peelings containing eyes!)

• Try leaving some potatoes exposed to light in your classroom and watch for the development of chlorophyll.

• Make potato chips, potato pancakes, and other potato snacks in the classroom. Create a potato cookbook.

• An ounce of potato seeds (50,000) is enough to plant an acre of potatoes. Have students find the average weight of a 2-inch by 2-inch potato piece and then estimate how much weight in potato pieces would be needed to plant the same acre. (Use seed catalogs to determine planting distances. An acre is 43,560 square feet.)

• Find out how many different types of potatoes are grown in South America, and how these South American natives have contributed to the production of our present potato varieties.

• Research the history of some other important food crops. Explore the relationships between food choices and culture.

What Did in the Dinner Guests?

When Queen Elizabeth's chefs cooked up potato plant stems, they were unaware that they contain large quantities of poisonous alkaloids. Potatoes themselves contain small amounts of these same substances, which are harmless when kept in the dark. Light, however, encourages potatoes to produce these toxic substances. Fortunately, light also triggers potatoes' production of chlorophyll, so green potatoes signal danger. Green skins can normally be peeled, leaving healthy potatoes.

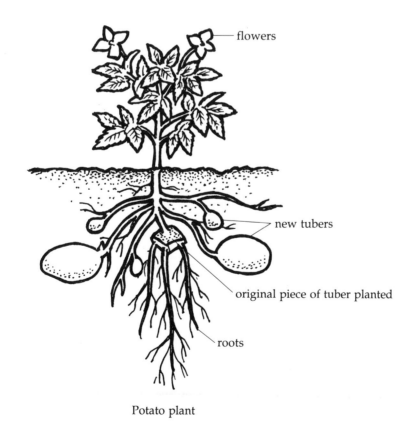

Potato plant

flowers

new tubers

original piece of tuber planted

roots

Chapter 3 | Diversity of Life

T hey come in all shapes and sizes. Some can withstand the desert heat; some thrive in the frigid tundra. They make their homes deep on ocean floors, under logs, in brick houses, or inside each other's bodies. More than two million different kinds of living things occupy the diverse habitats on this green planet.

It is largely because of these diverse habitats that the Earth is teeming with a fantastic assortment of living things. Since habitats range from vast savannahs to deep ocean trenches, one all-purpose type of organism couldn't possibly survive everywhere. Those individuals best suited, by chance, to meet environmental challenges survive and pass on the successful traits to their offspring. This "natural selection" results in the evolution of many different kinds of organisms, including nearly half a million known species of plants, inhabiting nearly every region on Earth.

Activities in the first section of this chapter explore some of the subtle and dramatic variations that exist among plants. Students will be challenged to develop systems to make sense of diversity. Activities in the second section of this chapter encourage students to look more closely at different ways plants are adapted to survive particular environmental conditions.

Diversity

*"Nature, in her blind search for life,
has filled every possible cranny
of earth with some sort of fantastic creature."*

—David Cavagnaro, Photographer

L iving things compete with one another to survive and reproduce in a wide range of environmental conditions. Adaptations are features that help living things survive and reproduce in their particular environment. In the desert, succulent cactus stems have spines that keep thirsty animals away. High atop tropical mountains, fine white hairs shield silversword plants from dangerous ultraviolet radiation. Because there is such a wide range of conditions and potential roles to fill, an incredible diversity of life has evolved on Earth. For more explanation about adaptations and their role in diversity, see page 188.

No two dogs, people, lettuce plants, or grapes are exactly alike. We all have behaviors and other characteristics that are special, unique, and distinguish us from the rest of the bunch. In the activity **Plant Private Eyes**, students look closely at and creatively describe variations between plants. In **Diverseedy**, students sort and grow a mixture of seeds to recognize that different plants grow from different seeds. In **Lettuce Be Different**, your students will grow different types of lettuce to explore the subtle differences that exist among even closely related plants.

Making Sense of Diversity

If you entered a supermarket to find frozen peas shelved between cat food and detergent, would your sense of order be undone? Humans are unique, in part, because we develop systems to organize things. From library books to zip codes, grouping things helps us make sense of our world.

To keep track of the vast assortment of living things, we group them according to specific characteristics. More than 2,000 years ago, Aristotle divided living things into plants and animals. Today many scientists distinguish five major groups, or **kingdoms**.

One classification system used today is based on the work of Carolus Linnaeus, an eighteenth-century Swedish botanist. In this system, organisms are divided into a hierarchy of categories: **Kingdoms—Divisions—Classes—Orders—Families—Genera—Species**, with each successive category based on more specific structural similarities. For example, humans are animals with backbones and thus belong to the phylum Chordata, along with other animals with backbones, such as reptiles and birds. Today, technological advances allow us to look also at biochemical and evolutionary ties. For example, we've learned that reptiles and birds share much closer genetic similarities than members of another phylum without backbones, such as sponges. In the activity **Order in the Class,** your students will create their own systems for organizing living things.

Plant families are distinguished from one another largely on the basis of their flower structure. In **Mystery Family Ties,** students will compare plant characteristics to determine which plants belong to the same families.

The Importance of Diversity

A healthy, resilient ecosystem results from the complex web of roles played by a diversity of organisms. Plants, for instance, supply food for consumers and help provide our atmosphere's gas mixture, which supports all life on Earth. Animals die, decompose, and provide materials to support plant life. Bacteria recycle nutrients that help to maintain healthy plant life. Consider what the Earth would be like if the only things living were decomposers!

When there are many different kinds of organisms in an ecosystem, they don't have to compete as fiercely for resources as they would if they had similar needs and adaptations. For instance, some birds nest in trees and perch on branches, while others nest on the ground and wade in the water. Some pasture plants have tap roots, while others have fibrous root systems.

How Humans Depend on Diversity

Humans take advantage of natural genetic diversity in many ways. The first farmers planted, harvested, and saved their favorite seeds, thus purposely selecting for specific desirable traits. All of our staple food crops reflect centuries of work by plant breeders. Many medicines originated with the traits of wild species, manipulated by humans. Relatively recently, however, humans have begun to "design" crops to meet our "needs," such as consumer tastes, nutritional values, or harvesting and shipping requirements.

In the activity **Designer Crops**, your students grow and compare two plants of the same species that have been bred for very different characteristics.

The benefits of plant breeding do not come without trade-offs. Some tomatoes, for example, have been bred for toughness to withstand mechanical packing and shipping, and have consequently lost flavor and appealing texture. We rely heavily on "high performance" crops, and this dependence makes us vulner-

Gopher It!

To communicate better with scientists around the world, we give organisms Latin genus and species names, such as *Homo sapiens* for human beings. Imagine how difficult it would be if we used only local, common names. For instance, how would we know whether a Florida "gopher" (a turtle) is different from a Kansas "gopher" (a rodent), or distinguish among the more than 100 known species of raspberries?

able. When only one variety of crop is planted and then hit by a disease, for instance, the entire crop can be wiped out. If the people depend on that crop as a food staple, its loss can be a catastrophe—like the potato blight that led to the Irish Famine in the 1800s.

When we rely heavily on specialty crops, we often lose track of or discard other varieties. These lost varieties may have great medical or agricultural virtues. Once lost, this valuable genetic information can never be recovered. The chart on page 176 presents an overview of different types of human manipulation of plant genetics. Share the information with your students, as appropriate.

Preserving Diversity

Some ways people can help to preserve genetic diversity include:

• setting aside areas representing major ecosystems to protect wild species in their natural habitats;

• preserving genetic information, e.g., saving seeds or semen;

• moving organisms to captivity, e.g., botanical gardens, aquariums or zoos.

Progress has been made in conserving the genetic resources of many of the world's most important crops. Seeds, for example, are being stored in gene banks, preserving thousands of species. Many gardeners are saving and exchanging seeds of old plant varieties, to keep them from vanishing (see Appendix F for addresses of seed-saving organizations). Protecting original habitats, however, is the most comprehensive and successful way to preserve threatened genetic resources. In the activity **Rainforest Stories**, students will have an opportunity to simulate a tropical rainforest in the GrowLab as a springboard to learn about this complex and diverse ecosystem. They'll explore its role as an invaluable genetic resource, examine the reasons for and consequences of rainforest habitat destruction, and begin to consider how they can personally help protect these diminishing tropical treasure chests.

"If we cannot end now our differences, at least we can help make the world safe for diversity."

—John Fitzgerald Kennedy

Overview: Students explore plant variations by creating descriptive clues to help classmates guess the identity of a "mystery" GrowLab plant.

Time:
Groundwork: 30 minutes
Exploration: 40 minutes
Making Connections: ongoing

Materials:
• miscellaneous plants
• blindfolds or brown paper bags

Background: Page 154

Plant Private Eyes

Laying the Groundwork

Objective: To observe and creatively describe plants.

1. Pass a few plants around the class and encourage students to use all of their senses—except taste—to examine the plants, paying great attention to detail. Ask each student to share one observation with the rest of the class, e.g., "The stem has little bumps all over it" or "Its leaves are soft and fuzzy."

2. Then ask questions that stimulate students to describe their observations more creatively. For example: *Does the stem feel like anything else you've ever touched? What? Have you ever noticed that the stem feels sort of like a pipe cleaner? What shape do the leaves remind you of?* Read some incomplete sentences and have students creatively complete the sentences based on their observations. For example:

"The leaf feels like _____."
"The color of the flowers reminds me of _____."
"The plant smells like _____."
"It's as tall as a _____"

Exploration

Objective: To explore plant variations by describing a "mystery" plant well enough for another student to figure out its identity.

1. Choose one student—the "Private Eye"—to turn his or her back (or put a brown paper bag or blindfold over his or her head) while you select a "mystery" plant from the GrowLab. Have several students use all of their senses and their imaginations to describe the "mystery" plant to him/her. For example:

"The smell reminds me of a spring day."
"The leaves feel like velvet."
"The color makes me think of pea soup."
"Its leaves feel smooth and fuzzy."

2. After a few minutes, return the plant to the GrowLab. Then the Private Eye must use her/his senses to find which plant the rest of the class was describing. After the mystery is solved, invite another student to be the Private Eye.

   If appropriate for your students, divide the class into Private Eye partners and have them play the same game in pairs.

 Just budding in: Advise your students to handle plants very carefully during this exercise. Excessive touching could damage the plants.

3. Develop a Plant Private Eye "big book" in which Private Eyes draw pictures of their plants while you write the descriptive words they used in identifying the mystery plants.

Making Connections

1. Possible discussion questions:

• *How did the imaginative clues help you? Which clue helped you the most? Why?*

• *After you found your plant, could you think of any other words to describe it that weren't used? Which ones?*

• *From your observations, how do you think all of these plants are the same? Even though they are all plants, how do they seem to be different?*

• *What other things can you think of that come in many different shapes, sizes, textures, etc.?*

2. Have students tell, write or draw a "What if..." story about a world without diversity. For example, What if you woke up one day and everyone looked the same? ...the only food sold in grocery stores was liver? ...the only plants were spinach?

Branching Out

• Look at and describe GrowLab plants with and without hand lenses and notice how each description differs.

• To enhance observation skills, have one team (Team A) of students change positions of plants in the GrowLab while another

Classroom Herbariums

If you want to keep an attractive and useful record of the different kinds of plants you grow in your GrowLab, why not create a classroom herbarium? You can press whole plants or any plant parts, e.g., flowers or leaves. Lay each specimen flat in between a thick layer (about four to five sheets) of paper towels or newspapers. Place the layers of specimens and absorbent papers under any heavy object such as a telephone book or a big stack of books. Carefully replace the papers after a few days. In about a week, the plants should be dry enough.

   Glue the plants on construction paper and coat with a clear lacquer or plastic adhesive. Don't forget to label them! Display the pressed and mounted plants around your classroom herbarium or store them for later reference.

team (Team B) has their backs turned. Have Team B figure out what's been changed before teams switch roles.

• Play a circle memory game, using plant descriptions. Have each person in the circle briefly describe her/his plant and recall the descriptions of everyone preceding them. For example, "My plant has dark green leaves." "My plant has sharp thorns and Simon's has dark green leaves." "My plant has velvety petals, Dylana's has sharp thorns, and Simon's has dark green leaves."

• Have one student (A) draw a picture of an exotic, make-believe plant and then describe the plant to Student B. Without looking at the original picture, Student B tries to draw a picture of the same plant—based only on the description. Compare pictures and switch roles.

• Use analogies to describe the flavors of edible parts of plants.

• Grow an herb or flower garden in the GrowLab. Creatively describe the unique colors, textures, and smells.

• Grow a rainbow garden in your GrowLab.

red zinnias
orange marigolds
yellow cucumbers
green lettuce
blue alyssum
purple pansies

Diverseedy

Overview: Students sort seeds from a birdseed mixture, then observe and compare plants that grow from these seeds.

Time:
Groundwork: 40 minutes
Exploration: 40 minutes setup;
   3 weeks ongoing observations
Making Connections: ongoing

Materials:
• 2 cups birdseed mixture
• paper cupcake liners
• small planting containers,
 e.g., milk cartons, paper cups
• potting mix
• "My Plant Journal" reproducible,
page 285

Background: Page 154

Laying the Groundwork

Objective: To sort seeds and understand that there are many different kinds of seeds.

1. Divide the class into pairs. Have each pair of students fill a paper cupcake liner with 2 to 3 tablespoons of commercial bird-seed mixture. Ask: *What do you think is in the mixture? Where do you think the ingredients came from (besides the store!)? In what ways do you think all seeds are alike? ...different? How are the seeds in your birdseed mixture alike? ...different? How many different type of seeds do you think make up your birdseed mixture? How could we find out?*

2. Have students sort the seeds by putting similar ones together in groups. When students have sorted about five seeds into each group, have them return the extra seeds. Ask: *What do you think will happen if we plant the birdseed mixture together in one pot? What do you think we'll get if we plant the separated seeds by themselves? How many different types of birds do you think will grow from these "birdseeds"?! Why do you think birdseed contains a mixture of different seeds?*

Exploration

Objective: To recognize that different plants grow from different seeds.

1. Prepare enough planting containers so students can plant one with each type of seed they've sorted. Also prepare a container for planting some of the mixture. Have students follow general planting instructions and set up an exploration as follows:

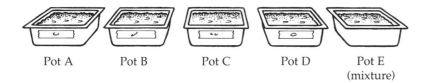

Pot A   Pot B   Pot C   Pot D   Pot E
                                     (mixture)

Tape a sample of each seed to the container in which it's planted.

2. Have students tape a sample of each seed onto their "My Plant Journal" reproducibles and then make predictions about what will grow. For example, ask them to put an X on the seed they think will grow the biggest plant, underline the seed they think will sprout first, or draw a circle around the seeds they think will grow into the same type of plants.

Focus on students' predictions. Ask: *Do you think the plants grown from different seeds will be the same or different? Why? Do you think all of the plants grown from the same type of seed (in one pot) will be exactly same? Why? How do you think plants grown from the mixture will compare with those in the other pots?*

3. Have students make daily observations, recording drawings and/or written descriptions of what emerges from each pot. To record height, have students cut paper strips sized to match the tallest plant in each container. Label appropriately and arrange the strips to form a bar graph by size.

While the mixtures are growing, hand out another 2 to 3 tablespoons of birdseed mixture to pairs of students. Have them sort and glue seeds on paper to make a graph illustrating the numbers of different types of seeds in the mixture. For example:

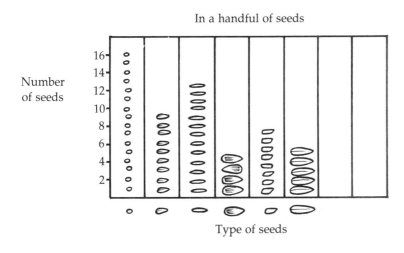

In a handful of seeds

Number of seeds

Type of seeds

4. Discuss findings. *Did all seeds sprout at the same time? Did all seeds in any one pot sprout at the same time? Which seeds sprouted first, second, ...last? What is the height of the tallest plants? From which seeds did these grow? Are all plants in any one pot the same height?* How else are the plants the same or different (e.g., color of leaves, shape of leaves, type of stem, rate of growth)? *Are any two plants exactly the same?*

> **What to expect:** Many birdseed mixtures contain sunflower and grass family seeds that germinate in a few days. Most of the seeds will grow very quickly. After a few weeks, remove plants from the GrowLab, since most plants grown from bird-seed will not mature indoors.

Making Connections

Possible discussion questions:

• *How did your predictions compare with what actually happened?*

• *Are there any pots, besides the one labeled "mixture," that have more than one type of plant growing in them? How do you think that happened?*

• *Which plants from the separate pots can you find in the mixed pot? Try matching up the plants growing in the mixed pot with the seeds in the birdseed mixture.*

• *Were you surprised that so many different kinds of plants grew from these seeds? Why or why not?*

• *What other types if seeds can you think of? Do people ever eat seeds? What types of seeds have you eaten? Can you think of some different ways people prepare seeds to eat (e.g., popped corn, puffed wheat, boiled rice, ground peanuts)?*

• *How would your life be different if the only seeds you ate were bean seeds?... if the only kind of plants that grew from seeds where you lived were cacti?*

Branching Out

• Try to grow some of the birdseed plants to maturity indoors and outdoors.

• Build bird feeders out of classroom, household, and natural materials, e.g., pine cones and peanut butter or dried-out gourds.

• Research what types of birds like each kind of seed in the bird-seed mixture and find out how birds digest seeds.

• Create birdseed collages.

• Plant a bird's nest in a large pot to find out if seeds are contained in the nest (and if they'll grow). Discuss how the seeds might have ended up in the nest.

• Prepare different edible seed snacks and have a seed party!

• Have students bring in empty boxes of their favorite breakfast cereals. Read the ingredients and graph cereals by seed type.

Overview: Students compare their own similarities and differences. They then grow and compare several varieties of lettuce plants to explore variations within the same type of plant.

Time:
Groundwork: 40 minutes
Exploration: 30 minutes setup;
  4 weeks ongoing observations
Making Connections: ongoing

Materials:
• seeds from three different lettuce varieties (e.g., red leaf, green leaf, buttercrunch)
• pots
• potting mix
• "My Plant Journal" or "Observation Journal" reproducible, pages 285 and 286
• "Lettuce Be Different" reproducible, page 271

Background: Page 154

Lettuce Be Different

. . . and from the Romaine side of the family- Uncle Augustus, inventor of the Caesar salad.

Laying the Groundwork

Objective: To recognize that different qualities make each human unique.

1. Have students sit in a circle and play the Let Us Be Different circle game as follows:

Have one student share one way s/he is the *same* as the person to her/his left. That student in turn should share one way s/he is the same as the person on her/his left. Continue once around the circle in this fashion, then switch and have each student tell one way s/he is *different* from the person to her/his right. Encourage students to think about ways they are alike or different that include how they look, what they do, and other traits that make them special. Specific traits, e.g., hair color, should be used only once.

2. After the game, have students consider how their lives might be different if people were all the same. For instance, ask: *What do you think a baseball game would be like if every player were a good* *pitcher and nobody knew how to bat well? What would the world look like if we all had green eyes?*

We've found that human beings can be alike in many ways and still have many differences. Is the same true for plants? Isn't any lettuce plant just like any other lettuce plant? Have students describe the kinds of differences they might find in any one type (species) of plant, e.g., lettuces, apples, tomatoes, or beans.

Exploration

Objective: To appreciate variations within species by growing and comparing different types of lettuce plants.

1. Give students three different types of lettuce seeds (see materials list) to compare and describe. Then have students plant the three varieties of lettuce in separate pots. As the plants grow, have students make and record regular observations of the lettuce in each pot on their "My Plant Journal" or "Observation Journal" reproducibles. At the end of four weeks, have students complete the "Lettuce Be Different" record sheet, comparing each of the lettuce types.

2. Discuss findings. Ask: *How are all of the lettuce plants in the different pots similar? How are they different? Are all the plants in any one container exactly the same? How are they different?* Compile responses on a large class chart.

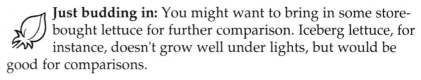 **Just budding in:** You might want to bring in some store-bought lettuce for further comparison. Iceberg lettuce, for instance, doesn't grow well under lights, but would be good for comparisons.

Making Connections

1. Using the class chart for reference, help students write a short class poem, describing each type of lettuce plant. For instance, a haiku poem (five, seven, and five syllables) about red leaf lettuce might be:

Red and curly leaves,
Thin and light, very fragile,
Seven inches high.

2. Possible discussion questions:

• *Are all golden retrievers or all tomatoes exactly the same? What other living things can you think of that come in variations?*

• *What other vegetables or fruits can you think of that come in different varieties* (apples, beans, melons)?

•*Do you think variation in food, pets, friends, plants, etc. makes your life more interesting? Why or why not?*

Branching Out

• Cut mature lettuce leaves at the soil surface. Continue caring for the plants to observe how the different types of lettuce continue growing.

• Graph class responses to such questions as: *Which lettuce is your favorite to look at? Which lettuce tastes best* (during a blindfolded taste test)? *Which lettuce would you rather have in your salad? ...on your sandwich?* Bring in several different varieties of apples or oranges and repeat the taste test.

• Grow and compare different varieties of beans or other plants.

• Make a lettuce plant catalog that advertises the unique characteristics of the different lettuce types.

• Conduct a Supermarket Survey. Call or visit grocery stores in your area to find out how many different types of lettuce are available in each store. Graph results.

• Count the number of different varieties of lettuce, apples, tomatoes, or other vegetables/fruits advertised in seed catalogs. Discuss why there are so many varieties.

• Discuss what the title "Lettuce Be Different" means to you.

• Create collages highlighting variations in one particular trait, e.g., different kinds of human noses, dog fur, or bird beaks.

Mystery Family Ties

Overview: Students observe the growth and development of some mystery plants while trying to determine which plants have the closest family ties.

Time:
Groundwork: 45 minutes
Exploration: 8 to 10 weeks ongoing observations
Making Connections: ongoing

Materials:
• bean, pea, marigold, and zinnia seeds (six of each)
• four 6-inch pots
• potting mix
• magazines with pictures of plants and animals
• assorted plants—GrowLab plants, houseplants, or plants gathered outdoors
• cardboard
• tape or glue
• "Observation Journal" reproducible, page 286
• "Mystery Family Ties" reproducible, page 272

Background: Page 154

Advance Preparation:
One week prior to this activity: Secretly plant six seeds of each type of plant (bean, pea, marigold, and zinnia) in separate pots. Label each pot with a code so that you alone know its identity. Thin to three plants per pot.

> *"... a great deal can also be discovered by looking at living animals, watching what they do, examining the ways they are constructed, and working out, from their similarities and differences, which group is related to which."*
>
> —David Attenborough, Science Writer

Laying the Groundwork

Objective: To appreciate how people classify living things.

1. To practice grouping plants and animals according to physical characteristics, first have each student cut out a magazine picture of an animal, mount it on cardboard, and hang it around her or his neck.

Choose a team of students to sort the "animals" into two separate groups, based on one way members of each group are similar to one another and different from the other group—e.g., number of legs or means of moving around. The rest of the class should try to guess what the "animals" in each group have in common. Team members should then join appropriate groups.

2. Select other teams of students to divide each group into two more subgroups, following the same instructions. Ask the class: *What characteristics were used to determine which animals belong in the same group? Was there only one possible way to divide the animals? What types of characteristics might you use for grouping plants?*

3. Using GrowLab plants, houseplants, plants gathered from outside, or pictures of plants, have students try to sort plants based on common characteristics, e.g., leaf shape, stem thickness, or flower color.

Exploration

Objective: To discover that plant families are largely distinguished by their flower structure.

1. Show students the Mystery Family Ties pots you had already planted (see Advance Preparation). Tell students the pots contain seeds of plants in two different families and that plant families are based on certain structural similarities. Have students record observations of the plants on their "Observation Journals" during the next six to eight weeks, until plants in all four pots have flowered. Challenge students, if and when they have enough information, to guess which plants belong to the same families and record their guesses on the "Mystery Family Ties" reproducible.

Peas

2. After six to eight weeks, discuss findings. Ask: *Which plants do you think are most closely related? Which clues led you to your conclusion? At what point did you feel most confident about your conclusion? What were the most dramatic differences between plants? ...similarities?*

Although students may notice a number of differences and similarities over time, share with them that the main criterion for grouping plants in the same families is flower structure. After students have drawn their own conclusions, relay the information from What to Expect, below.

Beans

What to Expect:

Family:	Legume	Composite
Plants:	peas, beans	marigolds, zinnias
Approximate Time to Flower:	4-5 weeks	7 weeks
Flower Structure:	irregular, butterfly-shaped flowers	many tiny flowers growing together in one composite flower often with tiny tubelike 'disk' flowers surrounded by longer, flat 'ray' flowers resembling petals
Fruits:	non-fleshy	non-fleshy, one-seeded (won't appear in time allotted)
Other Common Examples:	clovers, lupines, peanuts, soybean	sunflowers, daisies, dandelions

Marigolds

Zinnias

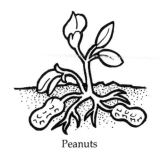

Peanuts

Mystery Family Ties 167

Making Connections

Possible discussion questions:

• *What other common flowers look as though they might also be in the same family as marigolds and zinnias* (daisies, black-eyed Susans, mums)?

• *What characteristic(s) do you think might make pine trees and maple trees less closely related than, for example, maple trees and oak trees?*

• *What characteristic(s) do you think might distinguish animals in the feline (cat) family from those in the canine (dog) family?*

• *Why do you think people classify living things in groups? Other than by physical/structural similarities, can you think of a different way to classify living things* (e.g., behaviors, where they live, what they eat)?

Branching Out

• Research and grow some other plants in each family. Try peanuts in the legume family! (See the "Plant Products Chart", page 236.)

• Try "inoculating" some beans or peas with rhizobia bacteria and look for evidence of nitrogen-fixing nodules (see sidebar). Experiment to see what conditions promote nodule development.

• Find out to which plant families your GrowLab crops belong.

• Grow different plants in the mint family, such as spearmint, basil, and oregano. In addition to flowers, try to guess what structure is similar in most plants in this family (square stems!).

• Use wildflower and tree guides to identify plants found around your school. Find out to which family each plant belongs.

• Research and compile a list of plants and animals that have different common names in different parts of the country or the world, e.g., skunks and polecats. Discuss the origins and benefits of scientific names.

• Design a wall chart of common plant families found around the school. Press plants and/or include pictures and descriptions of the plants and their characteristics. (See the "Classroom Herbarium" sidebar, page 158.)

• Research the reasons scientists once classified living things into two kingdoms and now classify them into three to five kingdoms. Discuss what led to altering the classification criteria.

What a Good Relationship!

Many plants in the legume family have a special symbiotic relationship with particular bacteria, rhizobia. These rhizobia, which form and live in small nodules in the roots of legume plants, can turn nitrogen in the air into a form usable by plants. Because of this nitrogen "fixing," these legumes require very little additional nitrogen fertilizer and can even be used as soil enrichers.

Although these bacteria can be found naturally in many soils, farmers and gardeners wishing to ensure their presence often "inoculate" moistened seed with a dormant, dried form of the bacteria before planting. You can try this in your classroom by purchasing a pea and bean inoculant at a garden center or through a seed catalog. Apply the inoculant to moist peas and beans before planting. When the roots of the mature plants are examined, students should be able to see the small round nodules that have developed.

Order in the Class

Overview: To try to make sense of diversity, students create systems to classify both their classmates and seeds.

Time:
Groundwork: 45 minutes
Exploration: 45 minutes
Making Connections: ongoing

Materials (per pair of students):
• 15-plus assorted seeds (old seeds are fine)
• large sheet of paper
• hand lens, optional

Background: Page 154

Laying the Groundwork

Objective: To develop systems to organize and classify class-mates.

1. Have each student share one thing he or she can think of that is divided into groups—e.g., addresses, library books, football teams, or foods in the supermarket. Ask: *What reasons might people have for organizing things into groups? If you had to divide living things such as animals into groups, what characteristics might you use to organize them?*

2. Challenge students to consider how they might divide their classmates into groups. Have volunteers present their systems to the rest of the class.

To illustrate one method of classification sometimes used by scientists, have one student divide her or his classmates into two groups based on one specific characteristic, e.g., "boy" or "not boy." The "classifier" should not reveal the category used. After the class is divided into two groups, encourage the rest of the class to try to guess the category used by the "classifier". Have them share what clues helped them "crack" the system.

3. Select another student to choose the next characteristic(s) for subdivision and separate the two groups into two more sub-groups. Again encourage the class to guess why they were placed in certain groups. Repeat until the class is broken down into small subgroups.

Have one student be the class recorder, writing the system down after each group subdivision. For example,

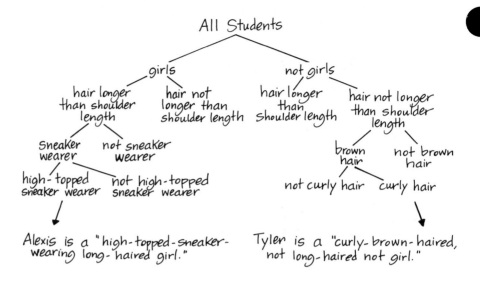

All Students
├── girls
│   ├── hair longer than shoulder length
│   │   ├── Sneaker wearer
│   │   │   ├── high-topped sneaker wearer → Alexis is a "high-topped-sneaker-wearing long-haired girl."
│   │   │   └── not high-topped sneaker wearer
│   │   └── not sneaker wearer
│   └── hair not longer than shoulder length
└── not girls
    ├── hair longer than shoulder length
    └── hair not longer than shoulder length
        ├── brown hair
        │   ├── not curly hair
        │   └── curly hair → Tyler is a "curly-brown-haired, not long-haired not girl."
        └── not brown hair

4. At the end, have students "identify" themselves, using the system the class developed. For example, Alexis is a "high-topped-sneaker-wearing long-haired girl" while Tyler is a "curly-brown-haired, not long-haired not girl".

5. Repeat Steps 1 to 3 above, using different students to choose the characteristics, thus creating a new system each time.

Try a variation in which one student (or teacher, principal, etc.) is out of the room. After the class has been broken down into small subgroups, ask each "guest" to place him/herself in the correct group and explain why. For example, "I belong here because I'm a long-haired, not sneaker-wearing girl."

Exploration

Objective: To create an original system to classify seeds.

1. Hand out ten or more assorted seeds and a large sheet of newsprint to pairs of students and read the following aloud:

Newsflash!!!!

Seeds For All, a world health organization responsible for distributing vegetable seeds to the world's undernourished countries, has experienced a major calamity. Thousands of seeds have been accidently mixed together. If the seeds are not identified, they can't be distributed to the correct countries. It is believed that millions of people may be be without food unless local citizens can help devise a system to organize and identify this mixed bag of fortune.

2. Challenge each pair of students to use the classification skills they just practiced to organize their seeds. Then have students create new names to represent the unique qualities of the seeds in terms of their classification system. For example,

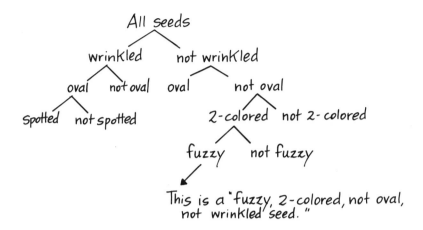

Making Connections

1. Have pairs of students try to identify other pairs' systems by only looking at their classmates' sorted seeds.

2. Possible discussion questions:

• *Why do you think each pair of students classified the seeds differently?*

• *How are the classification systems useful to you? Why do you think it's helpful to have such systems for everything from birds' nests to mushrooms? What aspects of your life might be different if we didn't have systems for organizing and classifying things?*

• *What characteristics might you use to develop a classification system for plants? (Look at your GrowLab plants for ideas.) If there's time, develop such a system.*

• *Name some possible groupings or classifications of outdoor plants (e.g., plants that keep their leaves year round/plants that lose leaves, flowering/nonflowering plants).*

Branching Out

• Group seeds (or GrowLab plants, leaves, pebbles, etc.) into sets and subsets, based on similar characteristics. Surround each set with string loops. Note how many different sets, subsets, and intersections can be found.

• Use field guides to identify some local plants such as trees or wildflowers.

• Research the life and accomplishments of Carolus Linnaeus, the eighteenth-century Swedish botanist and developer of modern taxonomy.

• Write a simple computer program for classifying something in your classroom, e.g., books, students, furniture, or plants.

• For a blindfolded partner, develop a classification system based on the sense of touch or hearing rather than sight.

• Survey people in your community to find out how things are grouped, e.g., at the hardware store, post office, or library. Write a creative story or make an illustration detailing how our world might be if humans didn't classify or organize things into groups.

• Discuss how we tend to group ourselves and other people in this society and/or around the world, such as by race or religion. Consider the implications of such classification, economically, socially, and ethically.

Designer Crops

Overview: Students grow and compare two plants of the same species that humans have bred for very different characteristics. They consider some of the reasons for and implications of human intervention in plant reproduction.

Time:
Groundwork: 30 minutes
Exploration: 40 minutes setup; 6 weeks ongoing observations
Making Connections: ongoing

Materials:
• sliced tomatoes
• 12 Fast Plants seeds, growing containers, wicks, fertilizer (see Appendix D)
• turnip seeds
• potting mix
• "Observation Journal" reproducible, page 286

Background: Page 154

Laying the Groundwork

Objective: To consider why humans might want to develop different types of plants.

1. Pass around some tomato slices for your students to eat while you play a game called What Bugs Us About Tomatoes. Encourage students to let their imaginations go wild as they brainstorm a list of complaints people might have about tomatoes, for example:

What bugs us about tomatoes?

* They're not salty enough.
* They take too long to get ripe.
* They make a mess when they're sliced.
* They're too small to fit on a burger.
* The color makes me nauseous.
* They're too acidic.
* The seeds are too slimy.

2. Share with students that they've just generated a list of possible reasons people might want to change tomatoes' characteristics. Explain that plant breeders are scientists who develop new varieties of crops with different characteristics in response to humans' needs and interests. The "new, improved" tomatoes might be able to resist a certain disease, for instance, or they might contain fewer seeds.

Exploration

Objective: To discover how different plants can be developed to have qualities that suit our purposes.

1. Tell the class you'd like them to grow seeds from two different plants that are very closely related (in the same species). Explain that plant scientists have specially bred both plants so they have different traits and uses. The goal of the Exploration is for students to try to figure out for which traits each of these plants has been bred.

Have the class plant four 2 1/2-inch pots with "Mystery Seed A" (turnips) and four 2 1/2-inch pots with "Mystery Seed B" (Fast Plants). Plant three seeds per pot, thinning to one plant per pot. See Fast Plants directions, Appendix D. Tell students that the true identity of the seeds will remain a mystery until the Exploration is complete.

Just budding in: In order for turnips to form strong roots, you'll need to hill up the potting mix around the base of their stems when they are one to two weeks old, and continue to do so as the roots develop.

2. Have students record observations in their "Observation Journals." Encourage students to compare such things as seeds, size of plants, growth rate, leaf appearance, root structure, and flowering. At the end of six weeks, allow students to remove plants from the pots to make final observations of the entire plants. Have students summarize their observations and data, making a class chart of findings of similarities and differences between both types of plants.

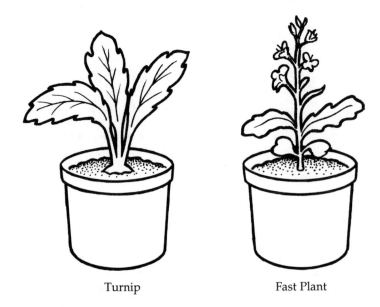

Turnip   Fast Plant

> **What to expect:** Students should find that plants grown from Seed A form a swollen root, while those from Seed B grow and flower very quickly, but have little root swelling. Turnips, Seed A, were specifically bred for their swollen roots which are storehouses for starch, used by humans as food. The Fast Plants from Seed B have been bred to complete a life cycle rapidly. These plants are used in breeding experiments since they can so quickly produce new generations. Fast Plants are also used in classrooms to teach students about plant life cycles in a short time.

Making Connections

1. Possible discussion questions:

• *At what stage did you first notice differences between the two plants?*

• *For what traits/uses do you think plant breeders may have developed each of these plants?*

• *What other crops can you think of that have been dramatically influenced by plant breeders? Why do you think the changes were made?*

2. Initiate a debate. Tell students that plant breeders have developed a tomato that is fairly hard and square-shaped, so it can be picked mechanically and shipped, without damage, across the country. At the same time, however, the new tomato has thicker skin, less flavor, irregular color, and more seeds. Debate the pros and cons of this agricultural "advance" for different groups.

Branching Out

• Compare other plants in the same species, e.g., broccoli, brussels sprouts, and cabbage, and discuss what traits each plant has been selected for.

• Research genetic engineering and prepare a debate on the question: "Should humans have the right to alter living organisms genetically?"

• Grow and compare a wild plant such as a wild carrot with its cultivated relative in the GrowLab.

• Read through seed catalogs and identify some of the "specialty" characteristics for which different varieties were bred.

• Write to seed companies and ask how they hybridize plants.

• Design original "mystery plants" and have the rest of the class try to guess for what purpose the plant was designed.

Human influence on plant genetics: An overview

	Plant Selection	Hybridizing	Genetic Engineering
What is it?	In nature, those plants best suited to a particular environment survive to produce offspring with similar characteristics. For 10,000 years, humans have taken advantage of this by saving seeds from plants with desirable traits (e.g., large tomatoes) to replant. Over time, we select and continue to reproduce the variety that has the traits we want.	This occurs when humans manually cross-pollinate two distinctly different plants to achieve a mix of desirable traits.	Transferring specific genetic material from one organism to another (e.g., splicing certain bacteria into strawberrries to prevent frost or splicing weed-controlling substances into a crop plant).
Potential Benefits	Low labor and cost. Seed can be saved from year to year. Plants are well adapted to the environment. Useful new offspring can emerge.	Offspring often more uniform, earlier, more disease resistant, higher yielding. Those holding patents make a lot of money.	Increased human control, potential for increasing productivity.
Potential Problems	Less uniformity. Takes time to select particular mix of traits.	In breeding for particular traits, other desirable traits (e.g., flavor) are often lost. More labor intensive and expensive. Our dependence has led to loss of diversity as older varieties, no longer used, vanish. Seed collected from hybrids will not grow the same crop.	Expensive for small-scale farmers. Might cause other genetic changes (e.g., in nutrient content) or have far-reaching environmental impact. We don't know full effects.

Tropical Rainforests

"Lakes fill with mud and turn to swamps inside decades; plains turn to deserts inside centuries; even mountains are worn down by glaciers within millennia. But hot, humid, tropical rainforests have been standing on the lands around the world's equator for tens of millions of years. This very stability may be one of the causes of the almost un-believable diversity of life that exists there today."

— David Attenborough, Science Writer

Tropical Treasure Chests

Imagine an area, covering approximately 7 percent of the earth's surface, that is home to more than 40 percent of all of the plant and animal species on Earth. Imagine going into this area—teeming with life—and finding an insect not yet discovered by scientists. Imagine that this area contains 70 percent of the known plants with anti-cancer properties and countless other medicinal and useful plants. It hosts many migratory songbirds every winter and, over the past 400,000 years, has supported the evolution and development of many complex, specialized relationships among living organisms. Now imagine this area being destroyed at the rate of 43,000 square miles per year—roughly the size of Pennsylvania—with almost 100 species becoming extinct every day.

Far from being imaginary, this is an accurate description of our planet's tropical rainforests. What makes these areas able to support such rich ecological diversity? Being located near the equator, the environment changes hardly at all from season to season. It stays moist and warm, supporting an abundance of plant growth which, in turn, supports many animals. The typical conditions of the tropical rainforest include:

Average rainfall:	60–200 inches/year
Temperature range:	70–90 degrees F (day and night)
Sunlight:	12 hours/day year round
Humidity:	70%, daytime; 95%, nighttime

In the activity **Rainforest Stories,** students will simulate a tropical rainforest in the GrowLab as a springboard to learn about these complex and diverse ecosystems.

Life in the Rainforest

In one 25-acre tropical rainforest in Borneo, there are 700 known species of trees. That's as many species of trees as are found in the six billion acres of North America! One rainforest tree was found to have 43 species of ants living on it—more than the total number of ant species living in Great Britain! It is estimated that two and a half million species of plants and animals inhabit tropical rainforests.

The diversity in tropical rainforests has resulted, in part, from the adaptations that enable living things to live in the different layers or **stories** of the forest. The main stories and some of the plants that inhabit them are described on the next page.

The canopy. The uppermost story is the continuous leaf canopy formed by trees 60 to 100 feet tall. The tallest trees, sometimes referred to as the **emergent layer,** tower 100 to 250 feet above the rainforest floor. Vines and plants such as orchids grow on the tree trunks, branches, and leaves. The trees are adapted to endure the most intense impacts of sun, wind, and rain. Water continually falls through the sub-canopy to the forest floor from this level. Many of the leaves are adapted with pointed tips, called **drip tips**, to shed water and prevent mold growth. The canopy's shade also greatly reduces the rate of evaporation from the lower levels.

The understory. In this level, beneath the canopy, are found plants less than 15 feet tall. Since only 2 to 5 percent of the sunlight reaches this layer, many plants here have large leaves to absorb the limited sunlight; others are climbers with aerial roots. The air is very still, and humidity is high (above 70 percent).

The forest floor. Here the air is cool and still and humidity is almost always above 70 percent. Little light reaches this level, so the sparse vegetation is composed of seedlings, fungi, mosses, ferns, algae, and other plants that are adapted for surviving with low light. While people tend to think of a rainforest floor as a tangled jungle of vegetation, that description is accurate only where the forest has been cleared and a new second growth has developed. The forest floor is actually a very open, still habitat, often described as "cathedral-like," while a great diversity of life grows and towers overhead.

A complex web of animal and plant partnerships (for pollination, seed dispersal, etc.) has evolved over hundreds of thousands of years in the rainforest. This diversity of plant life thrives even though the rainforest soil is very nutrient poor. When plants and animals die, the heat, moisture, specialized fungi, and bacteria cause rapid decomposition. The nutrients released by decomposition are immediately taken up and stored in new plants. The decaying processes are so fast that hardly any nutrients soak into the soil or are washed away by heavy rains. Rainforest plants have developed adaptations which enable them to support themselves on the poor soils.

Although rainforests are diverse systems, they're not necessarily tough—there is a fragile balance between every organism in the interdependent web. A change in any one species could affect the whole intricate system.

Rainforest Products

The rainforest is a virtual pharmacy, as many of our most important drugs are derived from its plants. Botanists are continually discovering rainforest plants containing substances that can help fight disease or soothe pain. Many of our staple agricultural crops have wild relatives in the rainforest. These relatives are critical to food supplies, since many have traits that, when bred with cultivated crops, can help make them strong and healthy (providing disease or drought resistance, for example).

Other rainforest products that we use in our daily lives include:

- coffee
- chocolate
- bananas
- many spices—cloves, vanilla, black pepper
- chewing gum
- oils—coconut, camphor, sandalwood
- rubber—tires, erasers, balloons
- many houseplants—African violets, orchids
- exotic hardwoods—mahogany, balsa, teak
- rattan and bamboo
- fibers—burlap, ramie

Tropical Rainforest Destruction: Why?

About five billion acres on Earth were once covered with tropical rainforests. Only half of that original acreage exists today. Some researchers estimate that we're losing roughly 50 million acres of tropical rainforest every year—an area equivalent to the size of Great Britain! If the trend continues at this rate, how old will your students be when the last piece of rainforest is gone?

A number of factors contribute to the deforestation of tropical rainforests, including:

Inequitable land distribution. In many tropical countries there is often a lack of farmland due to inequitable land distribution and population pressures. As people are transplanted from overcrowded cities, they burn large areas of the forest to clear land for farming. Once cut down, it is very difficult, if not impossible, for a rainforest to regenerate. Without any cover the already fragile soils easily lose nutrients and/or are washed away. Because the soils are so poor, farmers have to move on and cut down more forest.

Logging operations. High demand exists for certain tropical woods (e.g., mahogany and teak) for furniture and other uses in the U.S. and Europe. While there are tremendous numbers of different species of trees in the rainforests, there are relatively few trees of the same species living close together. When loggers want to remove a few select trees, they also ravage much larger stands of the other trees in the way. Logging equipment and roads tear up the fragile soils, resulting in erosion.

The hamburger link. It is estimated that, each year, millions of

---

Tropical Pharmacies

Some of the useful drugs that originate with plants from tropical rainforests include:
- Ipecac, used to treat dysentery, is made from the roots of a Brazilian plant.
- Quinine, used to treat malaria, was made from cinchona bark.
- A drug used to treat childhood leukemia and Hodgkin's disease is made from the rosy periwinkle plant.

Perhaps tropical rainforests hold the cure for cancer or AIDS. As tropical rainforests are being cut down, what potential medicines are we eliminating.

acres of tropical rainforest are burned to make room for agriculture, much of it for raising cattle. When rainforests are first burned, nutrients are released that promote good grassland growth. Soon, however, nutrients are depleted, and pounding hooves and rains wash soil away. New areas of rainforest must constantly be burned as old areas are used up. Much of the inexpensive beef used in U.S. fast food chains originates in these cleared areas of rainforest. Each year, the U.S. imports over 120 million pounds of beef from Central America alone. Valuable rainforest land continues to be lost for each hamburger produced.

International politics. Many of the problems plaguing the rainforest have economic or political roots. Countries with rainforest land, for instance, eager to pay back their national debt, often receive outside financial support for special projects such as dams, which will eventually generate income. However, these projects often suffer from poor planning and short-sightedness, resulting in greater long-term environmental problems.

Effects of Rainforest Destruction

A forest that may have taken 100,000 years to establish may be destroyed in a matter of days. The delicate balance of complex relationships formed over thousands of years cannot be recreated in a short time. Some of the results of rainforest destruction are easily documented, while others are, no doubt, beyond our comprehension. Some of the potential impacts include:

• **Loss of species**. Plant and animal species, many of which have potential value to us (medically, agriculturally, etc.), are being lost forever at an unprecedented rate. Only one percent of identified tropical rainforest plants have been analyzed by scientists; those few plants are the source of more than one quarter of the medicines produced today.

• **Loss of habitats.** As habitats diminish, pressure increases on smaller areas. Migratory songbirds are among the more obvious animals suffering from a loss of their winter habitat.

• **Destruction of indigenous cultures.** An estimated 140 million indigenous people live in the rainforests. Destroying their habitat leads to destruction of their cultures. Along with development and new settlers come new diseases and potential for violence.

• **Increase in CO_2/global warming**. As rainforests are burned, CO_2 locked up in plant material is released into the atmosphere. In addition, fewer trees are available to use CO_2 in photosynthesis. The excess of CO_2 traps heat in the atmosphere and results in global warming.

• **Worldwide changes in climate.** Largely because of their abundance of vegetation, rainforests significantly affect climate both locally and worldwide. As trees transpire and lift water up through their massive structure, they absorb 70 percent of the solar radiation and act to cool the environment. The water re-

Silent Spring

Among the animal species at home in the rainforest are many favorite songbirds. The rich diversity of food and habitats make rainforests a prime winter residence for many migratory birds. Some effects of deforestation may have far-reaching environmental implications that we haven't even imagined. Consider, for instance, the implications of losing winter feeding grounds for songbirds. Fewer songbirds might, in turn, lead to an increase in insect populations (bird prey), which might lead to agricultural destruction and food shortages worldwide.

Water, Water Everywhere

Water is constantly being recycled. The water in your perspiration could have once flowed as part of the Nile River. The water your GrowLab plants transpire could someday be soaked up by roots in a tropical rainforest. Transpiration plays a key role in the water cycle. An average birch tree (with about 200,000 leaves) will transpire 4,560 gallons of water through its leaves in one summer. One acre of lawn transpires 27,000 gallons of water each week all summer!

leased has a dramatic effect on relative humidity, cloud formation, and rainfall. It is estimated that 50 percent of the rainfall in tropical rainforests is due to transpiration. Cutting down significant portions of rainforest, it is predicted, could dramatically alter climate worldwide.

• **Loss of topsoil.** Deforestation can result in severe topsoil erosion. When soil is washed away, rivers and dams become clogged, which interrupts income-generating hydroelectric projects, and disturbs habitats.

Addressing the Problem

There are many encouraging efforts taking place within countries that have rainforests. One of the most important approaches is to provide financial reasons *not* to destroy rainforests. For example:

• **Tourism.** Countries with extensive rainforests are attempting to build up their tourism industry, often setting up "rainforest parks" to attract visitors. This not only brings money into the country, but also provides a way to raise awareness about problems of the rainforest.

• **Debt for nature.** Conservation groups and other non-profit organizations are buying part of a developing country's debt (at a reduced rate) from banks. The developing country then works out a deal with a local conservation group to preserve the tropical forest land.

• **Environmental impact evaluation.** Big banks are beginning to evaluate the environmental impacts of proposed projects in developing countries before approving loans.

• **Environmental/agricultural education.** Many groups, concerned about the rainforest, are helping local people to develop ways of using the rainforest sustainably, rather than destroying these precious resources.

• **Other efforts.** These include researching how to restore certain habitats, setting up special areas to extract resources without destroying a large area, and designing programs to protect specific species/resources.

While these may all sound like large-scale solutions, there are things that we can all do to help. See the Branching Out section for some ideas on how we can all get involved in helping to save our precious resources—the tropical rainforests.

Rainforest Stories

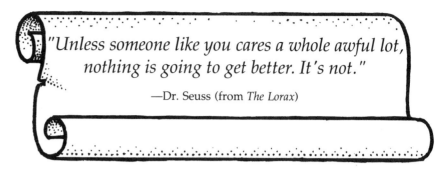

"Unless someone like you cares a whole awful lot, nothing is going to get better. It's not."

—Dr. Seuss (from *The Lorax*)

Overview: Students simulate a tropical rainforest in the GrowLab and compare it to conditions in a real tropical rainforest. They are introduced to these unique and endangered ecosystems, which support an incredible diversity of life.

We recommend conducting this long-term horticultural project as a centerpiece for a comprehensive study of tropical rainforests. The Branching Out section offers interdisciplinary suggestions for learning about tropical rainforests.

Time:
variable (long-term project, minimum 2 to 3 months)

Materials:
• globe or world map
• crayons, markers, or colored pencils
• potting mix
• pots
• assorted plants and seeds (e.g., mimosa seed, houseplant cuttings, ginger root, moss)
• *optional:* containers for water, heating cable (see page 112, *GrowLab: A Complete Guide to Gardening in the Classroom*), thermometer, hygrometer
• "Rainforest Stories" reproducible, page 277

Background: page 154, page 177

Laying the Groundwork

Objective: To develop an overview of tropical rainforests.

1. To uncover students' ideas about tropical rainforests, have each student create her or his own word web using "tropical rainforest" as the central theme. Ask students what images or words are conjured by this phrase. When making word webs, students should try to "connect" these images in some way that physically "maps" their perceptions.

For example:

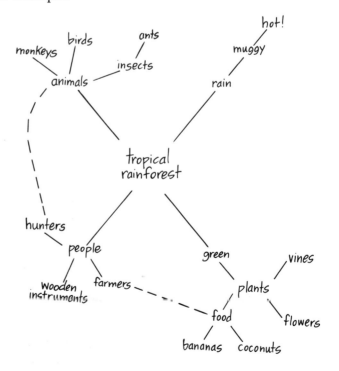

Display word webs around the classroom.

2. After students have looked at each others' webs, share with them the "Tropical Treasure Chests" section of the Tropical Rainforests background, page 177.

Display a world map or globe, and have students try to identify the location of tropical rainforests. As a homework assignment, consider having students research where the world's tropical rainforests are located.

3. Hand out the "Rainforest Stories" reproducible. Have students color in each rainforest "story" as you share the "Life in the Rainforest" information from the background, page 178. Discuss how the different stories help contribute to the diversity of tropical rainforests.

Exploration

Objective: To try simulating a tropical rainforest in the GrowLab. To become aware of the complex relationships of a rainforest by comparing it with a simple GrowLab simulation.

1. Referring to the information obtained in Laying the Groundwork, have students generate a list of conditions that characterize tropical rainforests. Ask students to identify those conditions that they can simulate in the GrowLab. Ask: *To what conditions are plants in tropical rainforests adapted to survive? Do you think we can simulate or recreate a tropical rainforest in the classroom? What problems do you think we might encounter in trying to simulate the rainforest ecosystem accurately?*

Solicit suggestions on how to simulate particular rainforest conditions. For example:

Rainforest conditions	How to simulate in GrowLab
very high humidity	keep base moist; mist plants 3-4 times/day, enclose in tent
75-85 degrees F day and night	heating cable on continually
"tropical plants"	snake plant, philodendron, mimosa, citrus, ginger, ferns, moss
12 hours of sunlight 12 hours of dark	leave timer on 12 hours

2. While the GrowLab "rainforest" is growing and students are making regular observations of plant growth, try some of the following:

• Take two cuttings from a houseplant and lay one on top of a moist pot of soil in the simulated rainforest. Lay the other cutting in a moist pot of soil on a windowsill. Predict what will happen. Ask: *Under which conditions do you think a cutting might root more quickly? Why?* (The warm, moist conditions and high humidity in a rainforest environment encourage rapid rooting and fast, lush

_____

Become a Rainforest!

Divide your class into several groups, representing the different stories they learn about. Have some students, representing the canopy, carefully stand on secure chairs or desks, while the sub-canopy species stand on the floor. Other students, the understory species, can kneel on the floor, and students representing the forest floor should lie down on the floor. You might consider having some students represent some other living things in the rainforest, e.g., decomposers (fungi) or consumers (ants, monkeys, anteaters, jaguars). Have each student share information about his or her role in the rainforest.

_____

growth.)

• Plant a dry-weather plant (cactus) in the simulated rainforest to observe what happens when a plant is placed in a climate to which it's not well adapted.

• Compare transpiration from leaves in the GrowLab "rainforest" and leaves out of the GrowLab. Try comparing leaves with different surface areas. After 2 to 3 days of observations ask: *How can you explain the differences in the rate of transpiration?* Set up as follows:

Set in GrowLab   Set out of GrowLab

3. While the simulated tropical rainforest is growing, try to give your students a more comprehensive understanding of tropical rainforests, their promise and their problems. The background information, page 177, offers an overview of the main characteristics of tropical rainforests. Share this information, as appropriate. See Branching Out for ideas about how you can help save tropical rainforests.

Making Connections

1. Have students compare rainforest conditions with their Grow-Lab simulated rainforest. Their list of comparisons might include:

Rainforest	GrowLab
humidity higher	lower humidity
great diversity of species	fewer species
dramatic differences in layers	plants similar heights
little temperature variation	temperature varies more
plants root more quickly	plants take longer to root

Students may recognize that there are many conditions that are difficult to simulate (different canopies, complex microbial relationships, poor soils, etc.). That discovery is an important part of this exploration. Discuss those aspects that are difficult to simulate because of the limitations of the GrowLab, and those that are difficult because they require much time and involve many complex relationships. It's important that students discover that rainforests can not easily be recreated. A simple simulation can serve as a backdrop for further studies and for comparisons of tropical rainforests and less diverse forest systems.

2. Have students work in small groups to discuss the question: *Big deal, why should we save tropical rainforests?* Have each group report back to the class and put answers on a master chart. Remind groups that there are numerous reasons, and no one right answer.

3. Ask each student to choose the reason for saving rainforests that is most compelling to him or her, to do further research, and to write one paragraph supporting his or her feelings. Consider combining these writings into an illustrated class book, complete with a cover. Copies can be made and distributed to parents, community members, and local governmental groups.

4. Have students make new word webs about tropical rainforests. Compare the new word webs to the original word webs. Ask: *How did the classroom simulation help you learn about tropical rainforests? What couldn't you learn from the simulation? What new questions do you have about rainforests?*

Branching Out

How You Can Help

Please don't leave your students with a paralyzed sense of doom and gloom about rainforest destruction. We can all help! The following ideas and research projects will help your students understand that they can be part of the solution.

• Spread the word. Invite other classrooms, parents, and community members, and present what your research has taught you about tropical rainforests. Prepare refreshments with foods that originated in the rainforest. Include crops like peanuts, avocadoes, bananas, and chocolate.

• Write to your senators and representatives, or have them visit your classroom. Ask them to support efforts to protect tropical rainforests.

• Read about indigenous peoples who live in rainforests. Put on a dramatic presentation highlighting the experiences and interdependencies of different people, plants, and animals in the rainforest.

• Design and make T-shirts and posters presenting some of the most compelling issues about tropical rainforests.

• Survey your local fast food stands to find out where their meat originates. Let them know your feelings about cattle ranching on rainforest land. Consider whether or not you'd be willing to pay five cents extra per hamburger to preserve rainforest land. Figure

out how much it might cost you each year.

• Work in teams to develop a creative plan to help preserve tropical rainforests. Have each team present its plan to the rest of the class. Try to make your plans a reality.

• Find out about non-tropical rainforests and compare their diversity and the issues facing them with with those of tropical rainforests.

• Visit a tropical greenhouse (at a university or botanical garden) and look for adaptations of plants from tropical rainforests, e.g., epiphytic plants, drip tips on leaves, or adventitious roots on trees.

• Make a display showing the direct and indirect connections between our lives and tropical rainforests, e.g., climate and products.

• Write to an organization that is working to protect tropical rainforests (see below). Find out about the many ways these groups are making a difference, for example, by making it possible for students to "buy a piece of the rainforest."

The Children's Rainforest
P.O. Box 936
Lewiston, ME 04240

This non-profit organization promotes awareness of and education about rainforests, and channels donated funds to preserve tropical rainforest land in Costa Rica. Order the booklet "Rainforests: Educational Resources" for a listing of books for all ages, newsletters, teacher's guides, and audiovisual materials to help present the topic of rainforests.

World Wildlife Fund (Publications Department)
1250 24th Street, NW
Washington, DC 20037

The World Wildlife Fund has an education packet, "Vanishing Rainforests," for Grades 2-6 to accompany the Smithsonian Institution's traveling exhibit, "Tropical Rainforests: A Disappearing Treasure."

Marine World Africa USA (Education Department)
Marine World Parkway
Vallejo, CA 94589

Contact this organization for a 14-page booklet titled "Rainforests--Kids for Conservation", geared for Grades K–12. It contains interesting facts, maps, activities, flash cards, glossary, and a list of organizations.

National Audubon Society
645 Pennsylvania Avenue, SE
Washington, DC 20016

Write for a poster on tropical forests to use with a teacher's activity guide. Also available are "International Fact Sheets" that focus on tropical forests.

Adaptations

Diversity among living things occurs, in large part, due to adaptations to environmental conditions. Any particular trait that appears randomly through sexual reproduction (the combining of genetic information) may give an organism a better chance of surviving a particular environmental condition. Certain plants may have characteristics (e.g., slightly harder seed coats, hairier leaves, stronger odor) that increase their chances of survival in a particular environment. For example, if a seed has a harder seed coat that enables it to withstand harsh winters, the plant will survive to reproduce again, passing on the favorable trait to its offspring. Over many generations, these traits become more finely tuned and are known as "adaptations." Plants lacking these traits have a poorer chance of survival in that environment. Their descendants will eventually die out.

Characteristics such as flower color, shape, structure, and odor, for example, are adaptations that evolve over many thousands of years, in response to the vital need to have pollen transferred from flower to flower. In many cases, flowers and pollinators coevolved adaptations (e.g., long beaks and tubular flowers) for these specialized relationships.

Because we use the term "adapt," a common misconception is that individual living things can consciously develop adaptations to different environmental conditions. Remind students that adaptations are chance structural and behavioral features that an organism already possesses that enable it to survive and reproduce in its particular environment.

Specific Plant Adaptations

Every living thing is actually a conglomeration of many adapta-

It Pays to Be Short

The following highlights how several plant species developed adaptations to changes in environmental conditions relatively rapidly.

A pasture in Maryland was seeded with a mixture of grasses and clover and then divided in half. On one half, cattle grazed; the other half was protected from livestock. Only three years after the division, the blue grass, orchard grass and clover on the grazed half of the pasture were dwarfed and rambling, while the same types of plants on the ungrazed half grew tall and upright. How did this difference occur? On one half, the grazing cattle had devoured most of the upright plants, allowing only those individual plants that were low-growing to survive, set seed, and reproduce. These plants adapted to the conditions imposed by grazing. On the ungrazed half, upright growing plants were able to survive, set seed, and reproduce. Individual dwarf plants on that half could not compete successfully for light with taller plants, so the well-adapted tall plants continued to grow and reproduce under these conditions.

tions. All of those features that help plants meet needs and survive, as covered in other chapters (e.g., how plants transport water, produce food, or get pollinated), are actually adaptations. Activities in this section highlight some other specific types of plant adaptations.

Seed Dispersal. Some seeds fly on wings; some are naturally catapulted. Others hitch a ride on passing animals. Some seeds are eaten by animals, pass through their digestive systems, and are deposited in a new location. These dispersal strategies enable young seedlings to grow in a variety of sites without having to compete for resources with parent plants.

In the activity **Go Seeds Go!**, students play nature's part and invent seeds with "special" dispersal mechanisms.

Seed Germination. Most seeds will stay alive until they receive all the conditions necessary for growth, e.g., water, oxygen, and temperature. Some have adaptations that prevent the young seedlings from emerging when their survival is less likely. For instance, if tree seeds in northern climates sprouted in the fall, the young seedlings couldn't survive the cold winter. Germination is prevented in these plant seeds, therefore, until they've been frozen and then warmed, signalling the onset of spring. Many desert seeds will germinate only when large amounts of water are continuously available. What might happen if young cactus seedlings ran out of enough water to ensure continued growth?

In nature, many seeds are adapted to germinate only after their coats are exposed to freezing, decay by fungi or bacteria, fire, soaking in water, decay by acid fruit surrounding seeds, or digestion by animals. In the activity **Seed Busters**, your students can discover seeds' adaptations for withstanding—and requiring—these natural forces.

Leaves. Leaves come in as many shapes and sizes as the habitats in which they live. They have many adaptations that help the plant meet its needs. For example:

• To reduce water loss—thick waxy coating (jade plant); surface hairs (lamb's ears); fewer stomata (cacti); small surface area (evergreen trees)

• To provide supplemental nutrients—leaves adapted to catch and kill insects (pitcher, Venus flytrap, sundew)

• To transpire excess water easily—large surface area and more stomata (philodendron)

Leaves may also be adapted help protect the plant from browsing animals, e.g., by emitting poisonous chemicals or offensive scents. If you've ever run into stinging nettles, you have first-hand experience with a protective adaptation!

In the activity **Turning Over a New Leaf**, students examine variations in leaves and discover how different leaf adaptations help plants survive diverse environmental conditions.

Weeds. Weeds are plants with many adaptations that help them

Climbing Leaves

On some plants, special leaves are modified to form tendrils that help plants climb and compete for light. Plant some pea seeds in pots in your classroom, and allow students to observe the development of these tendrils (they should emerge in a couple of weeks). Try leaving one pot of peas with no support, and placing a stick in another pot. Tendrils will grab firmly onto the support as the pea plant works its way upward. Ask: *How do you think this leaf adaptation helps the plant meet its basic needs?*

compete with other crops. The term "weed" is very subjective. A plant is labeled a weed when it grows where we don't want it. Depending on one's perspective, a field of mustard can be an unwanted nightmare or a valuable cash crop. A violet can be a weed in a corn field or a wildflower in the woods.

Adaptations that help different weeds compete so fiercely and survive include:

- ability to grow in poor soil or in other harsh conditions;

- hairy leaves to reduce moisture loss;

- strong taproots or complex root systems that develop shoots each year;

- ability to reproduce sexually and asexually;

- production of enormous quantities of seeds;

- seeds lasting into the winter to be dispersed by winds;

- highly efficient seed dispersal mechanisms.

In the activity **To Weed or Not to Weed?**, students will consider the subjective classification of weeds and grow and compare weeds with cultivated plants.

Go Seeds Go!

Overview: Students explore various seed dispersal adaptations and invent their own creative seed modifications to disperse GrowLab seeds.

Time:
Groundwork: 1 to 2 40-minute sessions
Exploration: 45 minutes
Making Connections: ongoing

Materials:
• beans or other large seeds
• 6-inch pots
• *Seeds: Pop, Stick, Glide* (see Appendix E)
• miscellaneous materials—cotton, feathers, wool, toothpicks, rubber bands, springs, pipe cleaners, lemon juice, balloons, yarn, crepe paper, etc.
• egg cartons (optional)

Background: page 188

Advance Preparation:
Soak fifteen to thirty bean seeds overnight.

Laying the Groundwork

Objective: To discover many of the ways seeds travel.

1. Discuss whether students think seeds have the ability to move from one place to another. Ask, for instance: *Do you suppose people plant a lawn full of dandelions? How might the ability to move help a seed? How do you think they move? What examples have you observed in nature?*

2. Read the book *Seeds: Pop, Stick, Glide* with the class.

3. If time and your location allow, take students on a fall "traveling seed" walk. Observe mature plants. Look at the ground, water, the air, and animals in search of clues that suggest how seeds might travel. Collect some seeds to bring back to the classroom.

Back in the classroom, check socks and pant legs for seeds that might have "hitchhiked" with you. Have students observe their seeds and try to guess how each might be dispersed. (Also include some pictures of seeds.) Students can use egg cartons to sort seeds, with each cell containing seeds dispersed in a similar way. Consider having students glue seeds on a bulletin board, sorting them by the way they're dispersed.

When looking at a seed, we can't always tell what its dispersal method is. In many cases, for instance, the fruit plays the key part, by luring animals that eat and then excrete seeds. In other cases, tension builds up as fruits dry (e.g., in impatiens and touch-me-nots), causing the fruit to explode violently and expel the seeds.

People Moving Seeds

Discuss with students the many ways in which people may aid in seed dispersal. Ask: *What do you do with your apple or watermelon seeds when you're through?* Share that immigrants to this country purposely brought seeds from their own countries to plant, and accidentally brought additional seeds, in bales of hay, straw, or on articles of clothing.

A look at the origins of some of our common food crops highlights humans' role in moving seeds. Tomatoes and peppers, for instance, are native to South America; cucumbers hail from India; watermelon comes from Africa; and oranges and grapefruits originated in China.

4. Discuss and make a list of adaptations that seem to enable seeds to disperse in different ways. For example:

Method of travel	Possible adaptation	Some examples
stick to animal fur	hooks or barbs	burdock
eaten by bird or other animal and secreted	bright color/tasty fruit	cherries, tomatoes
carried by wind	fluff or feathers	dandelions, cattails
floats on water	can float	coconut
flung from parent	spring-like mechanism	touch-me-nots, pansies

Exploration

Objective: To demonstrate understanding of seed dispersal adaptations by inventing creative travel mechanisms for Grow-Lab seeds.

1. Challenge small teams to invent a strategy for dispersing one kind of GrowLab seed, for example, a seed (or fruit) that...

...hitchhikes on your wool sweater or on an animal for 10 feet.

...attracts a bird; the seed passes through the bird's acidic digestive tract and back to the soil. (Hint: Consider using acidic lemon juice in the simulation.)

...is thrown 5 feet from the plant by a special mechanism.

...is carried on the wind for at least 4 feet.

...floats downstream and is washed up on shore.

...(your own ideas)

2. Supply students with the miscellaneous materials listed on page 191. These materials should be used to modify seeds to help them reach, ultimately, a 6-inch pot. Bean seeds that have been soaked overnight will be the easiest to work with. Have teams first discuss their design, draw sketches, and decide on one design. (If you plan to grow the seeds in the GrowLab, each team should fill a pot with soil mix. Otherwise, leave the pots empty.)

3. Once teams have had a chance to test and modify their designs, have a Go Seeds Go! event. Invite each team, in turn, to demonstrate its seed dispersal mechanism. Have the team members first tell a short story to highlight the nature of the trip taken by their seed, explaining the natural conditions they simulated. Give each team three tries, allowing members to modify the setup, if necessary, in order to reach the pot.

 Just budding in: If students intend to plant the seeds, they'll have to cover them or push them into the potting mix to the appropriate depth once they've landed.

Making Connections

Possible discussion questions:

• *What portion of the dispersed classroom seeds actually reached a pot in which they would have been able to grow? How does this compare to seeds in real life? Why do you think many plants (e.g., dandelions) produce such a large quantity of seeds?* (This strategy ensures that at least some will survive and produce new plants.)

• *What do you think would happen if seeds did not travel away from parents? Imagine a tree dropping all of its seeds directly underneath. How might that affect the ability of each seed to thrive and grow?*

• *How do you think real-life conditions would be different from the simulations?*

• *How did the contribution of each member of your team help in the design of your invention?*

• *If you were a seed, what method of travel would you choose? Why? What do you think would be the pros and cons of that "lifestyle"?*

Branching Out

• When taking a walk in a meadow or overgrown field, wear old socks over your shoes. Back in the classroom, use a hand lens to examine the seeds that have "hitchhiked" on the socks. "Grow" the socks.

• Bring in a dandelion or other plant about to disperse its seeds. Have students calculate the number of offspring that one plant would produce if all seeds found new homes and survived.

• Research how the seeds of different fruits in your GrowLab are naturally dispersed.

• "Become a seed," and act out a certain dispersal method. Ask classmates to guess what type of dispersal adaptations the depicted seed has.

• Write creative travel stories from the perspective of a seed that has left its parent with the help of a natural force.

• Find pictures to compare seeds to human-made objects, e.g., maple seeds and helicopters; burdocks and velcro.

Seedy Feet

Charles Darwin once took a clump of soil from the leg of a dead partridge, watered it, and observed eighty-two different plants emerge. Suggest your students repeat Darwin's experiment, scraping off and "planting" mud from their boots or from their dog's paws. You and your pets are pretty efficient seed dispersers!

Seed Busters

Overview: Students invent ways to simulate forces of nature. They expose seeds to these forces and discover how seeds respond to different natural forces.

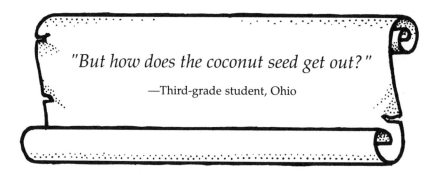

"But how does the coconut seed get out?"

—Third-grade student, Ohio

Time:
Groundwork: 45 minutes
Exploration: 45 minutes setup; 1 to 2 weeks ongoing observations
Making Connections: ongoing

Materials (per small group):
• three small growing containers (2-inch pots or small milk cartons)
• potting mix
• 12 seeds (tomato, marigold, radish, pea, or bean)
• *optional:* hot plate, freezer, matches, birthday candles, tweezers, vinegar, nail file
• "Seed Busters" reproducible, page 273

Background: Page 188

Laying the Groundwork

Objective: To consider how natural forces might affect seed germination.

1. Have students imagine that they are living things out in the wild. Brainstorm a list of the natural forces they think they might encounter. Ask: *How do you think animals would be affected by these forces—e.g., being crushed? ...frozen? ...burned? ...eaten by another living thing? ...cut open? ...buried? How do you think plants would be affected by these same treatments? What about seeds?*

2. From the list of natural forces, have students select those they can safely simulate in the classroom. Record students' predictions about whether seeds will germinate after being exposed to each simulation. For example:

Forces of Nature

Nature's forces	Classroom simulation	Will seed germinate?
Winter	Freezer for 2 days	yes
Flooding	Submerge in water	yes
Forest fire	Burn with match	no
Animal steps on it	We'll step on it	...
Scratched by rock	Scratch with rocks	...
Temperature changes	Oven, freezer, oven	...
Eaten by animals	Soak in vinegar (like stomach acid)	...
Drying out in sun	Leave on top/don't water	...

Exploration

Objective: To explore the effects of simulated natural forces on seed germination.

1. Divide your class into small groups. Have each group prepare three small growing containers for planting. Give half of the groups twelve of one type of seed (e.g., tomatoes) and the other half of the groups twelve of another type of seed (e.g., beans) to have adequate samples on which to base conclusions.

2. Have each group treat four seeds with one of the simulated natural forces, treat four seeds with a different simulated force, and keep four seeds as a control (no simulation). After the simulation, have each team plant their twelve seeds as follows:

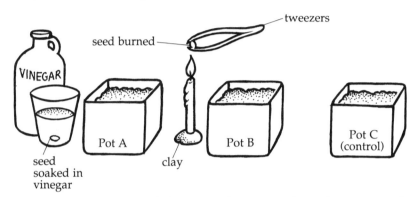

3. Have students record their simulations and predictions on the "Seed Busters" reproducible. A week after control seeds have germinated, have students compile their data on a class chart.

What to expect: Your students will probably find that many of the seeds germinate regardless of the treatments. Seeds soaked in water, however, germinate more quickly and seeds left in "drought" conditions may not germinate at all. Some more fragile seeds, like marigolds, will easily be damaged by harsh treatments, and may fail to germinate.

---

4. Discuss findings. *Which treatment(s) seemed to have the greatest effect on germination? How? How did the treated seeds compare to the controls? What did you notice about the way seeds from different plants responded to the same treatments?*

Making Connections

Possible discussion questions:

• *How did your predictions compare with your actual results? Were you surprised by any of your findings? Which ones? Why do you think many seeds fared well despite the simulations?* (Share the background information about seed germination adaptations on page 189, as appropriate.)

• *Calculate the number of offspring that would result if all the dandelion seeds from one flower survived to germinate. What would happen in the next generation? Discuss why living things produce more offspring than could possibly survive. What do you think the world would be like if all seeds survived exposure to natural forces?*

• *What kinds of results do you think we'd have if seeds did not have outer coats? Why?*

• *From this exploration, can you conclude that all seeds would respond the same way to these natural forces? Why or why not?* (Caution students against generalizing findings from one type of seeds to all other types of seeds.)

• *Why do you think we planted pots with untreated seeds?*

• *After reflecting on the data, what new questions do you have about how natural forces affect seed germination? How could you set up an investigation based on your questions?*

Branching Out

• Collect seeds found outside. Conduct experiments to find out how these seeds respond to simulated natural forces.

• Plant seeds that we know require certain treatment—e.g., soaking, scarring, or chilling—for germination. Compare germination of treated and untreated seeds.

• Try growing plants from bulbs with and without chilling. Discuss how different plants are adapted to require a cold period.

• Examine seeds that we treat and use as foods, e.g., popcorn, roasted chestnuts, and rice. Consider how the treatments might affect their protective coats. Try germinating treated seeds.

• Create and describe a "superseed" that could withstand all natural forces. Discuss implications of such a seed.

• Create a "Natural Force Obstacle Course" (or board game!)—in drawings and/or words—to depict the natural forces a seed might experience before germinating (see illustration).

Seed obstacle course

To Weed or Not to Weed?

Overview: Students examine the relative, subjective nature of the term "weed." They observe competition between "weeds" and cultivated plants.

Time:
Groundwork: 30 minutes
Exploration: 40 minutes setup; 2 to 3 weeks ongoing observations
Making Connections: ongoing

Materials:
• ryegrass seeds
• tomato seeds
• potting mix
• 4-inch pots
• "Problem Solving for Growing Minds" reproducible, page 283
• "Observation Journal" reproducible, page 286
• "Should Dandelions Be Considered Weeds?" reproducible, page 276

Background: Page 188

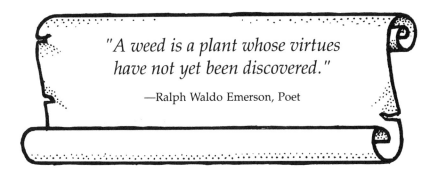

"A weed is a plant whose virtues have not yet been discovered."

—Ralph Waldo Emerson, Poet

Laying the Groundwork

Objective: To uncover conceptions about weeds.

1. Play a word association game to find out what students think of when they hear the word "weed." Divide students into pairs. Hand out a list of words to one student (A) in each pair, making sure the list includes the word "weed." For example,

dog	hot
love	weed
house	friend
leaf	red
soap	forest

2. Have Student A read each word on the list to Student B. After each word, Student B should share the first word that comes to mind and Student A should record the free-association responses. Students then change lists and switch roles.

3. Have students read aloud the images that were associated with the word "weed," while you list the responses on the board. Ask: *Why do you think you came up with so many negative images?* Ask students what they know about weeds. Add this information to the list.

4. Ask: *How do you think plants competing for resources such as water, nutrients, and light might affect each other? What plants have you observed that seem to be better survivors than others? What special characteristics did they appear to have?*

Explain to the class that any plant that is unwanted by humans in a particular situation is considered a weed. Weeds are plants well adapted to compete with other plants for basic needs. What one person might call a weed, however, someone else might value. Share some of the background information about weeds on page 189 with your class, as appropriate.

Exploration

Objective: To understand that some plants labeled "weeds" are successfully adapted to compete with other plants.

1. Tell the class that many farmers consider ryegrass a weed while others plant it as a crop. To investigate how weeds—in this case ryegrass—survive when competing for resources, have the class design and set up an exploration, or set up the following:

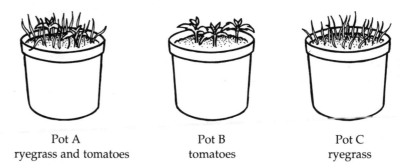

Pot A
ryegrass and tomatoes

Pot B
tomatoes

Pot C
ryegrass

    Fill three small pots with potting mix. In Pot A, plant a small handful of ryegrass seeds and three to five tomato seeds. In Pot B, plant only three to five tomato seeds, and in pot C, plant just a small handful of ryegrass seeds. Cover all pots with 1/4 inch of potting mix.

2. Following the Problem Solving for Growing Minds process, page 10, encourage students to predict how they think the plants in each pot will look in two to three weeks. Have students use their "Observation Journals" to record daily observations of the plants. Have the class define what characteristics they'd look for in a plant they considered to be a "weed" and then decide what to measure, e.g., average height of both the ryegrass and the tomatoes, and/or what to observe, e.g., overall color, leaf number, leaf size.

What to expect: When the tomatoes are forced to compete with ryegrass they are typically stunted, compared to the tomatoes grown by themselves. The ryegrass should thrive in both pots.

Making Connections

1. Possible discussion questions:

• *How did the growth of tomatoes in Pots A and B compare? ...the ryegrass in Pots A and C? How did your predictions compare with your results?*

• *Which plant would you consider a "weed"? Explain what observations lead you to this conclusion.*

• *If you were a gardener raising tomatoes, would you consider ryegrass to be a weed? Why or why not? If you were a farmer raising ryegrass, would you consider ryegrass a "weed"? Why or why not?*

• *In what situations might radishes, oak trees, or daisies be considered weeds? What other plants are sometimes valued and at other times considered weeds?*

• *How do you think the characteristics that make a weed a weed might also make it a useful plant? (See "Worthy Weeds" sidebar.)*

• *How or when might animals act like weeds?*

• *What adaptations do you think a dandelion might have for reproducing and surviving mowing, growing in sidewalk cracks, or being trampled on? (Dandelions have many lightweight seeds for wind dispersal, low growth withstanding mowing, and long taproots for obtaining resources most other plants can't reach.)*

• *Do you think dandelions are weeds? Why or why not?*

• *What do you think Ralph Waldo Emerson meant by, "A weed is a plant whose virtues have not yet been discovered"?*

2. To consider how one person's treasure can be another person's weed, facilitate a discussion in which students play various roles to address the issue: Should dandelions be considered weeds?

Cut the "Should Dandelions Be Considered Weeds?" reproducible into ten pieces describing the different characters and their opinions on dandelions. Have groups of 2 to 3 students randomly choose one of the characters. Before the class discussion, give groups time to cultivate their opinions, elaborating on the reasons suggested, and to develop the characters they'll be playing in the discussion.

Worthy Weeds

Many of our "weeds" were traditionally and still are used as nutritional or medicinal plants. Others move in and hold on to precious topsoil when an area has been cleared. Some weeds supply fruits and seeds for birds, and other food parts for rabbits, mice, insects, and other animals. They can supply nectar and pollen for birds and insects. They can protect the soil from wind and water erosion.

Many weeds provide a source of medicine for humans. Plant breeders continually search for wild plants ("weeds") that might have desirable characteristics such as natural disease resistance. They are used to breed new crops to help meet the world's food demands. Many of our current food crops are relatives of common weeds including Queen Anne's lace (wild carrot), deadly nightshade (a relative of the tomato), and wild mustard.

Branching Out

• Design experiments to test the effects of different types of mulches on weed growth, e.g., pencil shavings, shredded paper, leaves.

• Collect some soil inhabited by weeds. "Plant" the soil in containers in the GrowLab and investigate what emerges!

• Research the common weeds in your area. "Adopt" a weed in the wild, observe its life cycle, write a descriptive poem about it, and collect a few of its seeds to be planted in the GrowLab.

• Create a scavenger hunt to locate weeds with specific characteristics such as hairy leaves or taproots. Discuss how these adaptations help these plants survive.

• Draw or make models of fictitious weeds that are adapted to specific conditions, e.g., surviving in outer space.

• Observe insects and other animals that depend on certain weeds (e.g., monarch butterflies and milkweed.)

• Develop and conduct a survey to explore peoples' attitudes about weeds.

• Research ways people try to eradicate weeds. Debate the pros and cons of different methods of weed control.

• Develop sampling techniques to estimate the size of various weed populations. Try using sample grids of one square meter.

• Write a story from the standpoint of a weed trying desperately to convince a gardener of its virtues.

Weed Overpopulation?

An example of a weed with enormous seed production is flixweed, a weed related to common wild mustard. One flixweed plant weed can produce approximately 730,000 seeds in a single season. If all these seeds grew into plants, in three years flixweed would cover twice the Earth's entire land surface. Another weed, mullein, produces an average of 223,000 seeds per plant!

Many weed seeds have adaptations to lie dormant in soil for many years—even decades—and germinate when good growth opportunities arise. Try "planting" some "bare" soil from an old garden site or empty lot to see what and how many weeds emerge.

Turning Over a New Leaf

Overview: Students examine variations in leaves and consider how leaf adaptations can help plants survive in different environments.

Time:
Groundwork: 1 to 2 days
Exploration: 1 to 2 days
Making Connections: ongoing

Materials:
See materials listed at each station in Exploration
• "Turning Over a New Leaf" reproducible, page 274

Background: Page 188

Advance Preparation: Set up stations around the room as described in the Exploration. Whenever possible, use leaves collected by students during the Groundwork activity.

Laying the Groundwork

Objective: To recognize that leaves have many structural variations.

1. Set the stage by asking: *How would you describe a leaf? How are all leaves alike? What are some of the differences?* Generate a list of different leaf characteristics.

2. Initiate a Leaf Scavenger Hunt. Using the leaf characteristics generated by you and your students, create a scavenger hunt list (see below). Give each small group of students the list and a day or two to locate one each of as many leaves as possible on the list. Encourage them to look first in the GrowLab for the items, then check other classroom, house, and outdoor plants. To avoid defoliating classroom plants, encourage students to write or draw a description of the plant, rather than take a leaf, e.g., "pointed leaves = tomato plant." Have them write down where each leaf was found.

Leaf Scavenger Hunt

Description	Where found?
triangular leaf	
hairy leaf	
leave with no petiole (leaf stalk)	
hairy and pointy leaf	
spiny leaf	
fat leaf	
waxy leaf	
leaf with jagged edges	
leaf that looks like a hand	
leaf with smooth edges	

3. Once as many types of leaves as possible have been collected or described on paper, have students examine the collection. Ask:

How are all these leaves the same? How are they different? Why do you think there is so much variation among leaves? Which leaf characteristics do you think might be useful to the plant? How?

Exploration

Objective: To recognize that leaves have different adaptations that enable them to survive in specific environments.

1. Have pairs of students visit each of the five stations, in numerical order, during the course of a day or two. They can do so during free time or while the rest of the class is engaged in other activities. Let students know that each station focuses on one or more leaf adaptations. Have each pair of students use the "Turning Over a New Leaf" reproducible to record observations and respond to questions at each station.

2. After all pairs of students have had a chance to visit each station and respond to the questions on their worksheets, discuss student responses and share information under "Class Discussion" for each station.

 Just budding in: If your students are unfamiliar with transpiration and/or stomata, visit station 1 as a class, preliminary to the exploration.

> **What's Stomata?**
>
> The word "stomata" comes from the Greek word for mouth. Challenge your students to count the number of stomata on a leaf. Oops! What's the matter? One square inch of a typical leaf can have 1/4 million stomata!

Station 1

Materials: potted live plant, potted plastic or silk plant, plastic bags, twist ties

Setup: Set up two pots as illustrated a couple of days before beginning the activity. Water well. Water droplets should form on the inside surface of the bag containing the live plant. Leave a hand lens next to the plants.

Class Discussion: Have students share worksheet responses. Ask: *What did the setup help us to infer about leaves?*

As a basis for understanding many leaf adaptations, students should recognize that an important function of leaves is to transpire or release water. Share with them that water, necessary for photosynthesis, is absorbed by the roots and moves up through the stem to the leaves. Excess water is given off or transpired through the stomata in the leaves. These are minute openings in the leaf surface, surrounded by special guard cells that open and close to let water out and exchange air.

With microscopes or hand lenses, set up a station next to Station 1 to allow students to examine evidence of stomata. Pick a leaf from a wandering Jew or other plant in the spiderwort family. Paint a coat of clear nail polish on the underside of the leaf. Once dry, the polish can be peeled from the leaf and placed on a microscope slide or viewed through a hand lens. Impressions of the stomata should be clear.

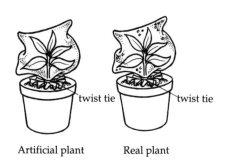

Artificial plant   Real plant

Station 2

Materials: jade plant leaf (Leaf A); lettuce plant leaf (Leaf B); 1 sponge (3" X 4" X 2"); 2 sponges (3" X 4" X 1"); one plastic bag.

Class Discussion: Have students share their worksheet responses. Ask: *Which leaf do you think can store more water? Why? Which do you think would dry out faster if left in the sun?*

To help guide thinking, focus on the sponges for comparison. Ask: *Do you think the thick or thin sponge could hold more water? How does the volume of the thick sponge compare with the volume of the two thin sponges laid side by side? If we wet them all, do you think the thick one or two thin ones would dry out faster? Why?*

If we put one sponge in a plastic bag, which do you think would dry out faster? Why? How can your observations and thoughts about the sponges help you answer the questions about leaves?

Share that many leaves found in dry environments are thick and fleshy. Thicker leaves, like thick sponges, can hold more water than thin leaves can. Although the two thin sponges laid side by side may have the same volume as a thick sponge, they have more surface area for water evaporation and will dry out faster. For the same reason, thin leaves will dry out more quickly than thick ones will.

Many dry-environment plants also have a waxy coating. The waxy coating (simulated by the plastic bag on the sponge) on many dry-climate leaves prevents water from escaping.

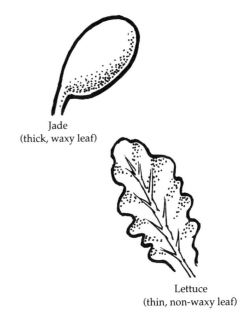

Jade
(thick, waxy leaf)

Lettuce
(thin, non-waxy leaf)

Station 3

Materials: cactus plant; ivy plant

Class Discussion: Have students share their worksheet responses. Ask: *How do you think having a large stem and spines instead of leaves might help a cactus-type plant survive in a dry environment?*

Share that cactus stems serve as storage tanks for water. They also carry out photosynthesis normally carried out by leaves of other green plants. Spines do not photosynthesize or have stomata, and thus water loss from the plant is reduced. Since the stem's surface area is relatively small compared to its volume, the stem transpires relatively little water.

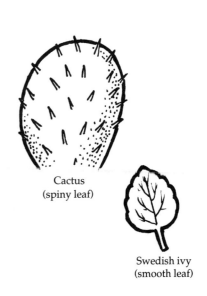

Cactus
(spiny leaf)

Swedish ivy
(smooth leaf)

Lamb's ear
(hairy leaf)

Lettuce
(smooth leaf)

Station 4

Materials: geranium, mint, or other aromatic plant; lettuce, radish, or other unscented plant

Class Discussion: Have students share worksheet responses and focus their attention on the aromatic plant. Ask: *How do you think a leaf's aroma might be an adaptation for survival? What examples can you think of in nature? Have you ever used an unscented bug repellent?*

Share that many plants produce scents that repel predators or attract pollinators.

Station 5

Materials: hairy leaf (e.g., bean, tomato, thyme, lamb's ear); smooth leaf (e.g., lettuce, pea, basil); hand lens

Class Discussion: Have students share worksheet responses. Focus on leaf hairs as an adaptation serving many different purposes in different plants. To help guide students' thinking, ask: *Do you think a bald head or a hair-covered head would dry out faster? How do people cope with extremes in climate such as cold and wind? How do you think leaf hairs might feel to an insect looking for a meal?*

Share that hairy leaves can help reduce water loss by providing an insulating layer, protecting from climatic extremes, and deterring leaf-eating insects. In addition, many leaf hairs have glands that secrete scents. Based on the discussion from Station 4, students should recognize why this would be a beneficial adaptation. Some plants have very specialized hairs. Venus flytraps, for instance, have stiff hairs that, when touched, trigger the closing of the leaves to trap insects. Slippery, downward-pointing hairs on the carnivorous pitcher plant allow insects to fall down but not climb back up to safety.

Making Connections

1. Possible discussion questions

• *Why do you think there isn't one generic, all-purpose leaf type?*

• *If you were a leaf living in the desert, describe how you might look and feel. Why?*

• *What adaptations do plants and animals have in common to help fend off predators* (bad smells; spines)?

• *What characteristics of pine needles do you think help trees live through cold winters?* (The small surface area reduces water loss; the narrow shape and waxy surface lessen drying by wind.)

• *Some rainforest plants have leaves that end in narrow points, com-*

monly called "drip tips." What purpose do you think these might serve? (They shed excess water.)

• *Why do you think some trees lose their leaves in winter?* (This prevents them from drying out when less water is being taken up by the roots.)

• *Many plants open their stomata only at night. Why do you think this adaptation might have evolved?* (Stomata lose less water at night than in the heat of day.)

• *In a drought year do you think moisture-loving plants can develop adaptations to survive the lack of water? If so, how do you think they could do that?* (Remind students that adaptations take many generations.)

2. Challenge pairs of students to "design-a-plant" adapted to survive certain conditions, by making a drawing with captions or constructing a model from classroom materials. For instance, students might create a plant whose leaves can:

• catch insects
• hold onto rocks in a river
• survive in a pasture
• live on a windy mountaintop

Branching Out

• Grow a mimosa or sensitive plant (see sidebar). Explore what stimulus (touch, wind, water, etc.) causes the leaves to fold up. Discuss to what type of environment the plant might be adapted.

• Grow carnivorous plants (Venus fly traps, pitcher plants, sundews) from seed or plants (see sidebar). Discover how their leaves are specially adapted.

• Explore how a plant adapted to a dry environment, such as a cactus, responds when placed in a very moist environment.

• After researching and observing leaf structure, make a "leaf sandwich" using classroom materials to simulate the layered leaf structure.

• Research human uses of plant leaves for such things as food, fiber, medicines, spices, and cosmetics. Consider how we make use of certain plant adaptations, e.g., for flavoring.

Nervous Leaves?

Some plant leaves have sophisticated "nervous systems" that enable them to transmit information and respond to stimuli quickly. A mimosa or sensitive plant leaf, for instance, if touched, will fold in half. This adaptive response likely helps these plants to survive life on windy ridges and to surprise insect predators. You can purchase mimosa seeds to raise in the GrowLab through the source listed in Appendix F. Challenge students to investigate what conditions cause plant leaves to respond by folding up.

Animal-Eating Leaves?!

Some leaves have adaptations to help plants obtain extra nutrients from insects and other animals. These plants are typically found in areas such as bogs with waterlogged soil, where nutrients like nitrogen are hard to obtain. The Venus fly trap, one of the better-known carnivorous plants, has two kidney-shaped lobes with bristles. If bristles of both lobes are touched, they'll snap shut on the victim. After 30 minutes, special glands secrete acids and enzymes to digest the victim, leaving all but the skeleton.

You can purchase Venus fly trap plants (and seeds, which are very slow to germinate) from the source in Appendix F, or from most science supply catalogs. These plants provide a fascinating focus for student-directed science explorations.

Chapter 4

Sharing the Global Garden

From human beings to microscopic bacteria, we are all connected in the great web of life. This chapter encourages you and your students to look more closely at how plants interact with other living things. The first section explores selected aspects of this interdependence, highlighting the role of decomposers in nutrient recycling. Students examine some ways in which humans depend on plants.

The second part of the chapter explores how human actions affect plants in the environment. Students investigate plants' responses to human actions and human-generated pollutants. They consider the environmental costs of our actions, and how we might minimize our negative environmental impact. Your GrowLab garden sets the stage for involving students in extended projects to explore some of our pressing environmental concerns.

Interdependence

No plant, person, bird, spider, bacteria, or moss is an island—we all depend on one another. Many types of relationships exist, at many levels and degrees of complexity. For instance, many plants depend on animals for pollination of flowers and/or dispersal of seeds. Animals, including humans, depend on plants for food, fuel, and shelter. Humans depend on intestinal bacteria to help digest food. Predators are directly affected by the numbers of their prey available, who in turn are affected by climate, food availability, and other environmental factors. Because of these interlocking relationships, a change in one element affects the whole.

Although it is difficult to explore complex relationships in an indoor garden, the activities in this section will help students begin to understand some important relationships directly involving plants. The section also highlights some important aspects of human dependence on plants.

The Energy/Nutrient Cycle

Green plants and algae turn the sun's energy into food, activating the cycle of nutrients that makes life possible on Earth. They are the **primary producers** in **food chains.** Food chains are composed of producers, consumers, and decomposers. Since most organisms have more than one food preference, these chains interlock to form complex **food webs.** Some consumers (such as aphids) obtain energy by eating producers, others (such as wolves) by eating other consumers, and some (such as humans) by eating both. All animals are both consumers and consumed, sometimes by other consumers but all, ultimately, by the decomposers.

Every time something is consumed, much of the original energy is lost in the transfer and in growth and maintenance. We are thus continually dependent on the sun for energy, and on green plants and algae to convert that energy into food.

Decomposers are the final links in food chains. These organisms use dead plants and animals as food, ultimately releasing

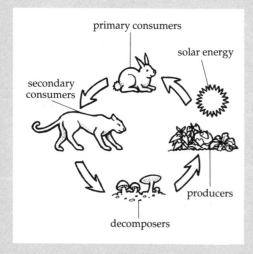

primary consumers

solar energy

secondary consumers

producers

decomposers

locked-up nutrients to be used again by plants. Among the decomposers are **fungi,** which include molds, mildews, mushrooms, rusts, and smuts. Because they lack chlorophyll and can't carry out photosynthesis, fungi feed on once-living materials, or act as parasites on living organisms. Some fungi can be seen by the unaided eye, but other decomposers, bacteria, are so small that a mere teaspoon of soil can contain billions of them.

In **FungusAmongUs,** your students will explore the ability of some decomposers to release nutrients from once-living matter, to be used again by living things.

Fungus Café

Earthworms help once-living materials decompose in a way that is easier to observe directly. Because they live right in the soil, their ability to recycle materials has an immediate impact on plant life. Extensive background information on earthworms can be found on page 214. In the activity **Getting Hooked on Worms,** your students will observe some of the special adaptations of these creatures, and examine how decomposers help once-living things return to enrich the soil.

Aphids, insects well known to many gardeners, consume plant nutrients and are in turn consumed by other animals. In **Aphid Pets,** students take advantage of the presence of aphids by exploring the habits of these garden visitors.

Humans depend on plants not only for oxygen and nourishment, but also for many forms of energy, medicines, clothing, building materials, and countless other uses. **Celebrating Salad** invites students, while growing a salad garden, to investigate food choices, and to explore how the nutrition in different plant foods helps us survive. **Plants 'R' Us** suggests ways of using the GrowLab to grow some important crops as a backdrop for exploring the wide range of roles plants play in our lives.

Overview: Students examine the process of decomposition and consider how living and once-living materials decompose to become part of the soil.

Time:
Groundwork: 1 week ongoing observations
Exploration: 30 to 40 minutes setup; 3 to 4 weeks observations
Making Connections: ongoing

Materials:
• clear gallon plastic bag
• GrowLab plant debris
• pieces of old fruit, cheese, and bread
• plastic bags or cups
• soil
• "Futures Wheel," page 292

Background: Page 208

Advance Preparation:
A week before starting the activity, place pieces of old fruit, cheese, and moist bread in a clear gallon plastic bag. Hang the bag on a bulletin board with a sign reading: "What do you think is happening in this bag?"

If your students have not yet explored soil, consider conducting one of the soil activities prior to conducting this activity.

FungusAmongUs

*Where would we be
with no FungusAmongUs,
But buried in waste to our waist?
Then why do some folks just think of the fungus
As "yucky" and of most poor taste?*

*Now is it because they see only death
And fear the cycle of life?
Or is it perhaps that they haven't yet learned
Decomposers prevent much strife?*

*In FungusAmongUs your students will learn
That life has its friends and its foes,
As they try to grow some fungus-among-them
They'll watch what was life decompose!*

Laying the Groundwork

Objective: To observe and begin to understand the process of decomposition.

1. Focus students' attention on the materials in the plastic bag hung ahead of time. Ask: *What do you think is in the bag? Do you think the contents are changing? How?* Have students record how they think the contents of the bag might change in one week ... in six months.

2. After an additional week of observing and describing changes in the contents of the bags, students will notice that the objects show signs of mold and other fungus growth. Ask: *How did the changes compare with your predictions? Where have you noticed this kind of change before? What do you think might be causing this change?*

Ask: *Where have you seen examples of once-living things changing and decomposing in the environment* (rotting logs, moldy garbage, roadkills, forest floors, compost piles)? *If leaves, twigs, old plant stems, and other natural materials are constantly dying and falling to the ground, why do you think we're not buried under them?* Explain that the same types of changes that took place in the bags constantly occur outdoors. Once-living materials are broken down by millions of microscopic bacteria, fungi, and other decomposers.

3. Focus on students' previous explorations of soil. Ask: *What, in addition to mineral and rock particles, is an important part of soil?* Discuss the importance of living and once-living matter in soils (see page 102). Share that soil also contains millions of microscopic fungi, bacteria, and other decomposers. Ask: *Based on what you saw happen in the plastic bag, how do you think these microorganisms might help create more soil? How could we explore this?*

Exploration

Objective: To understand that soil hastens decomposition of living matter which, in turn, becomes part of the soil.

1. Ask: *How could we set up an investigation to examine whether soil seems to help once-living things decompose?* Follow student suggestions, or set up two "decomposiums," as illustrated.

Decomposium A
(moistened materials mixed
with soil)

Decomposium B
(moistened materials
without soil)

Solicit student suggestions for materials to include in the decomposiums. Be sure to include some GrowLab debris (plant thinnings, clippings, old leaves). Also include some materials that students think won't decompose (marbles, styrofoam), and some about which they're not sure.

2. Have students predict how the materials in each container will change during the next three to four weeks. Ask: *Why do you think they'll change as you predicted?* During the next three to four weeks, students should regularly record observations of their decomposiums. Use hand lenses and/or microscopes to look for changes and organisms invisible to the unaided eye.

 Caution: Warn students not to inhale or ingest contents while examining. Some types of molds can be harmful.

3. Discuss findings. Ask: *How did the materials in each of the decomposiums change? Why do you think there might have been differences between the two? Did some materials seem to decompose more quickly than others? Which? Did some materials show no signs of decomposition? Which?*

> **What to expect:** Students should find that materials in both containers will show signs of decomposition. Depending on the content of your garden soil, once-living material may decompose more quickly in it than in the container without soil. Soil contains millions of microorganisms—bacteria and fungi—which help decompose organic materials. It may also contain animals such as worms, springtails, sowbugs, and flies which help physically break down organic matter.

Making Connections

1. Possible discussion questions:

• *Why do you think materials might break down quickly in soil? Based on your observations and experiences, what do you think happens to once-living things that decompose in the soil? How do you think these once-living materials might help support new life?*

Share that as decomposers break down these organic materials, they are releasing the nutrients back to the soil to be used by the next generation of plants, and the cycle begins again. Over time, the organic materials will actually become part of the soil, enriching it in the process.

• *Can you describe how you think a GrowLab plant could become part of a carrot, and then part of you?*

• *How do you think the Earth would be different if there were no decomposers?* (Use the "Futures Wheel" to help answer this question.)

• *What kind of materials do you think decomposers cannot break down? What do you think eventually happens to those materials?*

2. Have each student write a paragraph explaining what they think is meant by the following quote by Loren Eisley:

"Nature has no interest in the preservation of her dead; her purpose is to start their elements upon the eternal road to life once more."

Branching Out

• Investigate what conditions, such as moisture, temperature, and soil type, seem to promote the most rapid decomposition.

• Find out about some of the ways humans prevent foods from decomposing, such as refrigerating, drying, smoking, canning, and salting. Experiment with some of these methods.

• Try growing seeds or plants in the "compost" produced in your decomposiums.

• Research ways in which we benefit from fungi, bacteria, and other decomposers (antibiotics, foods, digestion, etc.).

• Prepare a large decomposium in a plastic garbage bag. Include things students think will decompose, things they think will not decompose, and things they have questions about. Include moist soil to provide adequate microorganisms. Inflate the bag with air, seal it, and bury it outside during warm weather. Dig up the bag in a month or two, and examine the ingredients.

• Find out what types of materials will not decompose for a very long time, if ever (plastics, styrofoam, disposable diapers, etc.).

The Secret Ingredient

One classroom expanded this exploration by comparing decomposition of organic materials in potting mix with decomposition in real soil. They discovered that the materials in the real soil began to decompose more quickly and completely. The real soil contained something that was missing from the sterile potting mix—millions of microscopic decomposers.

Find out how you can do your part to decrease the amount of these materials put into the environment, and to recycle what's already around.

• Estimate the number of disposable diapers that might be used in one year in your city or town. Calculate the volume of garbage resulting from these materials that don't readily decompose.

• Prepare edible fungi snacks (e.g., blue cheese or mushrooms).

• Write "oldy but moldy" songs.

• Develop a school composting program to create rich compost for your garden (see sidebar).

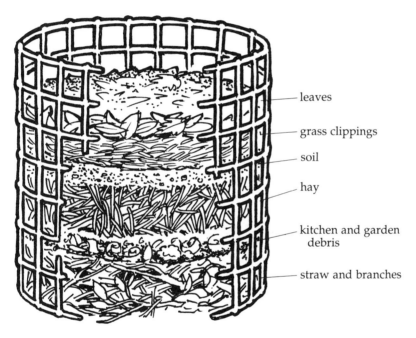

leaves

grass clippings

soil

hay

kitchen and garden debris

straw and branches

Compost pile

Getting Hooked on Worms

An outdoor garden ecosystem is alive with billions of organisms, constantly interacting and affecting one another and their environment. Although your indoor garden has relatively few of these living things, your students can recognize the importance of different community members in a healthy ecosystem. One creature that is vital to decomposition and recycling of organic materials is the earthworm. You can raise earthworms in your classroom to complement your indoor garden project. By trying some of the suggestions from the activity on page 218, you and your students should soon be **Getting Hooked on Worms**.

Earthworm Structures and Adaptations

Some of the most distinguishing features of an earthworm's body are the rings or **segments** along the length of its body. Each segment is surrounded by a set of muscles and connected to adjoining segments by another set of muscles. The alternating action of these two sets of muscles allows worms to lengthen, contract, and move and twist through the soil. Other features that help a worm move and anchor itself are the tiny bristles or **setae** on each of its body rings. Why do you think robins work so hard to pull out earthworms anchored in the soil!?

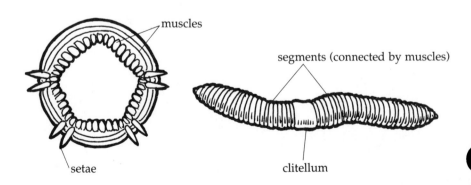

muscles

setae

segments (connected by muscles)

clitellum

While it may be hard to tell front from back, the narrow, slightly pointed end of an earthworm is the front end, which thickens to force soil apart. (If the soil's too hard, a worm can simply eat its way through!) Earthworms have mouths, but no teeth. As they feed on soil and all types of organic matter (leaves, grass, decaying animals, etc.) everything they eat is pushed through the digestive tract. There it is ground and worked by muscle action, tiny stones, digestive juices, and bacteria.

Although earthworms have no need for eyes underground and cannot see, they will move away from light, particularly when it is shone on their front end. Avoiding the light helps them survive by protecting them from predators and from becoming dried out by the sun. Earthworms can be found above ground primarily at night. People who use earthworms for fish bait take advantage of the fact that worms do not move away from red light.

Worms have special glands to maintain the skin moisture they need in order to take oxygen through their skin and into blood vessels. Because they breathe through their skin, however, excessive water can suffocate them. This is why earthworms stampede upwards after a heavy rain.

Each earthworm has both male and female reproductive organs, covered by a wide, whitish band, or **clitellum**, around its middle. During mating, any two adult worms can join together at this band, their heads pointing in opposite directions, to fertilize each others' eggs. The clitellum then secretes mucus which encases the eggs in the soil until the young hatch. If moisture and temperature conditions are right, they will hatch in about a month; if not, it can take up to a year. Look for small red or purplish "rice" or small pea-sized egg cases in your earthworm center.

Earthworms and Soil

Small pellet-like piles emerge after organic matter travels through the worm's digestive tract. These **castings** are a valuable fertilizer. The nutrients that were locked up in the dead organic matter, unavailable to growing plants, are recycled and usable nutrients are released. These castings not only provide nutrients, but they also prevent soil from crumbling or packing down hard. They improve the ability of the soil to hold water. The tunnels or burrows created as worms move soil particles (up to forty times their weight) also contribute to the loosening and conditioning of soil. The mixing and tunneling let in air and water necessary for animals and plants in the ground. As earthworms burrow, these little "soil plows" carry leaves and other materials into the soil, hastening decomposition, and bring nutrients and humus to the top. An acre of soil may house as many as a million earthworms!

Earthworms in the Web of Life

Like all other living things, earthworms are part of different food chains. While they eat and release nutrients from soil and organic matter, they in turn are eaten by such animals as birds, moles, turtles, and snakes. People who fish use worms to lure the fish we eat. When earthworms die, they're "consumed" by other decomposers, and their nutrients are released back into the soil.

Setting Up a GrowLab Worm Farm

You can easily set up earthworm centers in the classroom. Use a shallow container such as a plastic shoe box or wooden box, with air holes placed in the sides and bottom. Some teachers use the bottoms of gallon plastic jugs so that small groups of students can work with their own worm farms. Fill each container about halfway with a mixture of rich garden soil and sand. You can substitute shredded paper bags, shredded black and white newspaper, peat moss, or decaying leaves for the soil and/or sand. These **bedding** materials all provide a place for the worms to burrow. Moisten well. Add fifteen to twenty-five earthworms (see "Do You Dig Worms?", below) and cover with a thin layer of sawdust, rotted leaves, or hay to maintain moisture.

Worm Farm Materials

• plastic shoe box, wooden box, or other container
• bedding (soil, sand, shredded newspaper, etc.)
• garden debris
• earthworms or redworms

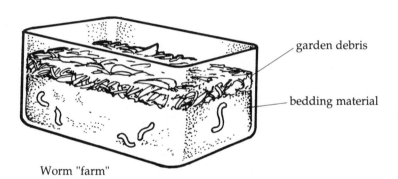

garden debris

bedding material

Worm "farm"

Regularly add indoor garden debris (old leaves, thinned plants, clipped grass) as well as coffee grounds, cornmeal, and vegetable scraps to the surface of the worm center. Keep the worm center under or near the GrowLab in a relatively cool (50-60 degrees F/15 C) spot. If your classroom is very warm, consider buying redworms (see next page), since they can tolerate warmer temperatures than earthworms.

Earthworms will immediately start burrowing and multiplying, and can be used for any of the explorations in the following activity, to continue to produce excellent compost for your GrowLab plants, to be placed in an outdoor garden, or to keep for company!

After two to three months, the bedding and castings will begin to look like rich soil. Since the castings create an unhealthy environment for the earthworms, push all of the material, including worms, to one side of the box. Add new bedding to the other side and begin putting garden debris and garbage scraps in with it. The worms will eventually migrate over to that side. Clean out the finished "compost" you pulled to one side, and use it in your indoor or outdoor garden. Replace with clean bedding and the cycle starts again.

Do You Dig Worms?

You can collect earthworms by digging for them in the rich, moist soil of a lawn or garden. Dig down approximately 20 cm (8 inches), lift the soil and use your hands to carefully sift through to find worms. Another way to find worms is to look on the ground after a warm, soaking rain, or to search for them at night, using a flashlight, under rocks, logs, or old boards. Have students mark or map the location of worms so they can eventually return them.

If earthworms are hard to find in your neighborhood, consider buying them from bait and tackle shops. If your classroom temperature is above 65 degrees F or so, purchase redworms from the sources below. They prefer warmer temperatures and are more likely to survive in a classroom environment.

Redworm sources:

Flowerfield Enterprises
10332 Shaver Rd.
Kalamazoo, MI 49002
616-327-0108

Cape Cod Worm Farm
30 Center Ave.
Buzzards Bay, MA 02532
508-759-5664

Earthworms and redworms can also be purchased from most school science supply catalogs.

Getting Hooked on Worms

Overview:
Students build a classroom earthworm farm and experiment with these important community members. They then investigate earthworms' relationship with plants and soil.

(Or, everything you always wanted to know about worms, but were afraid to touch!)

Time:
Groundwork: variable (2 days setup; ongoing observations)
Exploration: 40 minutes setup; 2-plus weeks observations
Making Connections: ongoing

Materials: (See background for worm farm materials)
• earthworms or redworms
• *optional* (see Laying the Groundwork): flashlight, red cellophane, ruler
• clear containers (e.g., milk jug or soda bottle bottoms)
• soil or potting mix
• organic matter (garden debris, cornmeal, etc.)
• black paper
• "Futures Wheel" reproducible, page 292

Background: Page 208 and page 214

Advance Preparation:
Construct a classroom earthworm center and/or collect worms as described on page 217. Consider doing **FungusAmongUs** to supplement this activity.

Laying the Groundwork

Objective: To discover some features of earthworms.

1. Have some worms available for students to observe. Ask: *What do you know about earthworms?* Generate a class list of things students know, or ideas they have, about earthworms. Ask: *Do you think earthworms affect us? How?* Add to the above list a column entitled "Questions We Have About Earthworms." Leave the list up for reference throughout this project.

2. Have the class set up an earthworm farm using the recommendations on page 216, or bring worms into the classroom solely for short-term observations and explorations.

3. Allow pairs or small groups of students to observe different structural and behavioral adaptations of earthworms by conducting some or all of the following mini-explorations. Consider setting up earthworm stations for each exploration. The mini-explorations will help lay the groundwork for examining how worms affect plants and soil.

Which end is up? Invite students to observe an earthworm closely. Ask: *Can you tell which end is the head and which end is the tail? What observations did you make to help you decide which end is which? How do you think its shape might help it move through the soil?*

The brush-off. Allow each student to run a gentle finger over an earthworm's underside. Ask: *What do you feel?* Have students use a hand lens to explore worms' bristly body surfaces. Ask: *How do you think the bristles might help the earthworm survive? Why do you think robins seem to have such a tug-of-war trying to pull an earthworm from its burrow?*

So sensitive! Ask students to find out how worms respond to changes in their environment—for example, by shining a flashlight at a group of worms on a smooth surface. Ask: *How do the* *earthworms respond? How do you think this response might help them survive in their environment?* Try covering the light with red cellophane to compare how worms respond to red light. Have students experiment to see how worms respond to sound vibrations. Ask: *How do you think this might help them underground?*

Inch worms? Challenge students to guess the length of an earthworm and then try using a ruler or tape measure to measure the actual length. Ask: *What problems do you encounter? After observing how earthworms move, why do you think it's hard to measure their true length? What do you observe about their bodies that might cause them to shrink and grow? How do you think this might help them survive?* Draw bar graphs comparing an estimate of a worm's length with its true length, both when stretched out and when shortened.

The worms crawl out. Ask: *Have you ever seen lots of worms on the sidewalk after a rain?* Explore this reaction in your worm center by placing worms in containers of soil, watering heavily, and observing how they respond to these simulated rain showers. Ask: *How do you think this response might help worms survive?*

Exploration

Objective: To examine how earthworms affect soils and infer how they affect plants. To appreciate the important ecological role of earthworms.

1. Ask: *How do you think earthworms affect soil? What have you observed that makes you believe this? How do you think they affect old leaves and other organic matter in the soil?* As a class or in small groups, set up an investigation to examine how earthworms interact with materials in the soil.

For each exploration, set up two clear containers (e.g., bottoms from milk jugs) with layers of soil or potting mix and organic matter, as illustrated. Place ten to twelve worms in one of the containers. Keep both slightly moist, provide airholes, and keep in a cool spot in the room. Cover containers with black paper.

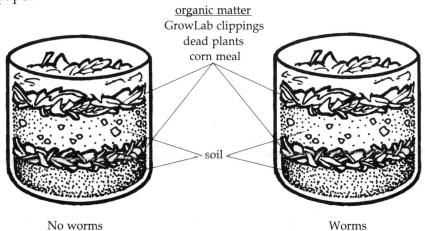

organic matter
GrowLab clippings
dead plants
corn meal

soil

No worms   Worms

2. Have students predict what will happen to the materials in each container over two weeks. Remove the black coverings daily for two weeks and record observations in pictures and/or words. Ask: *Have the layers changed? What evidence do you see of the earthworms' actions? How do you think worms might be helping the soil? How do you think their actions might affect other animals in the soil? How do you think they might affect plants? Why do you think we covered the containers with black paper?*

3. Share some of the background information about earthworms with students. Highlight their role as soil plows, improving soil structure with their burrows and castings. Describe their ability to recycle organic matter through their digestive systems and to release a nutritious, soil-improving fertilizer.

Making Connections

1. After making some of the Groundwork observations, sharing background material, and conducting the soil exploration, have small groups of students work together to create "Amazing Earthworms" reports for presentation to the class. These should creatively highlight what they've discovered about these creatures, using graphs, illustrations, poetry, etc. Students can include new vocabulary learned as well as data from experiments.

2. Possible discussion questions:

• *Based on your explorations, what role do you think earthworms might play in the soil in a forest?*

• *In what ways do you think our gardens, forests, lawns, and/or world might be different if there were no earthworms?* (Use the "Futures Wheel" on page 292 to record ideas.)

• *How do you think earthworms' burrows might help plant roots? ...other animals in the soil?*

• *What words of advice do you think earthworms might give gardeners to help them raise healthier gardens?*

• *List the questions you still have about worms. Decide which ones you can test in the classroom. How can you find answers to the others?*

Branching Out

• Conduct a taste test experiment (no, you don't have to taste the worms!) to find out what kinds of foods worms prefer to eat. Choose leaves from different GrowLab plants. See if they prefer food moist or dry, chopped or whole, fresh or decaying. (Worms will exhibit preferences for certain types of leaves!)

• Grow plants in soil with and without earthworms. Compare differences in plant growth and health.

• Find out what animals prey on earthworms. Draw how earthworms fit into food chains and webs.

• Calculate the reproductive rate of your worms. *How many worms do you predict you'll have in one month ... two months?* Calculate the money you could earn if you sold your own classroom-raised earthworms as bait or garden supplements.

• Build earthworm mazes from cardboard placed on a moist, waxed-paper surface. Record the amount of time it takes a worm to reach the end of the maze. *Will the worm learn, and decrease its time after several tries?*

worm "chow"

• Dig up a set volume of soil from a garden or area near your school. Count the number of earthworms found, and estimate the total number of worms in a prescribed area.

• Do a survey of other teachers, students, and parents on their attitudes about worms. Create a graph to present results.

• Imagine there were no earthworms. Devise a machine that people could use to do a worm's job. Draw an advertisement for the machine.

Aphid Pets

I f you garden, someday you're bound to meet up with aphids, or "plant lice." The piercing mouths of these soft-bodied, pale green, gray, white, or tan insects suck sap from a variety of plants. They're attracted to the undersides of leaves, stems, and flower buds, particularly of young, rapidly growing plants. The activity **Aphid Pets** encourages students to take advantage of the appearance of aphids by exploring these fascinating creatures.

Aphids are often found on the undersides of leaves.

Prolific Creatures

Aphids have complex life cycles and overwhelming reproductive rates. As each generation is born, sometimes as often as every seven to ten days, the next generation is already growing inside the newborns! With a good microscope, you can actually see aphids growing within aphids. Newborn aphids are normally wingless and similar to adults. When conditions become over-crowded, however, winged aphids, which can fly to another plant, are born.

     Females of one species of aphid give birth to at least ten female offspring every week. These offspring, in turn, do the same in another week. It's been estimated that if all offspring were to survive, one female could trigger the production of a quadrillion offspring per season! Disease, weather, limited resources, and predation prevent this from happening; but with reproductive rates like these, it's no wonder we need to be vigilant with these visitors.

Lions and Ladies and Cows, Oh My!

Like the rest of us, aphids are an integral strand in the great web of life. While aphids are munching away on plants, they are also an important part of other insects' diets. The voracious larvae of the lacewing fly, for instance, devour leaves and consume any aphids in their path. It's no wonder they are known as "aphid lions"! Ladybugs are also avid aphid consumers, as are certain tiny wasps that parasitize unsuspecting aphids.

Some hungry ants actually herd aphids. The ants "milk" aphids by stroking their bodies with their antennae, causing the aphids to release drops of sweet honeydew, a nutritious food source. Sometimes ants will carry these aphid "cows" underground where the aphids can feed on plant roots right in the ant colony nest.

An Ounce of Prevention

Just as we can resist disease when we're in good condition, healthy plants are most likely to resist an aphid attack. If they have been stressed by lack of water or by under- or overfertilizing, plants are more susceptible to aphids. They can become weakened, yellow, and misshapen, and may eventually die. This may be due, in part, to one of the many viruses that aphids transmit.

Some of the suggested means of getting rid of aphids, once they've appeared, include hand crushing, water or soap spray, and homemade repellents. For a large infestation, thorough hand crushing can be not only time consuming but also devastating to plants. Although a hard water spray will knock many aphids from plants, hardy individuals can crawl or fly back to plants. Soapy sprays, however, kill aphids on contact. See directions on pages 61 and 62 of *GrowLab: A Complete Guide to Gardening in the Classroom* for application of soapy sprays.

Some gardeners prefer homemade insect controls using recipes such as the following:

- 3 cloves garlic, chopped
- 1 onion, chopped
- 1 tablespoon cayenne powder
- 1 teaspoon soap flakes
- 1 quart warm water

Blend ingredients, and let sit covered overnight. Spray leaves with a mister. Rinse leaves with warm water the next day.

Aphid Pets

Overview: Students take advantage of the presence of aphids by exploring these fascinating insects.

Although this activity focuses on aphids, you can use a similar format for exploring other garden insects.

Time:
Groundwork: 30 to 40 minutes
Exploration: variable
Making Connections: ongoing

Materials:
• variable (aphids!, hand lenses, GrowLab plants, pots, etc.)
• "Problem Solving for Growing Minds" reproducible, page 283
• "Observation Journal", page 286

Background: Page 208 and page 222

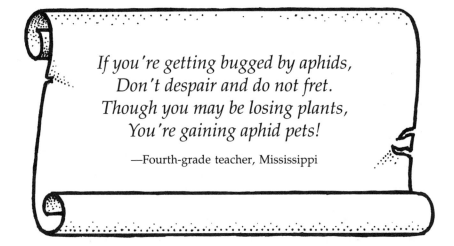

*If you're getting bugged by aphids,
Don't despair and do not fret.
Though you may be losing plants,
You're gaining aphid pets!*

—Fourth-grade teacher, Mississippi

Laying the Groundwork

Objective: To observe and raise questions about aphids.

1. If your vigilant plant detectives notice what appear to be "pests" in the GrowLab, have them observe the visitors closely with hand lenses. As a class, make a list of the things students can observe about the visitors. *What do they look like? Where are they most abundant? How do they seem to move around?* Refer to pages 60 and 61 in *GrowLab: A Complete Guide to Gardening in the Classroom*, to identify the insects.

Since aphids are the most common insect in the GrowLab, they're used as a springboard for this activity.

2. Ask each student to come up with one question about aphids, encouraging them to ask questions that cannot be answered by a simple yes or no. List the questions on a class chart. Questions that make viable classroom explorations include the following:

• What types and/or ages of plants do aphids prefer?

• What type of plant parts do aphids prefer?

• How fast do aphids multiply (and how do they do it)?

• What do aphids do to plants? How do they seem to do it?

• What would happen if we sprayed aphids with different "natural" insecticides?

3. Unless you're experimenting with methods for eradicating aphids, we recommend that you treat most of your infested plants as described in the background, page 223. Carefully quarantine one or a few sacrificial plants in a large jar or aquarium with a fine screen or a cheesecloth covering. Use this as your experimental chamber.

Exploration

Objective: To design and conduct simple explorations to uncover new information about garden insects.

1. As a class or in small groups, choose one of your aphid questions to explore. Students may choose to supplement their investigations with library research, or interviews with local gardeners, extension agents, or garden store staff. Use the Problem Solving for Growing Minds process, page 10 and the "Observation Journal" to help guide and record explorations.

Two sample investigations follow.

Question: *What type of plant leaves do aphids prefer?*

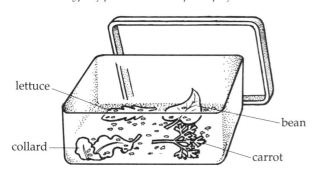

Question: *How will aphids respond to different natural insecticides?*

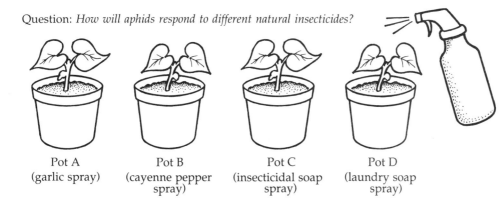

Pot A	Pot B	Pot C	Pot D
(garlic spray)	(cayenne pepper spray)	(insecticidal soap spray)	(laundry soap spray)

2. Discuss findings as a class. Ask: *In general, how do aphids seem to affect plants? Do they seem to prefer specific parts, types, or ages of plants? Which ones? What sparked your interest in the question you explored? How did you decide on the best method for answering your question(s) about aphids?*

Making Connections

Possible discussion questions:

• *How did your findings compare with your predictions? What might you do differently if you were to conduct this exploration again? Why?*

• *If we had conducted these investigations in an outdoor garden, what other things might have affected our results? What other organisms might have been affected?*

• If it were true that aphids preferred certain types of plants, how might this information help us develop a strategy for getting rid of them?

• Why do you think aphids are considered pests? Can you think of other animals that are sometimes considered pests and sometimes considered helpful (grasshoppers, birds, spiders, bees, etc.)?

• If aphids can reproduce so quickly, why do you think the earth isn't covered with them?

• Some aphids are born with wings. Under what conditions do you think this adaptation might help them survive?

• When you don't get proper nutrition or sleep, or when you put harmful things into your body, what is likely to happen? Do you think healthy or unhealthy plants are best able to resist insects and diseases? What, then, as gardeners, can we do to help prevent insect problems?

• What other questions about insects did your exploration raise? How might you go about answering them?

Branching Out

• Research biological control of insects (using predators or parasites). Purchase or capture some predators such as ladybugs or lacewings, and observe their interaction with garden insects.

• Based on a short-term study of aphid reproductive rate, estimate the number of aphid offspring from one plant that could be generated in one week, one month, etc. Graph this population growth.

• Research how aphids fit into different food chains and webs. Illustrate this or cut out pictures of the different links of a food chain that might include aphids.

• Research and discuss the costs and benefits (environmental, health, financial, etc.) of using "organic" (e.g., soap spray) compared with "synthetic" (e.g., DDT) insecticides.

• The best defense against garden pests is healthy plants. Write a "news article" relating this statement to human health.

• Identify and invent other words with the "ph" sound.

• Make papier-mâché masks of selected garden insects.

Celebrating Salad

Overview: Using a GrowLab salad garden as a backdrop, students conduct a survey of vegetable preferences and examine how various salad ingredients meet human nutritional needs.

Time:
Groundwork: two 40-minute sessions
Exploration: 40 minutes; ongoing salad garden
Making Connections: ongoing

Materials:
• assorted salad vegetables or vegetable pictures

Background: Page 22 in *GrowLab: A Complete Guide to Gardening in the Classroom*

Laying the Groundwork

Objective: To gather data on people's salad ingredient preferences by conducting a salad survey.

1. Prior to planting a salad garden, or as the plants in your Grow-Lab salad garden are maturing, ask: *What are your favorite salad ingredients? Why do you like those particular ingredients? What other things do people eat in their salads that we aren't growing in the Grow-Lab? Do you think everyone likes and dislikes the same salad ingredients? How do you think we can find out the salad preferences of our friends and families?*

2. Have students conduct a Salad Survey of parents, other relatives, neighbors, and friends. Primary students may prefer to make a simple survey, e.g., of favorite and least favorite ingredients. Older students may choose other survey methods: for instance, they might provide a long list of vegetables and have respondents rate each on a scale from 1 to 10.

3. After conducting surveys, combine survey results on a class chart. Individually or as a class, have students present results on a bar graph. Upper-level students can calculate percentages of different responses.

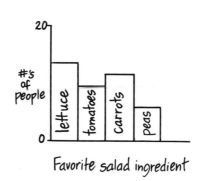

Favorite salad ingredient

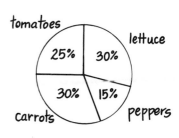

% people choosing each ingredient as favorite

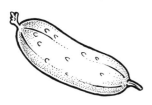

4. Discuss the survey findings. *Were there certain vegetables that people listed more often as most favorite? Which? As least favorite? Which? Were some vegetables listed that you'd never heard of or eaten? Which? Which would you like to try?*

Exploration

Objective: To understand how different salad vegetables help people meet nutritional needs.

1. Facilitate a discussion to find out what students know about different salad vegetables. *How do these different vegetables help us? Do you think that some may be more nutritious than others? Which?*

2. To develop a broader understanding of vegetables and human nutrition, invite the class to play Veggie Riddles. Have a supply of different vegetables or pictures of different vegetables available. Secretly choose one vegetable or picture and keep it hidden from the class. Challenge the class to guess the identity of the mystery vegetable, with the help of your riddle clues.

Using the "Salad Nutrition Chart," page 231, as your reference, give some clues that highlight the nutritional value of the mystery vegetable—for example, "Being high in vitamin C, it helps you resist colds." Add another clue about how this vegetable relates to the plant, such as: "It is the fruit of a plant" or "It helps the plant take in water and nutrients." Allow the class to make one or two guesses after each clue. Add one clue at a time, until the vegetable is identified.

3. Once the mystery has been solved, reveal the vegetable or picture. Review what was learned, through the clues, about that particular vegetable. Use the information to begin constructing a class chart like the one below. Consider adding other categories to the chart, such as "How We Eat It" or "How to Grow It."

Vegetable	Plant part	How it helps us	How it helps plant (Optional)
carrot	root	has vitamin A; helps resist colds; helps us see well	absorbs water and nutrients; stores sugar

Cute Cukes

When your cucumbers have just started to fruit, have a student gently carve a picture of a small dolphin on the immature cucumber. As the cucumber matures, watch that dolphin grow into a whale! Or grow a cucumber in a jar. When a tiny cucumber forms on the plant, gently insert it in a narrow-mouthed plastic soda bottle and let it continue to grow in the bottle. When the cucumber matures, it will really be in a pickle!

4. Once the students have a base of information, have them create their own vegetable riddles. They should use the class chart, their salad survey results, and their own observations and ideas to help them develop creative riddles. The riddles can be shared in pairs, or all riddles can be placed in a pile and handed out randomly.

Sample riddle:

I protect my hairy seeds,
Most people seem to love me,
I'm the tang in pizza pie,
I help you fight colds, so Who Am I?

New vegetable information provided by students' riddles can be added to the class chart.

Making Connections

Possible discussion questions:

• *Based on your surveys and the nutrition chart, do you notice any connections between the most popular vegetables and the foods' nutritional values? What, if any, connections exist? What are the nutritional values of your favorite vegetables?*

• *Many people choose certain foods because they taste good. What other reasons do you think people have for making food choices?*

• *Choose one vegetable. Using your imagination, describe some of the possible consequences if it were the only vegetable you ate.*

• *What is your favorite root to eat? ...fruit? ...leaf? ...seed?*

• **Extra challenge:** *Beans are very high in protein. Based on the part of the plant beans come from, why do you think they're so nutritious? (As seeds, they contain the nutrients necessary for the young plant.)*

Branching Out

• Learn about and make salads that contain proteins and carbohydrates. Include such things as bean salad and potato salad. Find out about the nutritional value of their ingredients. Also try salads from different cultures.

• Find out about food groups. Draw a diagram to trace how plants form the basis for every food group.

• Research the differences in nutritional value between raw, cooked, frozen, and canned vegetables.

• In a blind taste test, compare the flavor of GrowLab-grown and supermarket-bought salad vegetables.

• Using a nutritional chart, calculate the nutritional contents

By Bread Alone

While people cannot live by bread alone, many can and do lead healthy lives by eating primarily plant products. You and your students might want to find out about the cultural, moral, nutritional, financial, religious, and ecological reasons people become **vegetarians.** Learn about complementary proteins—how you can get all the protein you need just from plants. Research what kinds of diets people have had throughout history. Why not try a vegetarian diet for a week?

(vitamins, minerals, calories) of your GrowLab garden. Determine the mix of vegetables you'd have to eat every week to get all of the nutrients listed on your chart.

• Collect data on the school lunch menu for a week. Sort the food items offered, by nutritional groups. Explain how each item originates with plants.

• Design clever invitations and menus for a class salad party.

• Design an advertisement to convince someone why he/she should eat a particular vegetable. Be sure to include nutritional information.

• Draw an imaginary, completely edible plant, by combining edible parts from different plants.

Salad Nutrition Chart

Vegetable	Plant Part	Nutrients	Some Benefits to Your Body
Carrots	root	A potassium	promotes healthy eyes; helps resist infection helps muscles and nerves work
Spinach	leaf	A C calcium potassium iron	promotes healthy eyes; helps resist infection helps heal wounds and bones, resist infection promotes strong bones, teeth, muscles helps muscles and nerves work helps blood carry vital oxygen to cells
Peas	seed or fruit	A B vitamins iron protein	promotes healthy eyes; helps resist infection help body use food energy keep skin and digestive tract healthy help body make protein and blood helps blood carry vital oxygen to cells vital to overall growth and maintenance
Greens*	leaf	B vitamins C E K calcium iron	help body use food energy keep skin and digestive tract healthy help body make protein and blood helps heal wounds and bones, resist infection helps keep skin smooth and moist helps blood clot; keeps membranes healthy promotes strong bones, teeth, muscles helps blood carry vital oxygen to cells
Cabbage	leaf	C E	helps heal wounds and bones, resist infection helps keep skin smooth and moist
Peppers	fruit	C	helps heal wounds and bones, resist infection
Tomatoes	fruit	C	helps heal wounds and bones, resist infection
Lettuce	leaf	iron	helps blood carry vital oxygen to cells
Beans	seed or fruit	phosphorus protein	important in bone formation vital to overall growth and maintenance
Parsley	leaf	C	helps heal wounds and bones, resist infection
Cucumbers **Radishes**	fruit root		NO SIGNIFICANT NUTRIENTS

* "Greens" refers to the dark green leaves of many vegetables including turnips, beets, kale, collards, Swiss chard, and dandelions.

Fabulous Fiber

In addition to vitamins and minerals, most vegetables contain large proportions of water and fiber, or roughage. Fiber is the cellulose in plant cell walls. It is the part of foods that is not digested, such as bean husks, connecting tissues of greens, or apple skins. Fiber is helpful in "cleaning out" digestive tracts, and is believed to help prevent certain types of cancer.

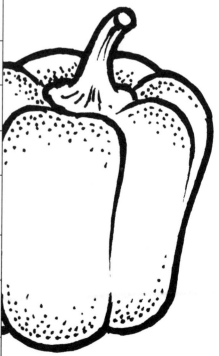

Plants 'R' Us

Overview: Students try to imagine life without plants, and recognize the tremendous variety of uses we have for plants. They then research and grow some important crops.

Time:
Groundwork: 45 minutes
Exploration: variable
Making Connections: ongoing

Materials:
• potting mix
• pots
• variable seeds (see Exploration)

Background: Page 208

Laying the Groundwork

Objective: To identify many of the ways, other than as food, that people use plants.

1. Read the following scenario to your class:

It is the year 2020. You have just learned that someone has developed an amazing new product—a special food substitute called Formula4Life. With regular fill-ups of Formula4Life, no other food is necessary! Kids around the world are thrilled, since they'll never again have to finish their lima beans or eat liver and onions on Thursday nights.

The creators of the Formula think their discovery is the greatest thing since Silly Putty. In fact, they intend to mass-produce the Formula so it can support colonies of people living in self-contained atmospherically controlled units (SCACUs) underwater, underground, or out in space. Until now, these SCACUs were not used because there was no way to raise food in such small units. The Formula, however, eliminates the need to raise food. Its creators feel sure that their discovery will enable humans to live healthy, happy, plantless lives.

2. Ask the class to reflect on the claims of the Formula4Life creators. Ask: *Do you think that creating alternate food sources would allow us to live in a world without plants? Why or why not? Close your eyes and imagine a world without plants. What do you think it would be like?*

3. To stimulate students to reflect on the role of plants in our lives, have small groups choose five activities they did during the day and then trace the materials involved in those activities back to their sources. Give some clues from the chart below as an example. Have students share their lists to be combined on a class chart with the following headings:

Activity	Materials used	Possible origin
washing face	soap	animal fat → animal → animal feed (plant)
		flowers (scent)
	water	rain clouds
	washcloth	cloth → cotton plant
riding bus	metal	under the earth
	plastic (seats)	oil → dead and decayed plants
	gasoline	dead and decayed plants

4. As a class, identify which of the materials originated with plants. Identify those materials whose origins students are fairly sure of and those about which students have questions. Share information about plant uses from the "Plant Products" chart, page 236. Ask: *Did any of the items originating with plants surprise you? Which?* Challenge students to consider how plant products that don't come directly from plants, such as wool and leather, are ultimately dependent on plants. Ask: *Other than as products, what roles do plants play in your life?*

Exploration

Objective: To explore some important roles of plants in our lives.

1. As a class or in small groups, choose some plants you'd like to learn more about and grow in the classroom. Use the "Plant Products" chart, page 236, to spark some ideas. Plants that can be grown in the GrowLab are marked with a superscript number (e.g., peanuts[3]) and have growing information on page 237.

Although students may choose a plant that cannot be grown all the way to maturity in the GrowLab, it can still serve as a useful starting point for researching the roles of plants in our lives.

2. While the crops are growing in the GrowLab, have students research how the plants are used or have been used by humans throughout history. Individuals or small groups of students could investigate specific aspects of a particular crop or different types of crops. Possible research questions:

• Where did your crop originate?

• What parts of the plant are used? Are they used by themselves or to produce other products?

• In what area of the world is this crop commonly grown and/or used?

• How have scientists changed this crop to meet human needs?

• Has the use of this plant changed over time? How?

• What is this crop's economic, cultural, or nutritional value?

• What would change in the world if we didn't have this crop?

• What area of land, number of plants, or amount of time does it take to produce certain products made from this crop (e.g., number of trees to produce one issue of *The New York Times*)?

Making Connections

1. Give each group the opportunity to present what they've learned about their GrowLab crop. Creative ways they might do this include the following:

• Demonstrate how this product is processed. For example, make peanut butter or soy sauce, mill cotton, or grind wheat grains into flour. (Since most of these crops won't grow to maturity in the GrowLab, and those that do will have small yields, you'll have to supplement the harvest.)

• Create a display of products made from this crop.

• Present a skit, ballad, or song, highlighting the importance of this crop to a particular region or culture (e.g., cotton in the South).

• Document, through drawing, dance, or interviews, the life cycles of these plants.

• Lead a class workshop on how these plants are used (e.g., making dyes from zinnia or marigold blossoms or carrot tops).

• If the crop is edible, serve foods made from it.

2. Ask students to "take a stand" on the following statements, by lining up in the room according to where they feel they belong on an imaginary continuum. Ask each student to explain why he or she chose that particular spot.

I...

(could easily)---(could not)

...live in a world without plants.

Soy What?

One group of students decided to grow soybeans. They presented a talk show where the special guest was Ms. Soybean. During the interview they asked her different questions about her life, family origins, and goals. The class learned a great deal about the importance of soy throughout the world. She even taught them how to make their own soy sauce!

Share Your Results!

The National Gardening Association and other GrowLab classrooms are eager to know the results of your "Plants 'R' Us" investigations. Consider having your class use the "GermiNation and Growth Journal," page 289, to share information about your growing endeavors.

Branching Out

• Explore the aesthetic roles of plants in people's lives. Collect and read quotes or selections from literature, poetry, or songs— and have students express their own feelings about the less tangible virtues of plants.

• Visit a botanical garden to explore some of the crops (coffee, bananas, etc.) that could not be raised in the GrowLab.

• Research products that replace plant-originated products, such as synthetic fibers, flavors, or oils. Discuss how the development of these products still depends on plants.

• Take an inventory of materials in the classroom, school, or home. Identify which ones originated with plants.

• Find out why paper bags and plastic bags are both dependent on trees.

• Develop a plan for school landscaping to present to school administrators. Raise plants in the GrowLab to carry out the plan.

• Draw pictures of a world without plants or draw a SCACU!

Plant Products

A superscript number next to a plant indicates that you'll find information on raising it in your GrowLab on page 237.

Product	Sources (examples)
Grains/Cereals/Flours[1]	seeds and fruits of rice, wheat, corn, oats, barley (grasses)
Vegetables[2]	stems of asparagus, roots of carrot, fruits of tomato, leaves of lettuce
Fruits	fruits of apple, kiwi, etc.
Peanuts[3]	seeds of peanut

Spices/Herbs/Flavorings[4]
  Cinnamon
  Pepper
  Basil
  Vanilla
	
	bark of cinnamon tree
	dried fruit of black pepper plant
	leaves of basil plant
	seeds of orchid

Tea	leaves of tea plant or loblolly bay tree
Coffee	seeds of coffee plant
Chocolate	seeds of cacao plant

Oils[5]
  linseed
  corn
  sunflower
  peanut
	
	seeds of flax
	seeds of corn
	seeds of sunflower
	seeds of peanut

Tobacco	leaves of tobacco plant
Animal feed	grasses

Medicines
  aspirin
  digitalis
  (heart stimulant)
	
	blossoms of spiraea plant
	leaves of foxglove plant

Fabrics
  cotton[6]
  linen[7]
	
	seed hairs of cotton plant
	stem fibers of flax plant

Natural dyes[8]	blossoms of marigold, zinnia, dahlia seed coat of black walnut skin of onion bulb
Cord, Rope	stem fibers of hemp plant leaves of sisal plant
Lumber	stems of pine, oak, maple trees
Rubber	sap (latex) of rubber tree
Cork	outer bark of cork tree

Fuel
    oil, coal, gas,
    wood
	decayed, metamorphosed remains of plants
	stems of trees

Bamboo	stems of bamboo plants
Turpentine	sap of pine and other cone-bearing trees
Varnish	resin remaining from turpentine production
Paper	wood pulp of tree (originally from Egyptian reed, papyrus)
Photographic film	cellulose from plant cell walls

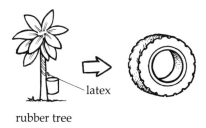

rubber tree

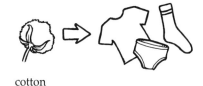

cotton

oats

Growing Information

1. Whole grains (wheat, oats, barley, rice, corn) can be purchased from health food stores. Sow these members of the grass family thickly, approximately 1 inch apart, in shallow containers. Although they won't grow to maturity in the GrowLab, they do grow quickly and will provide a good backdrop for investigations.

2. For information on raising vegetables in the GrowLab, see pages 86 and 87 of *GrowLab: A Complete Guide to Gardening in the Classroom.*

3. Peanuts are lovely plants which can be grown from seed to maturity in the GrowLab. See pages 86 and 87 in *GrowLab: A Complete Guide to Gardening in the Classroom*, for growing information. Seeds are included in the GrowLab Seed Collection, described in Appendix F, or can be purchased from sources listed.

4. Many herbs can easily be raised from seed in the GrowLab. See page 90 in *GrowLab: A Complete Guide to Gardening in the Classroom* for growing information.

5. Any of the seeds listed in this category can be purchased from seed catalogs or, unroasted and unprocessed, from a health food store. Only peanuts and soybeans can be grown to maturity indoors, although they both have long growing seasons.

6. Cotton can be raised to maturity in the GrowLab in six to eight months. Plant three seeds per 6-inch pot. Thin to one seed per pot when 1 inch tall. Bell-shaped flowers will emerge at around ten or twelve weeks. Later, fruits or **bolls** will develop. When mature, they'll open up to reveal the white seed hair fibers we know as cotton. Seeds are included in the GrowLab Seed Collection, described in Appendix F, or can be purchased from sources listed.

7. Flax seeds can be purchased at health food stores and planted like the whole grains, above. They also will not grow to maturity in the GrowLab.

8. Although not used for commercial dyeing, many of these plants are used on a small scale for fabric dyes. Marigold and zinnia seeds are included in the GrowLab Seed Collection, described in Appendix F.

Human Impact

> "...Whatever befalls the earth befalls the sons of the earth.
> If men spit upon the ground, they spit on themselves.
> This we know—the earth does not belong to man,
> man belongs to the earth. All things are connected
> like the blood which unites one family.
> Whatever befalls the earth befalls the sons of the earth..
> Man did not weave the web of life;
> he is merely a strand in it.
> Whatever he does to the web, he does to himself."
>
> —Chief Seattle

Although we are all part of the intricate web of life on Earth, we humans often act as though we're somehow separate. Many of our actions, however, disproportionately affect all other life on Earth. As our population rapidly increases, we are using up natural resources at an alarming rate. As we clear forests and employ poor agricultural practices, we are losing precious topsoil. Our personal and industrial wastes are polluting the Earth's land and water. Our burning of fossil fuels causes many air pollution problems, including disrupting the Earth's carbon dioxide balance and threatening to upset world ecosystems and agriculture. Personal and industrial use of chlorofluorocarbons (CFCs) in aerosols, coolants, and the production of styrofoam is destroying the Earth's protective ozone layer and threatening all living things.

While we can't live in the global garden without affecting the whole, it's important to recognize the impact of our choices and actions on other living things. We have the ability to consider tradeoffs and to conceive alternatives that are more environmentally benign. The indoor garden enables students to explore plant responses to changes in their environment, and provides a springboard for further explorations of some complex environmental issues.

Land Use

How we choose to use land can dramatically affect other organisms. Every new shopping mall, landfill, or hydroelectric dam alters the ecosystem and affects a wide range of living organisms —for example, by displacement, by changing resources such as water level or temperature, or by destroying food sources. Even when only a few living things are directly affected, they are part of the larger web of life and therefore the impact could be widespread.

U.S. Impact

Although the United States has only about six percent of the world's population, we use about forty percent of the world's resources and contribute an inordinate share of air, land, and water pollutants.

The activity **Grass Blast** encourages students to think very simply about how human use of land might affect other living things. A simulation of human impact on a container of grass provides a backdrop for considering how living things are affected by our actions and how we can lessen this impact.

Environmental Pollutants

We use natural resources and dispose of wastes in an effort to meet our own needs and preferences. In doing so, we create and release substances that harm the environment. Since plants are low on food chains, once they are damaged the impact can be magnified manyfold.

Environmental pollutants or toxins can take many forms. Even fertilizer, running off from farm fields, can cause unnaturally rapid growth of aquatic plants that then cut off the oxygen supply for other plants. Road salt running off a highway can damage nearby plant and animal life. Many pollutants weaken plants, leaving them open to disease and insect attack. Some air pollutants can damage protective waxy layers on plant leaves; others may more directly harm plant tissues or interfere with life processes. Systemic insecticides are taken up into plant tissues, and even though they don't harm the plant, they can harm the animal eating that plant, and the human eating that animal.

Many scientists are concerned about our ignorance of the potentially dangerous substances and reactions formed when different environmental pollutants are combined. Some contend, for instance, that acid rain and other air pollutants together can create even more dangerous substances and magnify one another's effects.

In the activity **Pollution Solutions**, students examine how some common pollutants can affect the growth and development of plants, and then consider how they can decrease their own contributions to pollution. In **PlantAcid**, students explore the effect of pH variations on plant growth, focusing on the problem of acid rain. **Global ReLeaf** highlights the issue of global climate change and challenges students to take steps toward helping to "cool the globe" by raising and planting tree seedlings.

Growing Awareness

The activities in this section won't result in your students understanding how specific actions or pollutants affect plants. There are simply too many variables interacting in the environment and no easy way to reproduce the effects of substances or actions on plants in the classroom. We hope, however, that as students reflect, devise simulations, conduct controlled experiments, and observe results, they will begin to recognize that plants can be harmed by substances in the environment. The explorations can provide a context for considering wide-ranging implications of our actions, and how each of us personally might act responsibly toward the environment.

"As crude a weapon as the cave man's club, the chemical barrage has been hurled against the fabric of life."

—Rachel Carson, Naturalist

Grass Blast

Overview: Students simulate human impact on grass and consider the environmental implications of our actions.

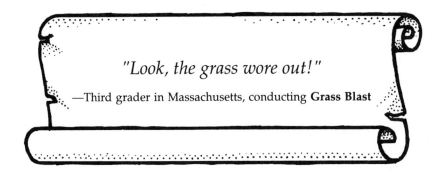

"Look, the grass wore out!"

—Third grader in Massachusetts, conducting **Grass Blast**

Time:
Groundwork: one to two 45-minute sessions
Exploration: 45 minutes setup; 3-plus weeks ongoing observations
Making Connections: ongoing

Materials:
• shallow planting containers (e.g., 5x7-inch flats)
• potting mix
• grass seed
• miscellaneous classroom materials
• "Observation Journal" reproducible, page 286
• "Futures Wheel" reproducible, page 292

Background: Page 238

Laying the Groundwork

Objective: To consider some ways in which humans affect their environment.

1. Ask: *How do people affect plants in their environment?* Generate a class list of how we or others affect plants. Students can include human actions that both help and hurt plants. The list might include such actions as tending a garden, building a parking lot in a meadow, cutting down trees, or littering.

2. If possible, take the class on a walk outside the school. Challenge small groups of students to search for and record clues that indicate human impact on plants. Is the grass trodden and worn on the playing field? Does a building sit where a field once grew? Is there a mall where a meadow used to be? Is there a flower garden where there once was bare soil?

3. Back in the classroom, combine findings from your walk, or use your list from Step 1, above, to fill out a chart like the one illustrated below.

How Humans Affect Their Environment

Observed effect/Action	Possible effects (on other living things)
grass worn (from playing baseball)	grass died, less grass for rabbits to eat, soil too hard for worms

As each item is put up on the chart, ask: *Did the human activity seem to help or hurt plants and other living things?* If the human action disturbed plants or other organisms, ask: *Could the same activity have taken place with less harm to the environment? How?*

Discuss with students that everything we do affects other things in the environment. Remind them that this is not necessarily bad, but it is important to think about the effects we might have, and realize that we have the ability to make choices.

Exploration

Objective: To consider some of the implications of human activities by simulating a simple disturbance of a plot of grass.

1. Ask the class to brainstorm ways in which their own activities might negatively affect a section of grass (e.g., bouncing balls, riding bicycles, playing tag, walking, digging holes, littering, or spilling soda).

2. Challenge small groups of students to choose one of the activities selected during the brainstorm. Discuss how they could conduct a simulation of that human activity on grass in the GrowLab. You may need to discuss what a simulation is, and offer some examples. For instance, they might simulate balls bouncing by dropping a marble twenty times a day in the same spot; create a "building" from blocks set on the grass; or "pave" a sidewalk with clay.

3. Have each group fill two shallow containers with moist potting mix. Scatter grass seed thickly over the potting mix and cover with 1/4 inch of mix. Water regularly to maintain moisture.

4. When the grass is 1 inch tall (just a few days after germination), direct students to begin simulating human impact in one of the containers, leaving the other as a control. Have them keep records on the "Observation Journal" reproducible.

 Just budding in: Grass will grow very rapidly in a Grow-Lab environment. Some classes choose to use scissors to "mow" the grass back to 1 inch every week.

5. After two to three weeks, summarize the investigations in a class chart, using drawings where appropriate.

Making Connections

1. Possible discussion questions:

• *How did the grass respond to different types of activities? Did some activities seem more harmful to the grass than others? What did you observe that led you to believe that?*

• *In real life, how could you do the same activity and be less harmful to plant life?* (Students could ride bikes on concrete instead of on grass, they could be careful not to litter, etc.)

• *Do you think it's possible to live on Earth without affecting plants and other animals? How?*

• *How long do you think it might take to plant and regrow a lawn? How about a forest? Do you think some environments are harder to re-create than others? Why?*

2. Using the "Futures Wheel" on page 292, have students show how other plants and animals (dandelions, earthworms, microbes, birds, bees, humans) might also be affected by some of the simulated actions.

Branching Out

• Read and discuss the environmental tradeoffs presented in Dr. Seuss's book *The Lorax* (see Appendix E).

• Have small groups of students research the environmental impact of different activities in the community (shopping mall, apartments, pool, parking lot).

• Take a class trip to a wildlife preserve. Discuss why these "sanctuaries" are important.

• After an outdoor walk, have students draw their vision of an area before human intervention and contrast it with a current drawing of the same area.

• Invite a local land use planner or interview the local planning board to discuss how decisions about land use are made in your city or town.

• Make a collage contrasting ways in which humans hurt and help plants.

• Explore how the land and other natural resources are regarded by different cultures, e.g., Native Americans.

Should We Mall the Trees?

For an extra challenge, ask the class to imagine that their town or city is trying to decide between building a shopping mall and saving that same area for a park. Divide the class into three groups. Ask Group 1 to pretend they are store owners; Group 2 to play themselves; and Group 3 to speak as members of a group called Defenders of Squirrels and Trees.

Give each group ten minutes to discuss their position on what should be done with the land. Have them come up with a list of reasons to support their views. Then as a class, use feedback from each group to create a chart with the headings: "Advantages of mall"; "Disadvantages of mall"; "Advantages of park"; "Disadvantages of park."

Facilitate a discussion of the situation. Stimulate thought by asking questions like: *How do you think different parts of the environment, including people, would be affected by each option? What do you think some of the long-term effects might be? Do you think one group's needs and interests are more important than another's? Why or why not? Can you think of a solution that might meet everyone's needs?*

Pollution Solutions

Overview: Students design and conduct experiments to investigate the effects of some common "pollutants" on plants, and consider how our actions can contribute to pollution solutions.

Pol-lute —To make impure.
To contaminate (an environment)
especially with human-made waste.

Time:
Groundwork: 40 minutes
Exploration: variable
Making Connections: ongoing

Materials:
• variable
• "Problem Solving for Growing Minds" reproducible, page 283
• "Observation Journal" reproducible, page 286

Background: Page 238

Laying the Groundwork

Objective: To consider what types of substances generated by humans could become environmental pollutants.

1. Before students enter the class, throw wads of paper, food containers, and other "garbage" around the room. Use the setting to stimulate a discussion about pollution. Ask: *How do we generally get rid of what we don't want? Where does this waste end up? What if this trash on the floor were actually an oil spill, toxic chemicals, or raw sewage? How do you think it could affect humans?... other animals?...plants?*

2. Brainstorm a list of common substances, generated by humans, that students think could adversely affect living things in the environment. Ask questions such as: *Where do you think salt spread on roads in the winter ends up? How do you think it might affect living things?*

Some examples:

Possible Pollutants

wood preservatives
water softeners
fertilizers
insecticides
sound
cigarette smoke
car exhaust

road salt
paint
detergents
cleansers
oil
sewage
garbage
industrial smoke

Ask: *Can you think of any subtle or indirect effects these pollutants might have in the environment? Have you seen evidence of pollutants in nature? What have you read or heard about any of these?*

3. Copy the following "stinging" telegram and read or tape the message to be played to your class.

TO (teacher's name here)'s CLASS.
I'm A. Pollutant and I'm here to say,
I affect your lives in many ways.
When you pass a landfill you say, "It stinks!"
But it's your garbage—so what did you think?

When foul waters close beaches for a day,
You complain—but how did it get that way?
When skies are smoggy and hard to breathe,
You shake your head and blame it on me.

You humans think you're so darn smart,
So why not accept the important part
That you folks play in making pollution—
Why, don't you know that you're the solution?
It's not my fault; you create me,
If it weren't for you, I just wouldn't be.

To explore pollution, I have some advice,
First look at how I affect plant life.
Without healthy plants, life on Earth's in trouble,
So investigate pollutants, on the double.

And please consider how I got here to start,
To prove that humans really can be smart.
If you do these things, I may start to fade away,
But not until you change the role you play.

R.S.V.P. (React Soon to Vile Pollutants),

A. Pollutant

4. Ask students how the telegram made them feel. *Do you agree with A. Pollutant's charges?* Encourage students to respond to A. Pollutant's telegram by investigating the effects of some pollutants on plant growth.

Exploration—Part 1

Objective: To understand that many common substances can affect plants' growth and development.

1. As a class, or in small groups, use the Problem Solving for Growing Minds process, page 10, to test the effects of a specific potential pollutant on plants. To simulate reality more closely, have students consider how their particular pollutant might reach plants (by wind, water, soil, etc.).

Some sample setups:

Question: *What will happen if plants receive different concentrations of salt water?*

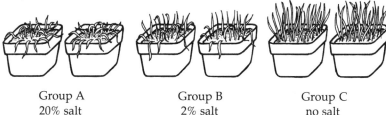

Group A
20% salt
(sprayed once a day)

Group B
2% salt
(sprayed once a day)

Group C
no salt
(control)

Question: *How will plants respond to cigarette smoke?*

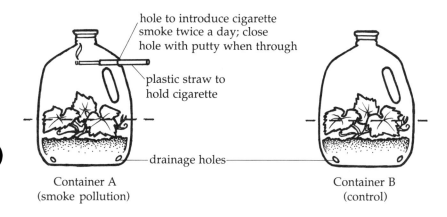

hole to introduce cigarette
smoke twice a day; close
hole with putty when through

plastic straw to
hold cigarette

drainage holes

Container A
(smoke pollution)

Container B
(control)

2. Review all proposed setups for safety. Have each group present its idea for setting up a pollution exploration to a Student Commission on Potentially Dangerous Experiments. If the Commission and the teacher decide that the experiment (setup, substances used, and disposal techniques) poses no risk in the classroom, the group will be allowed to proceed. Consider posting polluted pots with warning signs or symbols.

3. Each group should be responsible for ongoing observations and record keeping using the "Observation Journal". Recommend rotating observers and recorders within each group. Have groups set up a series of graphs and/or charts (see "Create-a-Chart", page 287 for suggestions) that will help them present their findings to the class.

4. As each group presents its findings to the rest of the class, the group members should address the following questions: *How did you treat your experimental plants? How did you decide on quantities and types of treatments? How did the plants respond to the pollutants? How did these results compare with predictions you made? What can you infer from your results?*

What to expect: Students' results, of course, will depend on many factors including their setup, their chosen "pollutant," and the plants used. Many of these substances, such as cigarette smoke or road salt, will, in certain concentrations, have dramatic effects on plant growth and health. It's important, however, not to overgeneralize conclusions. These simulations cannot exactly reproduce real-life conditions. It is helpful, however, for students to see that plants' health and growth can be seriously affected by substances in their environment.

Making Connections—Part 1

1. Possible discussion questions:

• *Do you think your experiment simulated a real-life situation? What factors might be different in the "real world"?*

• *To do a real simulation of the effects of your pollutant, how might you conduct your experiment differently? Consider length of time, types of plants, quantity of pollutants, different environmental conditions, how the pollutant really reaches plants, etc.*

• *What kind of pollution did we create during our investigations? Do you think the information you gained was worth the cost of producing pollution? Explain your answer.*

2. Use the "Futures Wheel" (page 292) to illustrate the effects polluted plants might have on other organisms. (A sample question: *What might happen if toxic pesticides drifted into a hay pasture?*)

Exploration—Part 2

Have students research and discuss "Pollution Solutions." Come up with a list of ways to eliminate or reduce the impact of the investigated pollutants on plant life. Consider the following questions:

• *How is this pollutant typically produced and/or disposed of?*

• *What substitutes could be used that would fulfil the function of this pollutant, but that would be less harmful to the environment?*

• *How might this product be disposed of in a less harmful way? How might it be recycled?*

• *How might I change my lifestyle and activities to cut down on the need for this pollutant?*

Making Connections—Part 2

Ask the class to "take a stand" on the following statement, with students lining themselves up across the room according to where they feel they belong on the continuum. Ask students to elaborate on why they chose to stand where they did.

I feel that my personal actions make a ...

(very big)--(very little)

...difference in creating solutions to pollution.

Branching Out

• Research the environmental effects of pesticides and other agricultural chemicals. Learn about different "organic" gardening and farming practices.

• Interview local businesses about their pollution production and solutions. For instance, have students survey area gas stations to find out how they dispose of used motor oil.

• Design and produce a button, bumper sticker, or T-shirt that cleverly admits you're a polluter and/or suggests a way to minimize polluting.

• Have students survey their homes for substances that may be toxic to plants if improperly disposed of. Research how to dispose of these products safely.

• Debate in support of or against the idea that some animals and plants pollute.

• Discuss the phrase: "If you're not part of the solution, you're part of the pollution." Illustrate with some examples.

• Visit a local dump or collect a week's worth of school garbage. Study and categorize the types of things that are thrown away. Discuss how these things contribute to pollution.

• Do a survey of soaps, cleansers, and shampoos in your local supermarket. Identify which have phosphates and which do not.

PlantAcid

From mustard to the fluid in car batteries, all substances in our environment are either acids, bases, or neutral. Acidity can be measured by the pH scale, which runs from 0 (most acidic) to 14 (most alkaline or basic), with 7 being neutral. The lower the number, the stronger the acid. Fruits, milk, soda, and coffee all have a measurable pH. Distilled water (not rainwater or tapwater) has a pH of 7 and is considered neutral. Anything with a pH above 7 is considered a base. Both acids and bases can be either weak or strong.

Since the pH scale is logarithmic, every whole number change increases or decreases the acidity tenfold. A substance, therefore, with a pH of 4, is ten times more acidic than a substance with a pH of 5.

Acid Basics

The acidity or alkalinity of a substance is determined by the concentration of hydrogen ions (H+) or hydroxide ions (OH-) produced when the substance is dissolved in water. The term pH reflects the concentration of hydrogen ions.

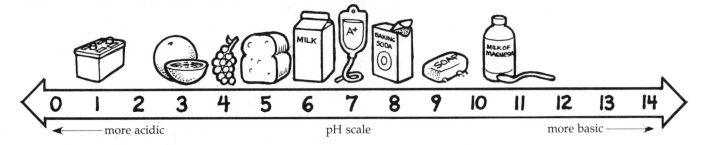

< 0 1 2 3 4 5 6 7 8 9 10 11 12 13 14 >

←—— more acidic   pH scale   more basic ——→

Acid Cavities?

Sugar doesn't cause tooth decay; certain acids do! Bacteria in your mouth produce acids that can dissolve tooth enamel. Eating carbohydrates (e.g., sugars) increases acid production. Have your students soak a tooth in cola and see what happens!

Although acids may sometimes get a "bum rap," they are not in themselves good or bad. Living things have a pH range for different functions that is optimal for health and growth. The strong acid in our stomach, for instance, is vital to digestion. Our blood has a pH of about 7.4. If the pH changed even a few tenths of a percent, serious illness or death could result.

How Can We Tell Whether Something is Acidic?

pH is often measured with an **indicator paper** which turns color when dipped into an acid or base. The color change, when compared with a standardized color chart, indicates pH. If you're measuring the pH of a wide range of substances, use a type of indicator paper that measures a wide range from pH 0 to 12 or 14. If you want more accurate measurements within a small range, use paper with a narrower range.

What is Acid Precipitation?

When fossil fuels, particularly coal, are burned for industry, automobiles, and electricity production, sulphur and nitrogen oxides are released into the air. As they float high in the atmosphere, they combine with water vapor and oxygen to form sulfuric and nitric acids. These acids fall to earth as rain, fog, or snow, and form **acid precipitation**. Although an average rainfall has a mildly acidic pH of 5.6, any precipitation that becomes abnormally acidic is commonly known as acid rain.

How Does Acid Precipitation Affect Plants?

Acid rain is a serious problem for all living things in the environment (see "Dead Lakes" sidebar). The activity **PlantAcid** focuses on its potential effects on plants. Acid is not necessarily bad for plants: most, in fact, grow best in slightly acidic soils and some, like blueberries and azaleas, prefer an even lower pH. Each type of plant, however, has an optimal pH range.

The chemical interactions that cause acid rain and its effect on living things are extremely complex and hard to document. This is due, in part, to the fact that it's hard to tell acid rain damage from other plant problems. Many scientists believe that other air pollutants interact with acid rain in ways that can increase the damage, but that are not fully understood. Some believe that plants can actually benefit from the extra nitrates in acid rain. Still other theories assume that acid rain activates certain **buffers** in the soil, which temporarily neutralize the effects of too much acid. Some theories on how acid rain harms plants state that it:

• removes many important plant nutrients from the soil;

• harms leaf surfaces and disrupts photosynthesis;

• dissolves plant tissues, making them susceptible to pest and disease problems;

• suppresses and kills soil organisms that help plants thrive;

• releases toxic metals, e.g., aluminum, which then interfere with nutrient uptake by plants and harm soil organisms;

• reduces earthworm populations, thereby reducing soil fertility;

• diminishes soil bacteria and fungi, slowing the rate of decomposition and nutrient recycling.

Addressing the Problem

As with most problems relating to environmental pollutants, an ounce of prevention is worth a great deal. Students should begin to recognize that, even without full agreement and firm theories from scientists, we can make personal choices that can help diminish the production of acid rain. An important point to note is that many of these choices, such as using less fossil fuels, conserving energy, and recycling, will also help address other serious environmental problems—other forms of air pollution, the greenhouse effect, solid waste pollution, and shrinking natural resources. Some specific measures that are being taken at the industrial level are instituting stricter air quality standards, using cleaner, low-sulphur coal, and employing "scrubbers" to remove sulphur dioxide emissions before they leave power plants.

Making a choice to follow any of these suggestions, of course, entails tradeoffs. Encourage your students, as they conduct **PlantAcid,** to discuss the implications of various proposed solutions and to consider how they personally might make a difference.

PlantAcid

Overview: Students explore acidity and experiment to examine how plants respond to changes in the acidity of their environment.

Simulation of actual acid precipitation would entail using caustic nitric and sulfuric acids. Instead, this activity recommends vinegar solutions. Although not a true simulation of effects of acid precipitation, this allows students to observe plant responses to different environmental conditions.

Time:
Groundwork: 45 minutes
Exploration: 45 minutes setup; 3 to 4 weeks ongoing observations
Making Connections: ongoing

Materials:
• bean plants
• white vinegar
• wide-range pH paper (0–12)
• "The Acid Test" reproducible, page 278
• "Problem Solving for Growing Minds" reproducible, page 283
• "Observation Journal" reproducible, page 286

Background: Page 238 and page 248

Laying the Groundwork

Objective: To explore the concept of acidity.

1. Find out what your students already know about acids by asking such questions as: *What common substances can you think of that are acids? Do you think acids are helpful or harmful? What have you experienced or read to lead you to believe this?* As a class, generate a list of things students think they know about acids.

2. Using the background, page 248, as a reference, explain to students how to measure the acidity of substances. Have students bring in different household substances (milk, water, lemon juice, cola, baking soda, etc.) that can be put in solution. Using wide-range pH paper, test the substances after predicting whether each will be more acidic, neutral, or basic. Record results on the "The Acid Test" reproducible.
   Ask: *Did any of your findings surprise you? Which? Did particular types of food tend to be more acidic or basic?*

3. Explain that acids are all around us, and that they're neither good nor bad, but that all living things (and systems) have a pH range within which they function best. When the pH changes, problems can result. Ask: *When have you ever been sensitive to acids in your environment* (e.g., acid indigestion)?
   Ask: *What do you know about acid rain? Can you tell if acid rain is falling outside? How? How do you think acid rain might affect living things in the environment? How could you find out?*

Exploration

Objective: To discover, after experimenting, that different levels of acidity affect plant growth and development.

1. Ask: *In the classroom, how could we find out if and how plants are sensitive to different levels of acidity?* Encourage students, in small groups or as a class, to design experiments to examine this question, using the Problem Solving for Growing Minds process, page 10. When designing experiments students might want to consider: whether and how best to simulate rainfall conditions; whether to test the effect of acidity on seed germination and/or plant growth; whether to test the effect of acidity on different plant parts, e.g., leaves and roots. Share that the pH of "normal" rain ranges from 5.0 to 5.6.

A sample setup follows:

Question: *How do seedlings respond to different levels of acidity?*

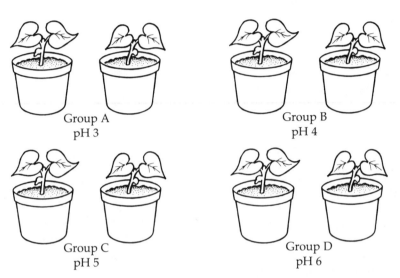

Group A
pH 3

Group B
pH 4

Group C
pH 5

Group D
pH 6

Step 1. Plant three bean seeds per 4-inch pot and thin to one plant per pot when plants are approximately 2 inches tall.

Step 2. Prepare solutions of different pH as described below. (Since the pH of tapwater varies, solution pH measurements will be approximate.) Test the pH of each solution with indicator paper so that actual values can be recorded and/or the solutions adjusted. In either case, the solutions will still allow students to examine results from large changes in pH.

Solution Preparation (assumes tapwater pH approximately 6.0; white vinegar pH approximately 3.3). Mix tapwater and vinegar in the following quantities:

pH:	Tapwater	Vinegar
pH 3:	none	1 quart (or 1 liter)
pH 4:	1 quart (or 1 liter)	1/2 cup (or 100 ml)
pH 5:	1 quart (or 1 liter)	2 tsp. (or 10 ml)
pH 6:	1 quart	none

Step 3. When plants have grown their first set of true leaves (3 to 4 inches tall), begin watering each with its respective acid solution. For each watering, spray part of the solution on the leaves with a spray bottle and use the remainder of the solution to water

the soil. Have students design a system to ensure that all plants are receiving an equal amount sprayed on the leaves and applied to the soil.

2. Students should use the "Observation Journal" to record observations and measurements of each plant group. Discuss what effects the different acid solutions seemed to have on plants. Ask: *Which pH level seemed to have the most dramatic effects on plant growth and development? When did you first notice the effects?*

> **What to expect:** The most dramatic effects of the more acidic solutions (pH 3 and 4) on plants will be evidenced by immediate discoloration, curling, and overall stunting, followed by the death of the plant.

Making Connections

1. Possible discussion questions:

• *Did your experiment reflect an accurate simulation of acid rain? If not, how do you think it varied from the real thing? How might you conduct a similar experiment to simulate the real thing more closely?*

• *What can you infer from this experiment about how the same type of plant in a garden, farm, or forest might respond to changing acidity in the environment? What additional factors do you think would affect plant response in an outside environment?*

• *How do you think acid rain might affect you, the dog next door, and a bald eagle?* (Consider using the "Futures Wheel," page 292, to explore this.)

• *What are some other ways in which plants are harmed by changes in environmental conditions* (e.g., road salt)? *What are some ways in which people can be harmed by changes in environmental conditions* (e.g., smog, drugs in our internal environment)?

2. Explain to students that scientists have many unanswered questions about the environmental effects of acid rain and other pollutants. Invite your students to "take a stand" on the following question by lining themselves up on an imaginary line. Ask each student to explain his or her reason for choosing a particular spot.

Should we wait until we have all the answers before we take action to reduce the types of pollution that we think cause acid rain?

yes---no

Set up an investigation, like the example illustrated below, to compare the effects of acid solution falling on leaves and acid solution taken up through plant roots. The investigation should help students recognize that plants will show signs of damage with both treatments. The combined effect—direct damage to leaves plus interruption of nutrient uptake and other processes in the roots —magnifies the problem of acid rain.

pH 3   pH 3
(water soil)   (water leaves)

Branching Out

• Explore how acid rain might affect other living and non-living things in the environment. Try applying acids to different materials such as seeds, granite, limestone, or bricks.

• Collect rainwater or melt snow at your school and determine pH. Apply the water to plants.

• Research soil pH. Test different soils to determine their pH. Find out how farmers and gardeners adjust pH in the soil.

• Experiment to examine what other factors influence how acid rain affects plants (e.g., age of plants, type of plants, temperature, soil type).

• Research and discuss what steps can be taken to reduce acid rain (e.g., restricting auto use), and what tradeoffs each step might entail. Debate whether the benefits of each suggestion would be worth the cost.

• Write letters to members of the U.S. Congress to find out the status of laws regarding waste products contributing to acid precipitation. Voice your opinion.

• Much of the nitric and sulfuric oxides produced in the U.S. end up as acid rain in Canada. Find out about international relations regarding acid precipitation.

• Correspond with students in another part of the country via mail or computer. Share acid rain data for your respective areas.

• Create a Concerned Student Bulletin Board highlighting articles about acid rain and other environmental topics.

• For a catalog listing interdisciplinary acid rain curriculum resources for Grades 4–12, write to:

The Acid Rain Foundation, Inc.
1410 Varsity Drive
Raleigh, NC 27606
(919) 737-3311

Global ReLeaf

Many scientists are becoming increasingly concerned about a phenomenon called the **greenhouse effect**, which seems to be contributing to a warming of our earth. Normally, the sun's light energy passes through our atmosphere to the earth as short-wave radiation. The earth then gives back this energy as long-wave radiation in the form of heat. Carbon dioxide (CO_2) and other naturally occurring gases (methane, nitrous oxide) trap this heat in our atmosphere just as glass retains heat in a greenhouse, making the earth warm enough to support life. CO_2 is the most plentiful "greenhouse gas."

During the last century, however, there has been a dramatic increase in the production of CO_2 and other greenhouse gases. Many scientists predict this will cause our atmosphere to have higher average temperatures—increasing by 2.7 to 8.1 degrees F —resulting in an overall global warming.

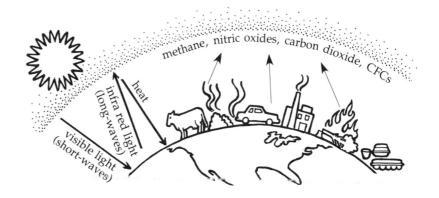

Who's Producing These Greenhouse Gases?

Although we all release CO_2 into the air every time we exhale, this isn't cause for alarm. Of more importance is the quantity of CO_2 and other gases released when fossil fuels are burned. Fossil fuels include coal, oil, and natural gas, formed over millions of years from deposits of ancient plant and animal remains. Because all living things contain carbon, CO_2 is a by-product of their burning. The release of all this "locked-up" carbon dioxide has increased rapidly since the Industrial Revolution. CO_2 levels increased 30 percent between 1850 and 1980 and are currently increasing at an even faster rate.

When we use automobiles, many electric appliances (electric power is often generated from fossil fuels), or plastic materials (their production requires fossil fuels), we contribute to increased greenhouse gases in the atmosphere.

Deforestation is another important contributor of carbon dioxide, since decay of organic material releases CO_2. When large forested areas (e.g., tropical rainforests) are burned, great quantities of CO_2 are released. Removal of forests also means that fewer trees are available to absorb CO_2.

In many areas forested land is cleared for agriculture. Agricultural fertilizers and manures contribute significantly to the production of greenhouse gases. As world population increases, so does the production of these gases.

Chlorofluorocarbons (CFCs), important factors in global warming, are chemicals used in refrigerators, air conditioners, aerosols, and styrofoam production. They not only contribute to global warming, but are also damaging the ozone layer that protects us from the sun's harmful ultraviolet rays.

What Might Result?

There is general agreement that greenhouse gases are increasing and that warming is occurring. Predictions of results, however, are not precise, since many factors are not fully understood. Some scientists, for instance, think that an increase in cloud cover, from evaporation, could actually cool the atmosphere.

Some of the predicted consequences of global warming include:

• Plants and animals won't necessarily adapt quickly to rapid environmental changes. Extinctions may result.

• Increase in evaporation could result in more cloud cover and dramatic changes in rain and snowfall patterns. This could have a major impact on agricultural regions.

• Human stress will intensify from increased heat waves.

• Certain air pollutants will increase with higher temperatures.

• Pests, diseases, and disease-carrying pests may increase.

• Ocean levels may rise as the polar ice caps melt, possibly causing coastal flooding and contamination of drinking water. Large populations living near coasts could be displaced or wiped out.

What Can We Do?

There are many ways that individuals can get involved to diminish their share of CO_2 released to the atmosphere. Some of these include limiting the amount of auto fuel used, conserving electricity and heat, and recycling resources. The only real solution to the problem is changing habits personally and globally to decrease the amount of greenhouse gases released.

In the meantime, some organizations are promoting planting trees as a way to raise awareness, cool the globe, and absorb some CO_2. The activity **Global ReLeaf** introduces students to the problem of global warming, and challenges them to raise tree seedlings in response to the "Newsflash," below.

> **Trees also produce CO_2**
>
> Trees, like humans, also produce CO_2 as a by-product of respiration. Since trees use more CO_2 during photosynthesis than they release during respiration, they ultimately remove CO_2 from the atmosphere.

Newsflash: Global ReLeaf Tree-Planting Project: Raise a Forest!

The American Forestry Association (AFA) and the National Arbor Day Foundation are mounting a campaign to involve citizens in helping combat the greenhouse effect. They believe we can all be part of the solution to environmental problems.

Since trees use carbon dioxide to live, planting new trees can help diminish the amount of CO_2 in the atmosphere. Trees are considered CO_2 "sponges." An average tree uses about 40 pounds of CO_2 per year, storing it in wood. If the wood is protected and not burned or decomposed, the CO_2 is "tied up"—not released. It's estimated that mature forests absorb CO_2 at an average rate of about three tons per acre per year.

The AFA is urging people in the United States to plant millions of trees, in an attempt to remove 18 million tons of CO_2 from the atmosphere each year. The shade provided by trees, particularly in cities, will further cool the environment, reducing the need for fossil fuels for cooling and air conditioning. As trees transpire, they also absorb a great deal of heat from the atmosphere.

Why not participate in this exciting national effort by raising some tree seedlings in your classroom garden? Plant them and make a difference in your community. At the same time, look at ways that you can decrease your own contribution of CO_2 and other greenhouse gases. Planting trees alone will not solve the problem.

Global ReLeaf

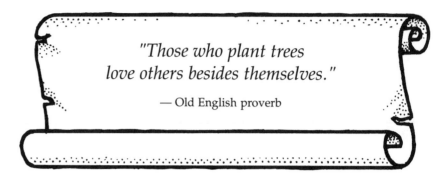

"Those who plant trees love others besides themselves."

— Old English proverb

Overview: This long-term, thematic project introduces students to the issue of global warming. By discussing the issue and raising tree seedlings, students realize they can personally respond to complex environmental problems.

Time:
Groundwork: 45 minutes
Exploration: ongoing class project
Making Connections: ongoing

Materials:
• 4-inch pots
• potting mix
• tree seeds (see Exploration)
• "What a Gas" reproducible, page 279
• "Futures Wheel" reproducible, page 292

Background: Page 238 and page 255

Laying the Groundwork

1. Ask your students what they know about global warming and the greenhouse effect. On the board, make a list of things students think they know about these topics, and things they'd like to find out. Share the basic information from page 255 on what causes the greenhouse effect.

2. Break the class into small groups and have them review the "What a Gas" reproducible. After reading the charts, ask each group to discuss the following questions: *Who or what is producing the largest quantity of greenhouse gases? Which greenhouse gas seems to be produced in the largest quantity? If carbon dioxide (CO_2) is something we breathe out every day, and drink in our soda, why do you think it's a problem? How much has the concentration of CO_2 increased in the last fifty years? In the fifty years before that? Why do you think it might be increasing at such a rapid rate? How do you think humans have affected that rate?*

3. Ask each group to develop a list in which each person shares three things he or she did or used that week that could have contributed to the greenhouse effect. Combine group lists on a class chart headed: "How We Contribute to the Greenhouse Effect." Save the chart for later reference.

4. As a class, use the "Futures Wheel" reproducible to brainstorm some of the possible consequences of an increase in global temperatures. Share some of the ideas from the background information, put forth by scientists.

5. Ask: *From what you've read and heard about global warming and the greenhouse effect, do you think scientists agree that global warming is occurring? Do you think they agree on its long-term effects? If not, why do you think they disagree?*
Share that although scientists agree that CO_2 and other

greenhouse gases are rising, they have conflicting opinions on what that means. Discuss that as we continue to learn new things, theories constantly change, but that we base our actions on the best information available at any one time. This is not always easy to do, since there are often multiple theories that conflict with one another.

6. Ask: *Although scientists aren't in agreement about global warming or its effects, do you think we should be concerned about its possibility? Why or why not?* Focus students' attention on their class chart of things contributing to greenhouse gases. Ask: *What types of things do you think we as individuals might do to help address the problem?* Brainstorm answers to this question, suspending all judgement and recording all answers. Responses might include:

- drive cars less often
- recycle more resources
- turn down the heat
- don't use styrofoam
- support efforts to reduce rainforest burning
- conserve electricity

If you're doing a long-term project, students might want to devise ways to implement some of these suggestions in their own lives and in your classroom.

7. If no one brings up the topic, ask: *How do you think trees might contribute to or counteract global warming? How do you think we might use trees in an effort to address global warming?* Have students consider how tree placement can affect the climate around buildings and thus influence the need for heating and cooling. Encourage them to think about the role of trees in the CO_2 cycle.

Share the "Newsflash" (page 257) describing the Global Re-Leaf tree planting project. Discuss how the class might use the GrowLab to participate in that project.

Exploration

Objective: To apply understanding of germination and growth needs to raise tree seedlings. To recognize that individuals can be part of the solution to the complex environmental problem of global warming.

1. Which trees to grow? Since different types of trees grow best in particular areas of the country, we recommend having students contact the local Cooperative Extension Service or Parks Department for information on the best types of trees for your area.

Consider the following when choosing trees to grow from seed: What trees are best for your climatic zone? Which types will grow relatively quickly indoors? What treatment do the seeds need to germinate? Which types will transplant outdoors easily?

We recommend **thornless honey locust** trees for classroom gardens. Their seeds, which must be scarred before they will germinate, provide an opportunity for students to explore seed

Honey Locust seedling

adaptations for survival (see sidebar). They germinate and grow quickly, grow well in almost any area of the country (even in polluted city air), and are tolerant of nearly any soil conditions. Honey locust seeds are included in the GrowLab Seed Collection, or can be purchased from sources listed in Appendix F.

2. Planting tree seeds. These directions are for honey locust seedlings. Research variations in treatment if you're using other types of seeds. If you start honey locust seeds indoors in the fall you can transplant them outside the following spring.

To prepare these hard seeds, vigorously rub the rounded ends with a nail file, until white shows through. Plant three or four seeds per 4-inch pot, to be thinned to one per pot when the seedlings are an inch tall. Water well, wait one to two weeks for germination, and then water and fertilize as you do your other GrowLab plants.

Just budding in: If you want to free up space in your GrowLab, you can place the seedlings on a windowsill after a month in the GrowLab. They may dry out more quickly there, however, and will have to be turned periodically as they bend toward the light.

3. Finding a new home—transplanting tree seedlings. If your honey locust seedlings were started in the fall, they should be ready to transplant outside the following spring when they are 6 to 12 inches tall. The following suggestions will help guide your transplanting efforts:

• Contact community members (parks department, school administrators, etc.) to find out what local areas might be appropriate for tree planting.

• Find a location with well-drained soil, protection from trampling by dogs and people, and full sun. If time and space allow, create a tree seedling "nursery" near the school. In a nursery, plant trees about 2 feet apart. After a year of careful nurturing, transplant each tree to a permanent location, 30 to 50 feet apart.

• Before transplanting tree seedlings, "harden them off" by setting them outside for increasing amounts of time each day to accustom them to the harsher realities of sun, wind, and cold outdoors.

• Dig a hole big enough to contain the entire root system, when stretched out. If available, line the hole with compost or rotted manure.

• Set the seedling in the hole, pack soil firmly around the roots, make a small water-holding basin around the plant, and water well. One of the main reasons for tree seedling failure is inadequate water. Continue to water and fertilize with manure or compost solution, or according to directions for your fertilizer.

Branching Out

Raising trees can become a thematic, long-term project, tying in a variety of subject areas. Some suggestions follow:

Science

- Experiment with different seed treatments. Try chilling, boiling, scarring, burning, and soaking in water or acid, and collect germination data.

- Research how trees affect climate by influencing wind, temperature, humidity, rainfall, and CO_2.

- Use your tree seedlings for other explorations, for example, of phototropism or fertilizer needs.

- Investigate differences between deciduous trees and evergreens.

Math

- Determine how tall your trees will be when you graduate, if they grow at an average rate of 20 feet every seven years.

- Chart the growth rate of your seedlings. Estimate when they'll reach 6 inches ... 1 foot ... 2 feet.

- Estimate the amount of CO_2 produced by some of your activities using the following rough estimates: Burning a gallon of gasoline produces 20 pounds of CO_2. Using one kilowatt-hour of electricity generated by a coal-fired power plant produces two pounds of CO_2. (Find out whether your power company uses coal.) Flying one mile in an airplane generates approximately one-half pound of CO_2 per passenger.

Social Studies

- Brainstorm a list of the values of trees and forests, in addition to their production of CO_2.

- Ask your local power company to play its part by helping to finance your tree-planting project or by providing publicity.

- Find out about National Arbor Day in your area. Plan an event to share your knowledge of trees, and/or highlight your project during a tree-planting ceremony.

- Develop a map to scale of the area(s) where the class plants trees. Mark each site and identify tree types and planting dates. Share these maps with families, community members, and local officials.

- Research and implement other ways to combat global warming such as cutting back on the number of miles driven by parents, conserving electricity in school, or recycling.

- Research and graph the amount of CO_2 emissions produced by different countries.

Language Arts

- Write local officials to inform them of your environmental concerns and about your project. Ask them to suggest public areas where you can plant trees.

- Read and discuss the stories *The Man Who Planted Trees* and *The Lorax*. (See Appendix E.)

- Write letters or develop a newsletter to distribute to other classrooms, challenging them to participate in the Global ReLeaf tree-planting effort.

- Present a talk to other classrooms, parents, or the school board entitled "What We Can Do to Help Combat Global Warming."

- Write a poem or short story that highlights the many values of trees.

- Write to one of the organizations in the sidebar on page 259 for more information and curriculum resources on global warming.

Appendix A: Specific Activity Reproducibles

Bingo Seedso 264
Yo Seeds, Wake Up! 265
Soil Sort 266
Puzzled by Photosynthesis 267
Flowers: Up Close—Part 1 268
Flowers: Up Close—Part 2 269
Slips and Snips Survey Results 270
Lettuce Be Different 271
Mystery Family Ties 272
Seed Busters 273
Turning Over a New Leaf 274
Should Dandelions Be Considered Weeds? 276
Rainforest Stories 277
The Acid Test 278
What a Gas 279

Bingo Seedso

smallest	most pointed	most wrinkled	fuzziest
biggest	rolls farthest	2 colored	floats
funniest	smoothest	most unusual	?!?

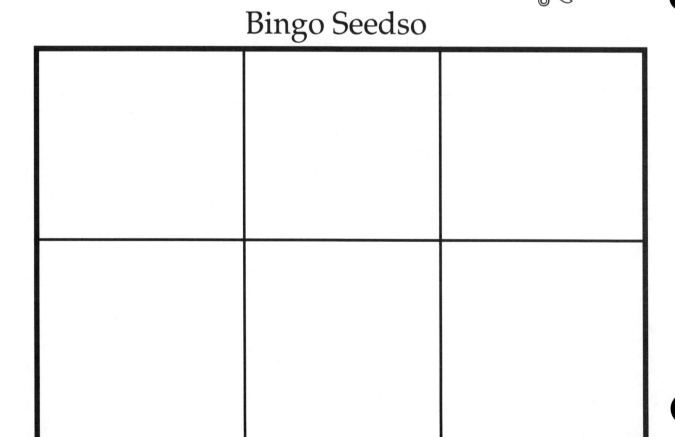

Bingo Seedso

Yo Seeds, Wake Up!

Name: _____ Date: _____

Draw your setups:

Condition: _____ Condition: _____

Number of seeds used:_____ Number of seeds used:_____

How many seeds have sprouted by... How many seeds have sprouted by...

Day 2	
Day 3	
Day 4	
Day 5	

Day 2	
Day 3	
Day 4	
Day 5	

Other observations: _____

_____

_____

_____

Soil Sort

Medical Chart

Name _____   Date _____

Pile #	Description

Dirty Drains
Setup:

Results:

Settle Down, Please!
Setup:

Results:

(Record other observations on back.)

Puzzled by Photosynthesis

Directions: Write the correct words on each puzzle piece.

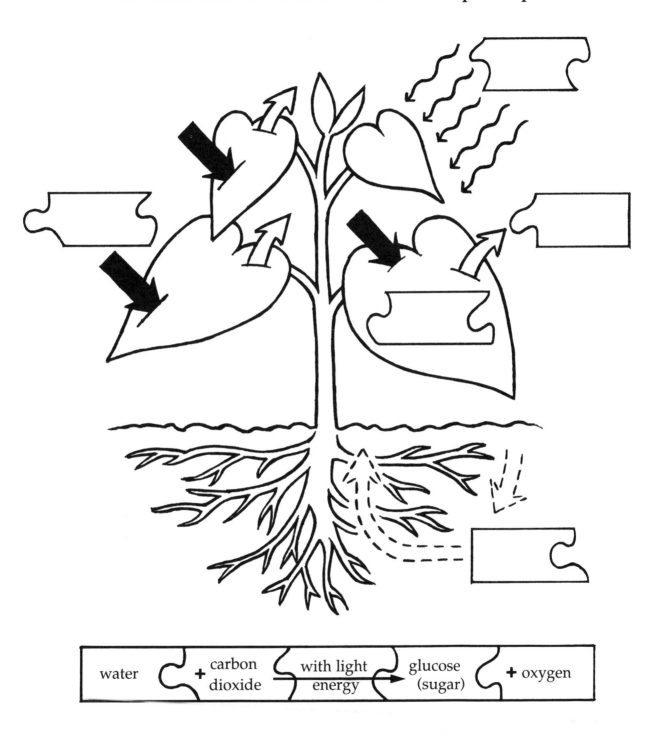

water ⌐ + carbon dioxide ⌐ with light energy → glucose (sugar) ⌐ + oxygen

Notes: _____

_____

_____

267

Flowers: Up Close—Part 1

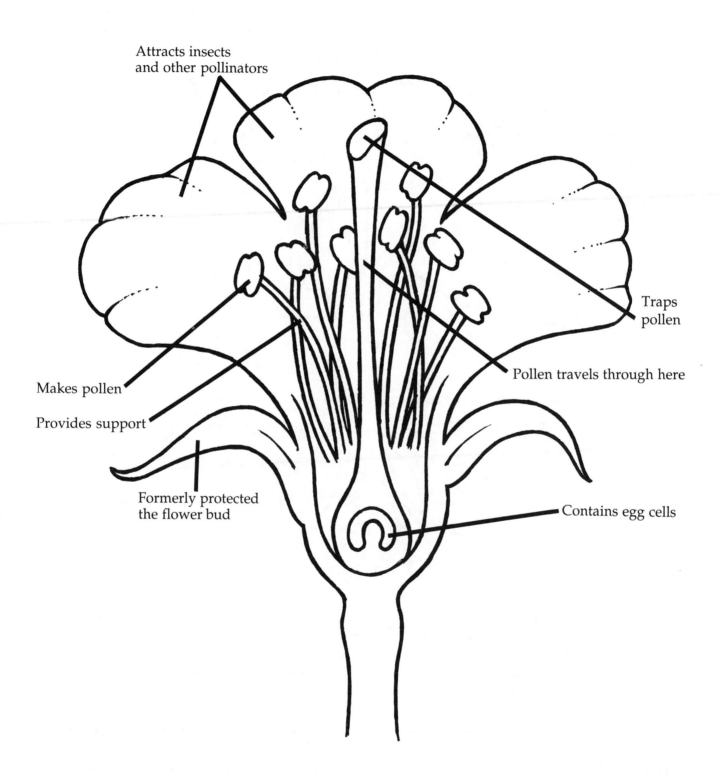

Attracts insects and other pollinators

Traps pollen

Pollen travels through here

Makes pollen

Provides support

Formerly protected the flower bud

Contains egg cells

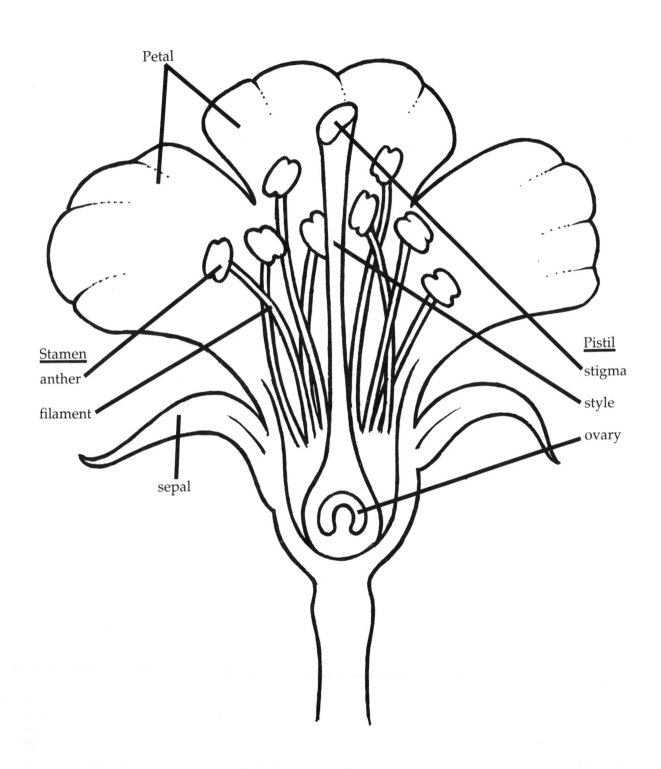

Petal

Stamen
anther

filament

sepal

Pistil
stigma

style

ovary

Slips and Snips Survey Results

Please share the results of your houseplant cutting survey and experiments with us. We're eager to share your findings with other indoor gardeners. Use extra paper, if necessary, and attach data sheets. Send to: **Slips and Snips Survey**, National Gardening Association, 180 Flynn Avenue, Burlington, VT 05401.

School Name and Address _____

_____

Teacher's Name _____ **Grade** _____

Survey Results

Classroom Experiments (Please describe your setups and results.):

Questions we have for students in other classrooms:

Lettuce Be Different

Name: _____   Date: _____

	Pot A	Pot B	Pot C
What do the *seeds* look like? (color, shape, size)			
What *color* are the *leaves*?			
How do the *leaves feel*?			
What *shape* are the *leaves*?			
How *tall* is the *plant*?			
How does it *taste*?			
What else do you *notice* about the lettuce?			

Mystery Family Ties

Name:_____

Which plants belong to the same families? Why do you think so?

Week:_____   _____
                _____
                _____
                _____
                _____

Week:_____   _____
                _____
                _____
                _____
                _____

Week:_____   _____
                _____
                _____
                _____

Seed Busters

Name:_____ Seed Type:_____

Date:_____ Usual days to Germination:_____ days

Experimental Group	"Forces of Nature"	Simulation	Dates and Numbers of Seeds Germinated		
			Predictions	Results	
				Date	Number
				Total Number of Seeds Germinated = ⬭	
				Date	Number
				Total Number of Seeds Germinated = ⬭	
				Date	Number
				Total Number of Seeds Germinated = ⬭	

Turning Over a New Leaf

Name: _____ Date: _____

STATION 1

Why do you think only Bag A has water on the inside?

Explain how you think the water got there.

STATION 2

Part A - Leaf A is from a dry environment plant (jade). Leaf B is from a plant not adapted to survive in a dry environment.

What two characteristics of Leaf A do you think help it survive in a dry environment?

Observations:

Part B - Use these sponges to simulate leaves to help you answer part A.

Do you think one fat sponge or two thin sponges would lose water faster?

Place a plastic bag over one of the two small sponges. Which do you think would dry out faster?

STATION 3

Plant A (cactus) is typical of many dry climate plants. Plant B is not adapted to a dry climate.

What characteristics of Plant A do you think help it survive well in a dry climate? How do you think they might do this? **Hint:** Plant A has spines in place of leaves.

STATION 4

Close your eyes and use your other senses to examine both plants. What is an obvious difference that might be an adaptation for survival?

How do you think that characteristic might help a plant survive in its environment?

STATION 5

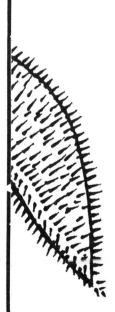

Closely examine both leaves. What seems to be the most obvious difference?

List several ways in which this difference might help a plant survive.

Should Dandelions Be Considered Weeds?

Character	Position	Reasoning
Nursery Owner	Yes	Dandelions make lawns ugly. Our business will boom if people want them removed from lawns.
Botanist	no	Dandelions have undeservedly bad reputations.
Landscaper	yes	Business will boom because people will want them removed.
Ecologist	no	Dandelions play an important role in the environment. For instance, they provide pollen and other food for insects.
Homeowner	unsure	The yard does look nice with them, but they blow seeds into the garden.
Road Crew	yes	Dandelion roots cause extensive damage to sidewalks and pavement.
Nutritionist	no	The leaves are full of vitamins and make a nice salad, the roots can be cooked as a vegetable or used as a coffee substitute, and the flowers make a nice wine.
Artist/Poet	no	Those who can't see the beauty and vitality in dandelions should be weeded from society!
Bees	no	Dandelion flowers are an important source of nectar for us.
Soil Scientist	no	Weeds pull up nutrients from deep in the soil and protect the soil from washing away in wind and rain.
Other	?	(You decide your position and reasoning.)

Rainforest Stories

Directions: As you and your teacher discuss each layer - or story - of a tropical rainforest, please color in that section on the illustration.

Emergents

Canopy

Understory

Forest floor

The Acid Test

Name: _____ Date: _____

Solution tested	Predicted pH	Actual pH (attach indicator paper)

Mark substances tested at the appropiate place on the pH scale.

← 0 1 2 3 4 5 6 7 8 9 10 11 12 13 14 →

What a Gas

Causes of Global Warming

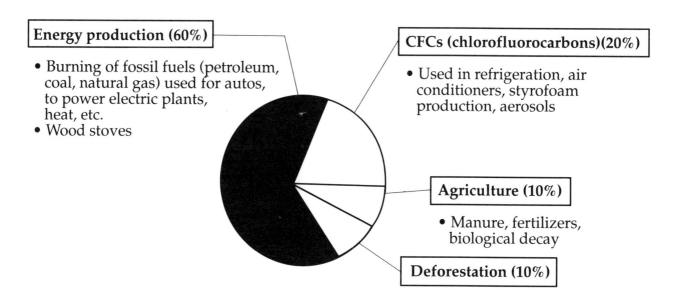

Energy production (60%)
- Burning of fossil fuels (petroleum, coal, natural gas) used for autos, to power electric plants, heat, etc.
- Wood stoves

CFCs (chlorofluorocarbons)(20%)
- Used in refrigeration, air conditioners, styrofoam production, aerosols

Agriculture (10%)
- Manure, fertilizers, biological decay

Deforestation (10%)

Culprit Greenhouse Gases

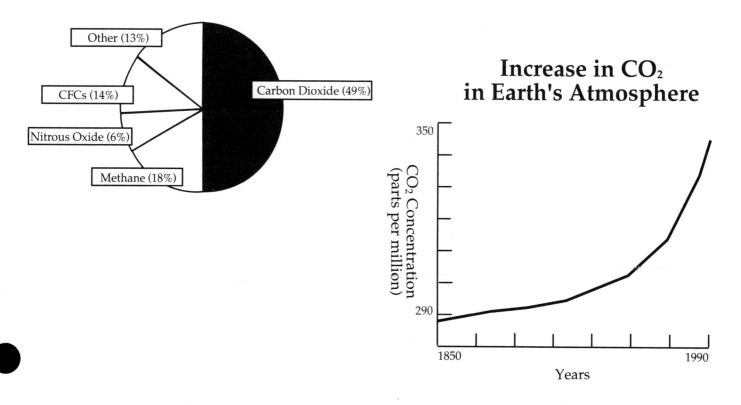

Other (13%)

CFCs (14%)

Nitrous Oxide (6%)

Methane (18%)

Carbon Dioxide (49%)

Increase in CO_2 in Earth's Atmosphere

CO_2 Concentration (parts per million)

350

290

1850   1990

Years

Sources: Adapted from Hansen et. al. 1988, Friends of the Earth.   Copyright © 1990 National Gardening Association

Appendix B: General Reproducibles

Plant a Question 282
Problem Solving for Growing Minds 283
My Plant Journal 285
Observation Journal 286
Create-a-Chart 287
Garden Calendar 288
GermiNation and Growth Journal 289
Futures Wheel 291

Plant a Question

Name:_____ Date:_____

What will happen if... _____

_____

_____

_____

_____

I predict... _____

_____

_____

_____

_____

This is what happened... _____

_____

_____

_____

Now I want to find out... _____

_____

_____

_____

Problem Solving for Growing Minds

Name: _____ Date: _____

Directions: Use this sheet to guide you through the stages of problem solving.

Plant a Question:

Sprout a Hypothesis:

I think... the more I water plants, the faster they'll grow.

Describe Your Growing Exploration:

Oh, I need to remember to change only one factor and keep the others constant!

What steps will I take to find the answer?

Let's see... what materials will I need?

I What will I observe? How often?

Which is the control group?

Did I remember repetition? Did I remember repetition?

283

Record Fruitful Observations:

(attach all record sheets)

Harvest Your Findings:

OnGrowing Review:

Cultivate New Ideas:

My Plant Journal

Name: _____ Date: _____

My plants look like this today:

Observation Journal

Name: _____

Activity: _____

Experimental Groups	Time (Day/Date/Week)	General Observations and Sketches	

Create-a-Chart

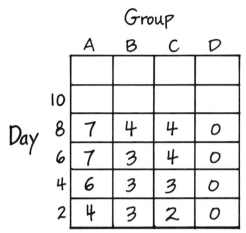

Average Plant Height (cm)/Group

		Height	#Leaves	Color	Other Notes
Week 1		Experiment-Control-			
Week 2					
Week 3					
Week 4					

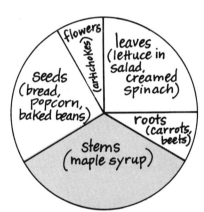

Percentage of Plant Parts Eaten in One Day

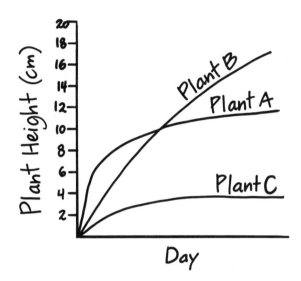

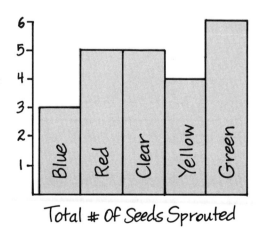

Total # Of Seeds Sprouted

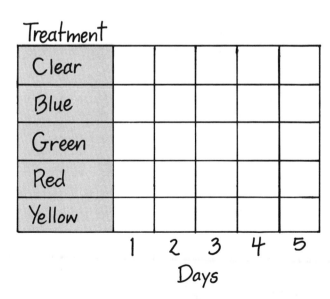

Total # of seeds sprouted

Garden Calendar

Sunday	Monday	Tuesday	Wednesday	Thursday	Friday	Saturday

288

GermiNation and Growth Journal

180 FLYNN AVENUE ■ BURLINGTON, VT 05401 ■ (802) 863-1308

Germination and Growth: Calling All Growing Classrooms!

Join a national network of schools conducting and sharing data about their growing experiences!!

Dear GrowLab Green Thumbs,

The National Gardening Association and other GrowLab classrooms throughout the country want to know about your growing experiences. For instance, Has anything worked particularly well — or poorly? What was your quickest method of germinating beans? Did you soak them first, or cover the container with plastic? Have you tried growing kiwis from seed from home, or orange trees from lunchbox leftovers? Have you discovered any surprises you would like to share?

Whenever you grow a new pot of plants, we invite you to record information on the enclosed GermiNation and Growth Journal and send it in to the National Gardening Association at the above address. Be sure to include your school name and address, teacher's name, classroom number, and other special information about your class. We'll share your information with students in other GrowLab classrooms nationwide. We're particularly interested in new and different plants. Have you collected and grown seeds from any weeds or other wild plants in your area?

Thanks for keeping the world green. We look forward to hearing from you and sharing information and new ideas!

Best wishes,

The National Gardening Association

289

GermiNation
and Growth Journal

What did you plant? (Describe seed type, variety, origin, etc.)

How did you plant the seeds and care for the plants? (Include pot size, kind of soil mix, planting depth, seeds per pot, special seed treatments, fertilizing routine, etc.)

What happened? (Include days to germination, growth rate graph, days to first flower, amount harvested per pot, etc.)

What would you like to find out from other classes?

Using a Futures Wheel[*]

A Futures Wheel can help your students use their imaginations to respond to "What would happen if..." questions. It will illustrate that every action or change has endless implications, both positive and negative. Many "Making Connections" sections suggest using this process to enable students to consider some of the implications of environmental change.

Directions for using a Futures Wheel:

1. As a class or in small groups, choose a "What would happen if...?" question. To practice the basic process, have students choose a topic that's relevant to their daily lives. For instance: *What would happen if kids brought their dogs to school?* Have a recorder write the question in the center of a piece of paper or on the board. This will be the "hub" of the Futures Wheel.

2. After reviewing the question for the class, ask for three to five quick responses. Tell students that they can think of both positive and negative consequences, and may want to label some as good (+), bad (-), or neither (o). Write down the responses in the space around the central question, circle them, and draw a single line or "spoke" connecting each of the responses to the central question. These are the first-level responses.

3. Then ask: "What would happen if..." to discover the consequences of each of the first level responses. Write the new answers around each first-level response, circle them, and connect each new answer to the first-level response with a double line. These are now the second level of responses.

4. Continue in this manner, asking "What would happen if..." regarding each of the second-level responses, connecting new answers with triple lines. You're limited only by your writing space and your students' imaginations.

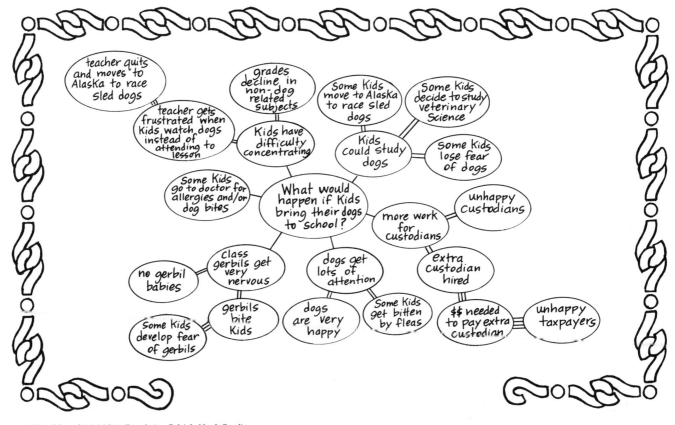

* Adapted from the Acid Rain Foundation, Raleigh, North Carolina

Futures Wheel

What might happen...? What if...? I wonder what...?

Appendix C: OnGrowing Ideas

While the plants are maturing in your GrowLab, consider the following interdisciplinary activity ideas.

As a class, create a "Big Book" with drawings of your plants and descriptive, sensory words for each one.

Make flip books illustrating the sequence of changes in plants.

Make a list of questions you would ask one of your plants if it could talk about its life. Consider how it would feel to be a germinating seed, a plant producing a flower, a plant producing seeds.

Develop a class experience chart about the growth of your plants. Use stickers or illustrations to highlight important events such as seed germination, first flower, or first fruit.

Use strips of construction paper to show changes in plant height over time. Glue them side by side, to form a plant growth graph.

Create a plant drama based on whatever you are studying. In an "underground drama," for instance, students can portray different roots and other living and non-living things they'd encounter in a newly planted garden.

Do abstract or realistic paintings of your GrowLab plants.

Look at and describe all of your plants with and without hand lenses. Compare how descriptions differ.

Measure plants using unusual instruments such as erasers or fingers.

Make a collage contrasting ways in which humans hurt and help plant growth.

Create a graph with blocks or Unifix Cubes showing how many seeds have sprouted each day.

Get to know leaves. Choose one or several leaves to observe every day. Sketch them; describe their color, texture, smell, size, shape; count and draw the main and smaller veins; measure the dimensions.

Record and graph the growth rate of one of your plants for two weeks. Based on your observations, estimate how tall the plant will be in another week. Graph your prediction and compare it with the actual growth rate.

Challenge students with some growth rate problems. For example, roots of young seedlings grow at .2mm to 1mm per hour. At the different rates, how long would it take a carrot root to reach the bottom of a 10-cm pot.

Use microscopes to observe different plant parts such as stomata, chloroplasts, pollen, root hairs, and soil. Make models of what you see.

Research the history of different GrowLab plants. Find out where the plant originated, how it's used in different cultures, and how humans have changed it for agricultural purposes.

Measure and weigh a plant once a week and determine whether there's a relationship between weight and height.

Prepare snacks using the plant parts you're studying (e.g., leaves, stems, roots, fruits).

Design and make garden calendars, illustrating or writing about different garden events such as germination, flowering, or fruiting on appropriate days.

Have an outdoor scavenger hunt to find different types of plants or plant parts.

Play twenty questions with plants in the GrowLab. After one student secretly chooses a plant, the others can try to guess by asking open-ended questions such as: *How do its leaves feel?*

Calculate the average heights and total weight of all plants in the GrowLab.

Appendix D:
Wisconsin Fast Plants™ in the GrowLab

Planting Instructions

Wisconsin Fast Plants are rapid growing members of the cabbage and mustard family (brassicas). They have been specially bred to have a life cycle, from seed to seed, of approximately 40 days! Scientists use them for plant breeding experiments because of their rapid life cycles. Now students and teachers can use these unique plants for classroom investigations.

If you do not have a Fast Plants Kit (see page 303 for Fast Plants ordering information), you will need to do the following:

1. Assemble materials:

• Fast Plants seeds
• small growing containers, e.g., empty plastic film canisters (puncture two holes in the bottom of each), egg carton cells, or pots (no wider than 2 1/2 inches)
• soilless potting mix
• soluble plant fertilizer with equal N-P-K (e.g., 20-20-20 or 14-14-14)
• reservoir - a shallow container to set pots in, e.g., roasting pan or plastic storage container
• wicks - cotton string or yarn for conducting water and fertilizer from resevoir to growing containers

2. Grow plants:

A. Planting Seeds. Plant 2-3 seeds per growing container (pot) and label pots. Set up as follows:

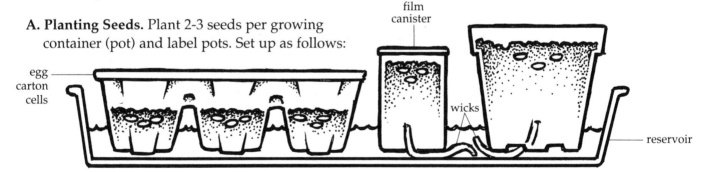

Until seeds germinate, cover pots with plastic to ensure proper moisture and warmth.

B. Watering. Following directions on fertilizer container, mix the maximum recommended dosage (e.g. for 20-20-20, use one full teaspoon per gallon of water). Fill up reservoir approximately 1/2 inch with fertilizer solution and gently mist the top of the pots with fertilizer solution. This will be the last time you water from above. Keep water reservoir filled 1/2 inch with fertilizer at all times!

Just budding in: If you're using cardboard egg cartons, you will not need wicks (as illustrated) as the cardboard itself provides the wicking action. The cardboard will get extremely soggy once the egg carton has been set in the resevoir, so do not attempt to move it. Because of the very moist conditions, you may find algae growth in and around the pots; it will not adversely affect the Fast Plants.

C. Lighting. Leave timer set to minimum 16 hour light cycle. Fast Plants grow most rapidly when receiving 24 hours of light, but 16 hours will allow you to continue to grow your regular GrowLab crops while the Fast Plants are growing. Place entire setup (resevoir, water, pots) in the GrowLab, 2–3 inches from the lights. You'll have to prop up the resevoir, e.g., by placing it on top of upturned pots. **Plants must stay 2–3 inches from the lights throughout their life cycles. Adjust light height accordingly.**

The Life Cycle

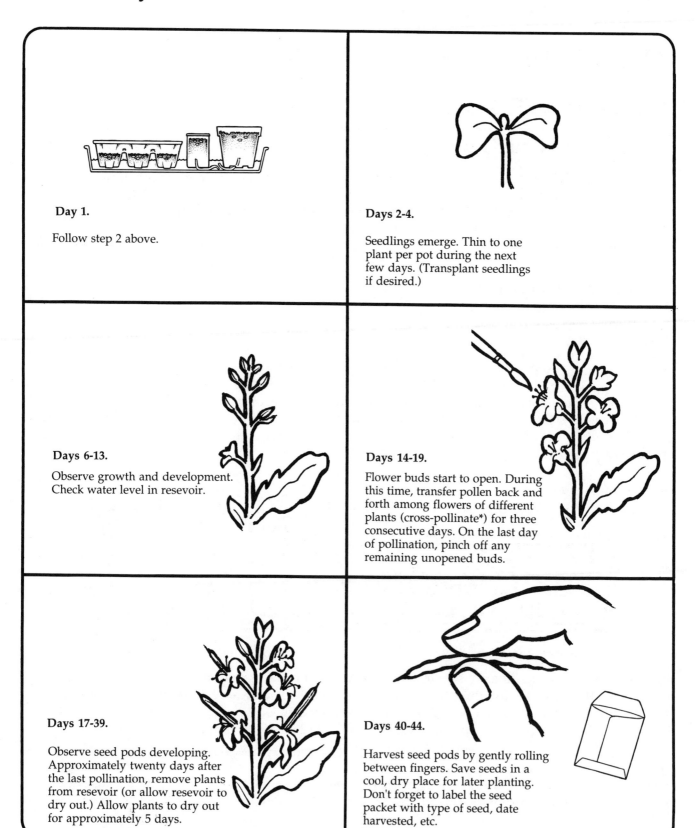

Day 1.

Follow step 2 above.

Days 2-4.

Seedlings emerge. Thin to one plant per pot during the next few days. (Transplant seedlings if desired.)

Days 6-13.

Observe growth and development. Check water level in reservoir.

Days 14-19.

Flower buds start to open. During this time, transfer pollen back and forth among flowers of different plants (cross-pollinate*) for three consecutive days. On the last day of pollination, pinch off any remaining unopened buds.

Days 17-39.

Observe seed pods developing. Approximately twenty days after the last pollination, remove plants from reservoir (or allow reservoir to dry out.) Allow plants to dry out for approximately 5 days.

Days 40-44.

Harvest seed pods by gently rolling between fingers. Save seeds in a cool, dry place for later planting. Don't forget to label the seed packet with type of seed, date harvested, etc.

* Fast Plants do not self-pollinate. To cross-pollinate, use a very fine paint brush, pipe cleaner, cotton swab, or bee thorax (from the Fast Plants Kit). See page 53 in *GrowLab: A Complete Guide to Gardening in the Classroom* for more about pollinating indoors.

Appendix E: Resources

This appendix highlights selected resource books for both students and teachers. See pages 119 to 124 in *GrowLab: A Complete Guide to Gardening in the Classroom* for additional annotated resource listings.

Student Resources

Fiction

79 Squares by M.J. Bosse. 185 pp. An 82-year-old ex-convict's garden becomes a way of teaching Eric, a young man on the outs with society, that he has a place in the world. New York: Crowell, 1979. **Gr. 6 up.**

Anna's Garden Songs by Lena Anderson. Translated from the Swedish. 31 pp. On the left-hand page, a simple and light-hearted poem about a garden vegetable faces a full illustration on the right. Anna is small enough to hide under a rhubarb leaf. New York: Greenwillow, 1989. **PreK-Gr. 2.**

The Carrot Seed by Ruth Krauss. 22 pp. A small boy plants a carrot seed; his family does not believe it will ever come up. But he continues to care for it and finally needs a wheelbarrow to haul his enormous harvest. Brief text and cartoon-like illustrations. New York: Scholastic, 1945. **Gr. K-3.**

"The Garden" from *Frog and Toad Together* by Arnold Lobel. 48 pp. In this brief story, Toad plants seeds supplied by his friend Frog. After yelling at them to grow, reading them stories, and playing music for them, Toad learns a "lesson" about seed sprouting. New York: Harper & Row, 1979. **PreK-Gr. 2.**

Garden Partners by Diane Palmisciano. 32 pp. Grandmother and granddaughter plant from scratch a vegetable garden in the country, sharing the hard work and the harvest. A quiet picture book with gentle illustrations. New York: Atheneum, 1989. **Gr. 2-3.**

Growing Colors by Bruce McMillan. 32 pp. Each color of the spectrum is given a two-page spread, with a full-page color closeup photograph of a fruit or vegetable on the right, and on the left a small photo of the entire plant with the name of the color in large letters. New York: Lothrop, Lee & Shepard, 1988. **PreK.**

Growing Vegetable Soup by Lois Ehlert. 30 pp. Bright pictures show a father and child sharing the simple joy of planting, watering, watching seeds grow, and making the harvest into soup. New York: Harcourt Brace Jovanovich, 1987. **Gr. K-1.**

The Lorax by Dr. Seuss. 63 pp. A classic Dr. Seuss book with a message that greed and lack of responsibility for our environment have a lasting effect. New York: Random House, 1971. **Gr. K up.**

The Man Who Planted Trees by Jean Giono. 52 pp. This award-winning fictional story was first published in Vogue and has been reissued with meticulous woodcuts in black and white. Elzeard Bouffier, a shepherd, plants one hundred acorns on the day the narrator meets him in 1913. The surrounding country is harsh, dry, almost deserted, but by the narrator's last visit in 1946, it is wooded and repopulated, with water again running in fountains and streams, and the new forest officially protected. Chelsea, VT: Chelsea Green, 1954, 1985. **Gr. 6 to adult.**

Miss Rumphius by Barbara Cooney. 32 pp. The narrator's great aunt, now an old lady, has lived an independent and adventurous life. We see her as the little girl Alice, the adventurer Miss Rumphius, even as That Crazy Old Lady, and finally, as she fufills an earlier promise to bring beauty to the world, as the Lupine Lady. New York: Penguin, 1982. **Gr. 3-4.**

Mr. Plum's Paradise by Elisa Trimby. 32 pp. Mr. Plum and his neighbors join forces to transform his dingy back yard into a public garden. Illustrations are in full color, attractive and detailed. New York: Lothrop, Lee & Shepard, 1977. **Gr. K–1.**

Plant Sitter by Gene Zion. 32 pp. One summer Tommy surprises his parents by starting a business caring for the neighbors' house plants in his home. The house becomes a jungle, for the plants flourish under his care. A good trim, with cuttings potted and given away, finally saves the day. New York: Scholastic, 1959. **PreK-Gr. 3.**

Pumpkin, Pumpkin by Jeanne Titherington. 24 pp. Jamie plants one pumpkin seed, watches it sprout, grow, flower, fruit. He finally picks the pumpkin and carves it—but he saves six seeds for next year. New York: Greenwillow, 1986. **PreK-Gr. 1.**

The Tenth Good Thing About Barney by Judith Viorst. 25 pp. A small boy describes his beloved cat Barney's death, cries, and delivers the funeral oration: nine good things about Barney. The tenth? .....that he will nourish the flowers in the garden in which he is buried. New York: Atheneum, Macmillan, 1971. **Gr. K-4.**

This Year's Garden by Cynthia Rylant. 32 pp. A three-generation family tells their garden's annual story, from spring planning to harvest and preserving until winter comes again. Their large country garden is meant as a major source of food. Scarsdale, NY: Bradbury, 1984. **Gr. K–3.**

Tiny Seed by Eric Carle. 32 pp. A tiny seed survives while its fellow seeds are eliminated by landing in the wrong place and other adversities. The resulting plant grows taller than houses; its flower in autumn disperses tiny seeds. Natick, MA: Picture Book Studio, 1987. **Gr. K–3.**

Top Secret by John Gardiner. 110 pp. Allen has an original idea for his fourth-grade science project: human photosynthesis. Persisting through adult skepticism and discouragement, he begins to turn himself into a plant - along with his bully of a science teacher. Boston: Little, Brown & Co., 1984. **Gr. 4-5.**

Indoor Gardening

Eat the Fruit, Plant the Seed by M.E. Selsam. 48 pp. How to grow plants from six kinds of fruit seeds, from avocado to citrus, step by step. Nicely illustrated. New York: Morrow, 1980. **Gr. 3-6.**

Kid's Garden Book by Patricia Petrich and Rosemary Dalton. 182 pp. An informal, brief introduction to many aspects of gardening indoors and out. Includes lots of project ideas. Text is hand printed, with colored illustrations done by children. Concord, CA: Nitty Gritty, 1974. **Gr. 4-6.**

Linnea's Windowsill Garden by Christina Bjork. 59 pp. Young Linnea introduces the reader to the plants she has grown in her apartment and gives instructions on how to grow them, as well as on general care and feeding. Includes avocado pits, carrot tops, scarlet runner, impatiens, lots of good ideas and

projects, as well as a little scientific background. New York: R & S Books, distributed by Farrar Straus and Giroux, 1978. **Gr. 4-5.**

Play with Plants by J. Wexler. 95 pp. How to grow plants from parts of houseplants as well as potatoes and beans. Clear directions. Explains how a seed grows. New York: Morrow, 1978. **Gr. 3-6.**

Potted Plant Book by S. Tarsky. 41 pp. The care and feeding of house plants; inviting text and illustrations, excellent ideas. Boston: Little, Brown & Co., 1981. **Gr. 4-6.**

Outdoor Gardening

The Garden Book by Wes Porter. Packaged in a mini-greenhouse for starting seeds, this book shows how to sow, grow, and explore the wonders of more than twenty plants. New York: Workman, 1989. **Gr. K-5.**

Gardening with Kids by Sharon MacLatchie. 207 pp. Covers outdoor gardens thoroughly; includes indoor projects and houseplants. Written for the inexperienced adult gardener, this guide focuses on ways to encourage the child's enjoyment. Emmaus, PA: Rodale Press, 1977. **Gr. K-6.**

Growing Things by Angela Wilkes. 24 pp. A brief introduction in comic-book format with information on planting trees, bulbs, three garden vegetables, and houseplants. London, England: Usborne, 1984. **Gr. 3-5.**

Herb Growing Book by R. Verey. 41 pp. Suggests project ideas and recipes for herb teas. Clear text and illustrations. Includes general gardening information. Boston: Little, Brown & Co., 1981. **Gr. 4-6.**

In My Garden: A Child's Gardening Book by Helen Oechsli. 32 pp. A good introduction to beginning an outdoor garden, with brief but clear instructions on soil, starting seeds indoors, weeding, thinning, com-

posting and directions for seven vegetables. New York: Macmillan, 1985. **Gr. 3-4.**

John Seymour's Gardening Book by John Seymour. 61 pp. A refreshing introduction to gardening, with a few pages each on digging, compost, tools, etc. and individual entries for over 25 vegetables. Zany and detailed illustrations. Useful tips from an expert whose enjoyment of gardening shines through. London: Whizzard, 1978. **Gr. 5-8.**

KidsGardening: A Kids' Guide to Messing Around In the Dirt by Kevin Rafferty. 87 pp. An attractive book with hand-printed text and amusing cartoon-like illustrations. A basic introduction to organic gardening, including compost and mulching, followed by a few projects using vegetables and flowers. An attractive book in a ring binder with hand-printed text and amusing cartoonlike illustrations; comes with packets of seeds. Palo Alto, CA: Klutz Press, 1989. **Gr. 4-7.**

A Kid's First Book of Gardening by Derek Fell. 96 pp. A clear, information-filled book on gardening, both indoors and out. Includes how to start plants from seeds, bulbs and cuttings, create container gardens, raise giant pumpkins or a tomato-potato! Philadelphia, PA: Running Press, 1990. **Gr. K-6.**

My Garden: A Journal for Gardening Throughout the Year by Louise Murphy. 160 pp. Arranged by month, with poems, stories, experiments, recipes, advice, and activities involving outdoor and indoor gardens. New York: Charles Scribner's Sons, 1980. **Gr. 4-6.**

Seeds/Flowers/Fruits

Bean and Plant by Christine Back and Barrie Watts. 25 pp. Color photographs show how a bean develops into a mature plant. Each stage is explained in simple language, with a bold heading for very young children and more detailed information for others. Morristown, NJ: Silver Burdett, 1984. **Gr. K-3.**

A First Look at Flowers by M.E. Selsam. 31 pp. Flowers and flower parts described and meticulously drawn in black and white. Encourages observing, identifying, and comparing. New York: Walker & Co., 1977. **Gr. 1-3.**

The Flower Alphabet Book by Jerry Pallotta. 32 pp. This beautifully illustrated book highlights interesting aspects of a different flower for each letter of the alphabet. Gr. K-4 (*The Icky Bug Alphabet Book*, in the same format, is also available.) Watertown, MA: Charlesbridge, 1988. **Gr. K-4.**

Flowering Plants by Alfred Leutscher. Action Science Series. 32 pp. Clear, colorful, realistic illustrations on every page and a text full of facts. Covers record keeping, parts of a flower, pollination, seed dispersal, etc., emphasizing activities and experiments the reader can do. New York: Franklin Watts, 1984. **Gr. 4-6.**

Flowers, Fruits, Seeds by J. Wexler. Excellent full color photographs and brief text follow the growth from flower to fruit to seed to plant again. Englewood Cliffs, NJ: Prentice-Hall Books for Young Readers, 1987. **Gr. K-2.**

From Flower to Flower; Animals and Pollination by P. Lauber. 57 pp. Large black and white photos complement a well-written text on pollination by small animals and insects, especially bees. New York: Crown, 1986. **Gr. 2-4.**

From Flower to Fruit by Anne Dowden. 56 pp. Beautiful drawings on almost every page help explain the transition from ovary to seed and again to fruit. Covers reproduction, fertilization, and distribution of seeds. New York: Crowell, 1984. **Gr. 5 up.**

Hidden Magic of Seeds by Dorothy E. Shuttlesworth. 44 pp. This

straightforward text with colored illustrations covers how seeds form, grow, spread, and are used. Suggests planting a garden, indoors or out, to be close to "seed magic," with brief directions for radish and tomato. Shows the variety of seed forms as well as seeds of familiar foods. Emmaus, PA: Rodale Press, 1976. **Gr. 3-5.**

How a Seed Grows by H. Jordan. Written to be read by beginning readers, explains that seeds differ and encourages readers to plant bean seeds for themselves. New York, Crowell, 1960. **Gr. K-2.**

How Plants Are Pollinated by J.E. Rahn. 135 pp. Accurate and concise, the text covers pollination, flower parts and, especially, means of pollination. Outstanding illustrations. New York: Atheneum, 1975. **Gr. 5 up.**

How Seeds Travel by C. Overbeck. 48 pp. Stunning close-up photographs help show the ways seeds move from their point of origin to find a new site. Minneapolis: Lerner, 1982. **Gr. 4 up.**

Look at a Flower by Anne Dowden. 120 pp. The evolution, structure, and reproduction of ten families of common North American plants. Readable, scientific text with detailed drawings. New York: Crowell, 1963. **Gr. 6 up.**

Lore and Legends of Flowers by Robert L. Crowell. 80 pp. Ten common flowers, from roses to dandelions, are gracefully illustrated. The text gives some history of the flower, including legends. New York: Crowell, 1982. **Gr. 6 up.**

Now I Know All About Seeds by Susan Kuchalla. 32 pp. A very simple introduction to what seeds are (beans, acorns), what they become, how they disperse and grow. Large colorful illustrations. Mahwah, NJ: Troll Associates, 1982. **PreK-Gr. 1.**

Plants, Seeds and Flowers by Louis Sabin. 30 pp. Straightforward,

informative guide to the life cycle of plants including pollination, germination, photosynthesis, and flowering. Color illustrations break up the text on every page. Mahwah, NJ: Troll Associates. **Gr. 4-6.**

Reason for a Flower by Ruth Heller. 42 pp. Bright, colorful illustrations and brief text cover kinds of pollination, seeds, and products from flowers, capturing some of the wonder of the transformation from flower to fruit. Full of odd facts. New York: Grosset & Dunlap, 1986. **PreK-Gr. 2.**

Seeds: Pop, Stick, Glide by Patricia Lauber. 57 pp. How the seeds of several dozen familiar plants travel, is shown for each plant in several step-by-step crisp black and white photographs. Includes both wild and cultivated plants. The text is well organized, pertinent, and informative. Includes index. New York: Crown, 1981. **Gr. 2-5.**

State Flowers by A. Dowden. 86 pp. Statutes proclaiming the state flower are given, along with some brief historical and general information. Arranged alphabetically by state. Each flower illustrated in its natural color. New York: Crowell, 1978. **Gr. 5.**

Watch It Grow, Watch It Change by J.E. Rahn. 88 pp. The growth of plants from buds to other stages is described and illustrated in detail. Familiar plants like lilac and peas are used as prototypes. New York: Atheneum, 1978. **Gr. 5 up.**

What Is a Flower? by Jennifer W. Day. 12 pp. Brief introductions to diverse groups of flowers: wildflowers, garden flowers, carnivorous flowers, grass, vines, etc. Each group is illustrated with several colorful examples. Racine, WI: Western, 1975. **Gr. 1-3.**

Wildflowers and the Stories Behind Their Names by P. S. Busch. 88 pp. Realistic drawings in color and black and white of fifty species. The text, by a science educator, gives customs and superstitions as well as botanical information. New York: Charles Scribner's Sons, 1977. **Gr. 4-6.**

Plants (General)

The Amazing World of Plants by Elizabeth Marcus. 32 pp. A question and answer book: What are conifers? Are these plants harmful? etc. Each question answered with a paragraph or two. Cartoon-like illustrations in color on every page. Mahwah, NJ: Troll Associates, 1984. **Gr. 4-6.**

Being a Plant by Laurence Pringle. 88 pp. Describes the life of plants and interrelationships between flowers, birds, insects, animals. Covers structure, reproduction, adaptation. Well written and researched, clear illustrations. New York: Crowell, 1983. **Gr. 5 up.**

Carnivorous Plants by Cynthia Overbeck. 48 pp. Explains how these plants are adapted to damp environments and reviews several species. Minneapolis: Lerner, 1982. **Gr. 4 up.**

Cotton by Millicent E. Selsam. 48 pp. An excellent introduction to cotton clearly written and well illustrated with photographs that range from a Peruvian cloth from 2200 B.C. to a closeup of pollen grains. Covers a brief history, growth of the plant, history of production machinery, and modern production methods. New York: Morrow, 1982. **Gr. 3-5.**

First Look at the World of Plants by M.E. Selsam. 32 pp. An excellent introduction to plants, from algae to flowering plants, and their classes. New York: Walker, 1978. **Gr. 1-3.**

My Own Herb Garden by Allan Swenson. 65 pp. Ten common herbs are introduced and well illustrated; we are told how to identify each one, and how to grow, use and store it. Includes indoor and outdoor growing. Emmaus, PA: Rodale Press, 1976. **Gr. 5-8.**

Mysteries and Marvels of Plant Life by Barbara Cork. 32 pp. Highlights such plants as the strangler fig, pitcher plants that trap animals, etc. Tidbits of information pack each illustrated page. Tulsa, OK: EDC Publishing, 1983. **Gr. 4-7.**

Plant (Eyewitness Books) by David Burnie. 64 pp. Bountiful, clear photographs and information-filled text highlighting plants as individuals and in the context of their use by humans. New York: Alfred A. Knopf, 1989. **Gr. 5 up.**

Plant Families by Carol Lerner. 32 pp. This nicely illustrated book examines twelve of the world's largest and most familiar plant families and tells how to recognize shared characteristics. New York: Morrow Jr., 1989. **Gr. 4-6.**

Plants Are Important. 15 pp. The simple text and color photos help young children distinguish the parts of a plant—roots, stems, leaves, flowers—and connect them with what the reader has eaten, from carrots to peas. Washington, DC: National Geographic Society, 1986. **PreK-Gr. 1.**

Plants That Changed History by J. Rahn. 144 pp. Highlights the adventures of grains, spices, sugar, potatoes, and coal, all plant products that have influenced our lives tremendously over the centuries. New York: Atheneum, 1982. **Gr. 5 up.** A second book, *More About Plants That Changed History* includes paper, rubber, tea, tobacco, and opium. **Gr. 6 up.**

Plants We Eat by M.E. Selsam. 125 pp. Beautiful black and white photographs accompany descriptions of many plants we eat. Some customs are highlighted. New York: William Morrow, 1981. **Gr. 4-6.**

Popcorn by M.E. Selsam. 48 pp. Outstanding photographs and well-written and -organized text cover history, structure, fertilization, growth, and the multiple uses of

corn. Encourages the reader to grow a popcorn plant. New York: William Morrow, 1976. **Gr. 3-5.**

Potatoes by Sylvia A. Johnson. 48 pp. A clear, factual scientific children's text. Many of the excellent color photographs were taken through a microscope. Shows the growth and development of the plant and gives information on it as an important food crop. Minneapolis: Lerner, 1984. **Gr. 4-7.**

Science Fun with Peanuts and Popcorn by Rose Wyler. 48 pp. Lots of simple experiments with clear directions and explanations especially for seeds and seedlings. Includes easy recipes and riddles and a few touches of history. Englewood Cliffs, NJ: Messner, 1986. **Gr. 3-6.**

Trees

Blossom on the Bough: A Book of Trees by Anne Dowden. 71 pp. Colorful drawings highlight the flowers and fruits of American trees, their parts and functions, forests, cycles, as well as conifers and forest regions of the U.S. New York: Crowell, 1975. **Gr. 5 up.**

Discovering Trees by Keith Brandt. 32 pp. An introduction to trees with a factual text covering growth from a seed, seed dispersal, coniferous and deciduous, etc. Mahwah, NJ: Troll Associates, 1982. **Gr. 4-6.**

Leaf and Tree Guide. Backyard Explorer Series. 64 pp. Part of a kit that includes a child's leaf collecting album. Extensive information about leaves and trees, with suggestions for kids' explorations and projects. New York: Workman, 1989. **Gr. 2-4.**

Look at a Tree by Eileen Curran. 32 pp. What do you see when you look at a tree? Bees, birds, fruit, tree house, ...me? One sentence to a page, each page an attractive drawing. Mahwah, NJ: Troll Associates, 1985. **Pre-K to Gr. 1.**

Man Who Planted Trees (see fiction section)

Once There Was a Tree (see ecology/environment section)

Ecology/Environment

Acid Rain: A Sourcebook for Young People by Christina G. Miller and Louise A. Berry. 115 pp. The book provides an overview of documented acid rain damage and offers a variety of simple experiments to learn more about acid rain. New York: Julian Messner, 1986. **Gr. 6-8.**

Amazing Earthworm by Lilo Hess. 48 pp. A fact-filled text and black and white photos on every page cover the life cycle of the earthworm, suggest a few experiments, distinguish the earthworm from other worms and distinguish worms as a group from insects. New York: Charles Scribner's Sons, 1979. **Gr. 4-6.**

Earth Calendar by Una Jacobs. 37 pp. Why the earth has climates, how soil forms, underground nests, animal habitats, recycling of nutrients, etc. are highlighted in text and illustrations. Morristown, NJ: Silver Burdett, 1985. **Gr. 4-6.**

Earthworms, Dirt and Rotten Leaves: An Exploration in Ecology by Molly McLaughlin. 86 pp. An introduction to ecology, with a focus on worms, that encourages observations and experiments. Highlights the role of earthworms in the food chain and soil improvement. New York: Atheneum, 1986. **Gr. 4-7.**

Ecosystems and Food Chains by Francine Sabin. 30 pp. A straightforward, factual text, complemented by lighthearted color drawings, defines ecosystems, explains food chains, and clarifies the damaging role pesticides can play. Mahwah, NJ: Troll Associates, 1985. **Gr. 4-6.**

The Little House by Virginia Lee Burton. 40 pp. The little house lives in the country surrounded by fields of daisies and apple trees dancing in the moonlight. First a highway, then tract housing, then skyscrapers replace the field and orchards, while the little house grows miserable and neglected. Finally rescued and moved, she watches the sun and moon and stars again. Boston: Houghton Mifflin, 1942. **Gr. 2-4.**

The Lorax (see fiction section)

Once There Was a Tree by Natalia Romanova. 28 pp. First published in Russia, this beautifully illustrated book shows the interdependency of insects, birds, animals, humans, and Earth. New York: Dial, 1985. **Gr. K up.**

Plants in Danger by E. Ricciuti. 86 pp. More than twenty thousand plant species are endangered. Covers history, remedial steps, and how individuals can help. Soft pencil drawings enhance a clear, well-organized text. New York: Harper & Row, 1979. **Gr. 5 up.**

Rainforest by Helen Cowcher. 35 pp. Colorful, inviting pictures and simple words tell the tale of a thriving, diverse rainforest changed drastically by human actions. New York: Farrar, Straus & Giroux, 1988. **Gr. PreK-2.**

Science Fun With Mud and Dirt by Rose Wyler. 48 pp. Suggests projects and activities to explore what dirt is made of, who lives underground, building with adobe and mud, dams, and erosion. New York: Messner, 1986. **Gr. 3-6.**

What Do You Want to Know About Earthworms? by Seymour Simon. An excellent, fact-filled text. Divided into nine small chapters, each the answer to a question such as, "Can Earthworms Learn?" The reader is eased into experimenting and observing. New York: Scholastic, 1969. **Gr. 4-6.**

Miscellaneous

How to Think Like a Scientist by Stephen P. Kramer. 44 pp. The author invites students to practice and understand in simple, real-life terms, how to solve problems, using a scientific method. New York: Crowell, 1987. **Gr. 3-6.**

Teachers' Resources

The resources listed here can supplement and extend your GrowLab efforts. Many widely available science curricula also have units that support the concepts and approaches presented in this guide.

Selected Curriculum Resources

Botany for All Ages by the New England Wildflower Society. Filled with a wealth of useful information and interdisciplinary suggestions for actively involving children in investigating the plant world indoors and out. Chester, CT: Globe Pequot Press, 1989. **PreK-Gr. 8.**

Botany: 49 Science Fair Projects by Robert Bonnet and G. Daniel Keen. Offers a wide array of botany project ideas for teachers and students, from composting to phototropism to hydroponics. Projects encourage the development of problem-solving skills. Philadelphia, PA: Tab Books Inc., 1989. **Gr. 3-8.**

The California State Environmental Education Guide. John Bateson, ed. Provides educators with creative classroom lessons to build a basic understanding of the environment. Many activities tie in plants, adaptations, soils, and other topics and concepts that complement a gardening program. Hayward, CA: Alameda County Office of Education, 1988. **Gr. K-6.**

Experimenting With Plants by Joe Beller. Provides detailed information for conducting controlled experiments with plants. Many are appropriate science-fair types of investigations. New York: Arco, 1985. **Gr. 6-8.**

Exploring with Wisconsin Fast Plants by Wisconsin Fast Plants. These plants can complete a full life cycle, from seed to seed, under lights in a classroom in about 40 days. Includes technical information for raising these plants in the classroom and outlines activities to explore all aspects of plant growth and development, while introducing students to the process of scientific exploration. Madison, WI: University of Wisconsin, 1990. **Gr. 4-8.**

The Green Classroom by Judith Salisbury. A comprehensive environmental science curriculum emphasizing hands-on experimentation and the development of a school garden. Lessons spring from the garden as well as covering agriculture and regional food systems. E. Falmouth, MA: New Alchemy Institute, 1989. **Gr. K-6.**

The Growing Classroom by the LifeLab Science Program. 400 pp. An exciting curriculum on establishing a garden-based science and nutrition program. Menlo Park, CA: Addison-Wesley, 1990. **Gr. 2-6.**

Growing Up Green by Alice Skelsey and Gloria Huckaby. This detailed resource book suggests many exciting activities for introducing gardening and the natural world to children. New York: Workman, 1973. **Gr. K-6.**

Ladybugs and Lettuce Leaves by Project Outside/Inside. This indoor/outdoor ecology curriculum covers the full growth cycle, from seed to plant to seed again, complete with bugs, weeds, flowers, compost, and climate. Washington, DC: Center for Science in the Public Interest, 1982. **Gr. 5-6.**

Looking at Insects by David Suzuki. Filled with background information and clearly described activities for exploring insects. Can be used by teachers with younger students or as a resource for older students. New York: Warner, 1986. (See *GrowLab: A Complete Guide to Gardening in the Classroom* for a description of *Looking at Plants* by the same author.) **Gr. 3-6.**

The National Gardening Association Guide to Kids' Gardening by Lynn Ocone with Eve Pranis. A comprehensive how-to guide covering planning and organizing a garden program, designing and maintaining a site, and raising money. More than seventy creative and educational activities. Formerly titled *Youth Gardening* Book. New York: Wiley Science Editions, John Wiley & Sons, 1990. **Gr. K-8.**

Naturewatch by Adrienne Katz. Abundant ideas for exploring gardens and the environment with children. Activities for indoors and out range from building caterpillar cages to raising bulbs and cooking with weeds. Menlo Park, CA: Addison-Wesley, 1986. **Gr. K-6.**

Project Seasons. This interdisciplinary guide helps you teach about time, growth, and change using the cycle of the seasons as a framework. Shelburne, VT: The Stewardship Institute, Shelburne Farms Resources, 1990. **Gr. K-6.**

"RainForests: Tropical Treasures." *Naturescope* magazine issue number 75044 (1989) The National Wildlife Federation, Washington, D.C. Abundant with creative activities, background information, and reproducibles to help students learn about tropical rainforests.

Seeds and Weeds by John Westley. Windows on Science Series. Contains 28 detailed lesson plans for stimulating problem-solving explorations in the world of seeds and plant growth. Sunnyvale, CA: Creative Publications, 1988. **PreK-Gr. 2.**

Selected Plant References

Blue Corn and Square Tomatoes by Rebecca Rupp. How do melons ripen? Why are peppers hot? This book not only answers these questions, but also tells the life stories and histories of twenty garden vegetables, including nutritional content. Pownal, VT: Storey Communications, 1987.

Green Immigrants: The Plants that Transformed America by Claire Shaver Haughton. Examines history, legends, and folklore of eighty-five familiar plants—how they were brought to this country and how they changed our nation and our lives. New York: Harcourt Brace Jovanovich, 1978.

Living with Plants: A Guide to Practical Botany by Donna N. Schumann. A comprehensive botany book highlighting the how and why of plants in simple language. Eureka, CA: Mad River Press, 1980.

Plant Watching: How Plants Remember, Tell Time, Form Relationships and More by Malcolm Wilkins. This botany book takes the reader on a fascinating journey through the inner workings of the plant world. Though somewhat technical, it's designed for the lay person. London, England: Roxby Reference Books, 1988.

Appendix F: Seed Sources

Because some of the seeds suggested in GrowLab activities are difficult to find at local garden centers, we've listed mail order sources below. Many of these seeds are also included in the GrowLab Seed Collection.

Cotton

Hastings
P.O. Box 115535
Atlanta, GA 30310

Mimosa pudica (sensitive plant)

Stokes Seeds, Inc.
P.O. Box 548
Buffalo, NY 14240

Thompson and Morgan
P.O. Box 1308
Jackson, NJ 08527

Peanuts

Hastings
P.O. Box 115535
Atlanta, GA 30310

Jung Seeds and Nursery
335 S. High Street
Randolph, WI 53957

Stokes Seeds, Inc.
P.O. Box 548
Buffalo, NY 14240

Thornless honey locust

Maver Nursery
Rte. 2, Box 265B
Asheville, NC 28805

F.W. Schumacher Co.
36 Spring Hill Road
Sandwich, MA 02563-1023

Frosty Hollow Nursery
P.O. Box 53
Langley, WA 98260

Venus flytrap (and other carnivorous plants)

Logee's Greenhouses
55 North St.
Danielson, CT 06239

Gardens of the Blue Ridge
P.O. Box 10
Pineola, NC 28662

Wisconsin Fast Plants™

Wisconsin Fast Plants seeds can be purchased separately or as part of a kit that includes a complete, specialized growing system from:

Carolina Biological Supply Company
2700 York Road
Burlington, NC 27215
(800) 334-5551

Rare Seeds

Seed Savers Exchange
C/O Kent Whealy
R.R. 3, Box 239
Decorah, IA 52101

This non-profit organization is dedicated to the preservation of rare varieties of vegetables and some fruits. Seed Savers Exchange consists of a network of home gardeners growing and saving rare varieties of vegetable seed for preservation and swapping with other members. They are also dedicated to educating the public about the role seed saving plays in preserving genetic diversity.

GrowLab Seed Collection

The GrowLab Seed Collection is available as part of the complete GrowLab Starter Kit, or by itself. It contains eighteen specially selected varieties for indoor gardening and for use with activities in this guide. Seeds include: tomato, lettuces, radish, carrots, cucumbers, beans, marigold, zinnia, basil, turnip, peanuts, cotton, honey locust, potato, and Fast Plants.
Available from:

National Gardening Association
Department B
180 Flynn Avenue
Burlington, VT 05401

GrowLab Program Resources

To enhance classroom indoor gardening efforts, the National Gardening Association has developed the following resources for teachers and other GrowLab supporters:

Teacher Resources

GrowLab Indoor Garden. This ready-to-assemble single- or double-level indoor garden comes with fluorescent lights, programmable timer, climate control tent, capillary watering base mat, plastic tray, and copy of *GrowLab: A Complete Guide to Gardening in the Classroom* (see below). Mobile stand is optional.

GrowLab Starter Kit. This contains pots, potting mix, labels, fertilizer, insecticidal soap, and a GrowLab Seed Collection for a full year of indoor gardening.

GrowLab: A Complete Guide to Gardening in the Classroom. This 128-page teacher's guide has a wealth of information on the "how-to" of indoor gardening, with many useful ideas for class projects and activities. It also includes plans for building your own GrowLab Indoor Garden.

GrowLab: Activities for Growing Minds. This 320-page, K-8 curriculum guide includes creative, interdisciplinary activities to help you stimulate science inquiry with an indoor garden. Includes reproducible student record-keeping sheets and a comprehensive, annotated resource section.

Growing Ideas **newsletter**. This newsletter, published three times each year, contains activity suggestions, indoor gardening classroom highlights, news and columns for sharing ideas with other indoor gardening teachers. (If you're not currently receiving the newsletter, contact us for a sample copy.)

Teacher Resource Videos. Whether you're new to classroom gardening, or have been at it for some time, our three videos will inspire and inform you. One presents a lively overview of garden-based science, another guides you through the technical "how-to's" of indoor gardening, and a third illustrates a range of instructional strategies to make plant-based science inquiry fun and effective.

Instructional Classroom Posters. This lively poster series will brighten your classroom and motivate your students with colorful illustrations, information and challenges. Includes "Salad Celebration," "Sensational Seeds," "Those Amazing Plant Parts," and "Plant a Question, Watch it Grow."

GrowLab Partners Program Resources

There is a growing network of individuals and organizations working in partnership with teachers to support GrowLab Program efforts. Such support can include: providing supplies or funding assistance; training teachers; providing ongoing horticultural and/or curriculum support; or working as classroom volunteers. Some groups that have established GrowLab partnerships include: Cooperative Extension (4-H and Master Gardeners), garden clubs, botanic gardens, science museums, environmental education centers, garden centers and nurseries, local businesses, and university educators.

To help support these partnerships, the National Gardening Association provides the following resources:

GrowLab Partner's Guide: Building Community/School Partnerships Through Indoor Gardening. This guide is a planning tool covering such topics as raising funds, initiating a GrowLab Program, working effectively with local educators or community groups, and training teachers.

GrowLab Regional Trainings. National Gardening Association staff offers trainings in selected regions of the U.S. for GrowLab partners and teachers. We are available for customized trainings as schedules allow.

National Network. Our national database of GrowLab users and supporters allows us to link individual teachers and schools with other educators and GrowLab partners in a given region.

Discounts. Discounts on GrowLab educational products and publications are available to qualifying organizations or individuals initiating or supporting multi-classroom GrowLab programs.

Fund raising. NGA can assist GrowLab partners to identify potential funding sources and by supporting grant-writing efforts.

For more information on current resources, training, or on starting a GrowLab Program, contact: GrowLab, Department B, National Gardening Association, 180 Flynn Avenue, Burlington, Vermont 05401. Phone: 1-800-LETSGRO.

Index

A

acid precipitation (acid rain) 248
acidity, environmental effects, 249, 251
acids, background, 248
adaptations (see also: diversity)
   background, 188
   flower, 118, 130
   leaf, 189, 201, 205
   seed, 29, 189, 191, 194,
adhesion, 54
algae, 50
annuals, 124
anthers, 118
aphids, 222, 224
asexual reproduction, 139, 145
assessment, student, 14
attitudes toward science, 12
auxins, 53, 55, 140

B

bacteria, 102, 114, 168, 209
basic needs, 39
bees, 119, 120, 129
biennials, 124
bird seed, 160
bulbs, 139

C

cabbage, as pH indicator, 249
cacti, 185, 189, 203
carbon dioxide
   and global warming, 181, 238, 255, 258
   and photosynthesis, 39, 74, 257
   and respiration, 75, 257
carnivorous plants, 189, 205
cells (plant), 77, 140
cellulose, 76
chlorophyll/chloroplasts, 74, 77, 85
classification systems, 154, 166, 169
clay, 101
clones, 139
coevolution, 120, 188
cohesion, 54
collecting soil, 102
composite flowers, 119, 167

composting, 213
consumers, 74, 208
cotton, 236
cotyledons, 28, 32
cross-pollination, 133, 295
crowding, 45
crowns, 139
cuticle, leaf, 77
cuttings, 140, 145,
cycles
   energy, 76, 208
   life, 118, 123, 124
   nutrient, 76, 208
   water, 181

D

dandelions, 276
decomposition, 102, 114, 210, 214
dicot, 28
differentiation, cell, 140
dispersal, seed, 122, 189, 191
diversity, 154
dormancy, seed, 199, 260
Dust Bowl, 68

E

earthworms, 102, 214, 218
embryo, 28
endosperm, 28
energy
   cycle, 76, 208
   source of, 74, 90
environmental impacts, 238, 239, 240, 243, 249
epidermis, leaf, 77
erosion, and roots, 54, 67
eutrophication, 50
evolution, 153

F

families, plant, 155, 167
Fast Plants, 295
fertilization, 118
fertilizer, 39, 49, 50, 215
fiber, 231
filament, 118
flowers, background, 118
food chains and webs, 208, 215, 223, 239,
food making, (see: photosynthesis)
footcandles, 91
fruits, 100, 121, 136
fungus, 102, 209, 210

G

genetic engineering, 176
geotropism, 53, 63
germination, 28, 34, 189, 260
   (see also: seeds, germination)
ginger, 73
global warming, 181, 239, 255
glucose, 74, 82
   (see also: sugar)
grass, 33, 240
gravity, and plant growth, 53, 63
greenhouse effect, 255
grouping, students, 13
growth needs, 39
guard cells, 77

H

herbariums, 158
honey locust trees, 259
houseplant cuttings, 140, 145
hormones, plant, 53
hybrids, 164, 176
hydroponics, 103
hydrotropism, 53, 65
human uses of plants, 232, 236
humus, 102

I

imperfect flowers, 119
indicator paper, 249
insects
   and pollination, 120
   controlling, 223
interdependencies, 208
iodine, 32, 81, 84

L

leaves
   adaptations, 189, 190, 194
   background, 76
   role in photosynthesis, 74, 76
legumes, 167
lettuce, 163, 231
life cycles, 118, 124
light
   background, 90
   plants response to, 87, 90
   role in photosynthesis, 74
loam, 102

M

microorganisms, 102, 114, 168, 209
minerals, 39, 74, 101

moisture, 28, 34
monocot, 28

N

natural selection, 153
nectar, 119, 129
needs, basic, 39
nutrition, chart, 231
nutrient cycle, 76, 208
nutrients, plant, 28, 39, 50
nutrition, human, 209, 227, 231

O

organic matter, 102, 211, 213, 215
ovary, 118
ovules, 118
oxygen, 28, 39, 74, 75, 85

P

peanuts, 167, 236
perennials, 124
perfect flowers, 119
pest control, 223
petals, 118, 128
petiole, 55, 73, 77, 80,
pH, 248, 251
photoperiodism, 91
photosynthesis, 39, 74, 81, 82
phototropism, 55, 87, 91
pistil, 118
planning, yearly calendar, 16
plant life cycles, 118, 123
"Plant Products Chart," 236
pollen, 118, 127, 296
pollination, 118, 127, 296
pollution, 238, 243, 246, 250
pores, soil, 101
potatoes, 139, 148, 151
potting mix, 103
problem solving, 8
producers, 74, 208
propagation, vegetative, 139, 141,
   144, 148

Q

questioning, 12

R

rainforests, tropical, 177, 183
reproduction (see also: propagation)
   asexual, background, 139
   sexual, background, 118

respiration, plant, 39, 75
rhizobia, 168
rhizomes, 55, 139
roots
   and erosion, 54, 68
   and soil, 102, 105
   and water, 52
   background, 29, 52
root view box, 62
runners, 139

S

salad, garden unit, 17
"Salad Nutrition Chart," 231
sand, 101
science
   attitudes toward, 12
   process of, 7
   teaching tips, 12
seeds
   adaptations, 29, 189, 191, 194, 199
   coats, 28, 189, 196
   dispersal, 122, 189, 191
   dormancy, 29, 188, 260
   germination, 28, 31, 37, 189, 260
   production, 119, 132
   saving, 121, 156, 103
   sorting, 30
   thematic unit, 21
sensitive plant (mimosa), 205
sepals, 118
sexual reproduction, 118
shoots, 29
silt, 102
soil
   artificial, 103
   background, 101
   collecting, 102
   drainage, 102, 108
   erosion, 54, 67, 199
   formation, 101, 114
   microorganisms, 102, 114, 168,
   209
   profile, 115
   properties, 101, 107
soilless potting mix, 103
species, 155, 164
sprouting (see: germination conditions)
sprouts, edible, 34
stamens, 118
starch, 32, 76, 82, 84
stems
   background, 54
   and phototropism, 55
stigma, 118

stomata, 74, 76, 202
style, 118
sugar, 83 (see also: glucose)

T

tap roots, 52
temperature, and germination, 28,
   35
tendrils, 189
test for starch, 83
tissue culture, 140
transpiration, 77, 79, 189, 181, 185
trees, seedlings, 257, 258
tropical rainforests, 156, 177, 183
tropisms, 53, 55, 63, 65, 87
tubers, 139, 148

U

uses of plants, 232, 236

V

vegetative propagation, 139, 141,
   144, 148
veins, leaf, 77
Venus fly trap, 205

W

water, 28, 39, 49, 52, 65, 74 (see also:
   transpiration)
water cycle, 181
weeds, 189, 197
wind, pollination, 121
worms, 102, 214, 218